Designing and Building
Colonial and
Early American
Furniture
with 47 Projects
2nd Edition

TAB FURNITURE WOODSHOP SERIES

No. 3014
$21.95

Designing and Building
Colonial and Early American Furniture
with 47 Projects
2nd Edition

Percy W. Blandford

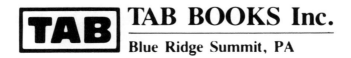

TAB BOOKS Inc.
Blue Ridge Summit, PA

SECOND EDITION
FIRST PRINTING

Copyright © 1988 by TAB BOOKS Inc.
First edition copyright © 1979 by TAB BOOKS Inc.
Printed in the United States of America

Library of Congress Cataloging in Publication Data

Blandford, Percy W.
    Designing and building colonial and early American
furniture, with 47 projects.

    Rev. ed. of: How to make Early American and
Colonial furniture. 1st ed. 1979.
    Includes index.
    1. Furniture making—Amateurs' manuals. 2. Furniture,
Early American. 3. Furniture, Colonial—United States.
I. Blandford, Percy W. How to make Early American and
Colonial furniture. II. Title.
TT195.B59 1988   749.214   88-2278
ISBN 0-8306-0914-8
ISBN 0-8306-9314-9 (pbk.)

Questions regarding the content of this book
should be addressed to:

Reader Inquiry Branch
TAB BOOKS Inc.
Blue Ridge Summit, PA 17294-0214

Edited by Suzanne L. Cheatle
Designed by Jaclyn Saunders
Illustrations by Grace Meyer

Contents

Introduction

THE FIRST SETTLERS from Europe arrived in America with a knowledge of furniture they had used in the old country, but with usually only a meager kit of tools and often very limited skill in using them. This meant that some of the first furniture was primitive, and that is the name applied to surviving pieces. These very early examples should not be dismissed as unworthy of attention, however; some have qualities worth reproducing.

Furniture that followed had more attention and skill given to it. The designers and craftsmen were in a different situation from others who had stayed at home among long-established ways. Instead, they were opening up a new field of furniture building based on new concepts. Fitness for purpose was a prime aim. This very desirable attribute of any furniture had been overlooked by some designers in Europe, where striving for novelty might have been the main aim.

Usually, anything designed to perform a task in the best possible way acquires a beauty of its own, without applied decoration. Obviously, there might be carving, veneering, inlaying, or other decorative touches, but if the design is wrong, no amount of decoration will make it right.

Furniture that best suits a particular purpose does not go out of date. Some of those early pieces of furniture can still be used in a modern home. In some cases, where the original use is no longer required, as with a washstand, the item will still serve for a new use—in this case as a side table in a bedroom, or maybe a buffet in a dining room.

The early craftsmen worked with basic tools. They did not have the luxury of power tools. Glues and metal fastenings were mostly of poor quality, so parts had to be properly jointed. This meant that their work was made in a craftsmanlike tradition, without shortcuts that go with mass-produced furniture today. Such work is ageless. A few modern cabinetmakers continue to make furniture in this way professionally, but such skill is expensive and the number of men able to engage in the work are few. This is where a keen amateur craftsman can keep a tradition alive, by making furniture in the time-honored way. What better examples to take than the furniture that is our own heritage? That is what this book is all about.

Furniture of the days of British rule is described as *Colonial*, while that made after Independence is *Early American*. There was no sudden change, however; furniture design evolved with steady progress. There are some influences from the other side of the Atlantic. Most settlers arrived with ideas from England and nearby European countries, but some groups wanted to make their furniture in a style they remembered from other countries, not necessarily very far apart. The Pennsylvania Dutch (German) with their bright painting may be particularly distinctive, and the Shakers produced the ultimate in simplicity, but there are other early characteristics of particular groups. In time there was more of a blending of designs, and the best features became adapted, so there was less distinction between the products of several areas.

News of furniture developments in the old countries came across the Atlantic. Designs were brought over. Particularly when special woods were imported, some of the European designs were followed and then adapted. By the time of Chippendale and other famous cabinetmakers, the best furniture in their styles was exceptionally good, but not of a type an amateur with limited skills could reproduce.

This book is about the furniture that led up to those days. I believe that an amateur woodworker of moderate skill, and with only a modest tool kit, should be able to find examples to make that will be within his skill and enable him to progress to some of the more ambitious types.

The furniture described forms a selection only. It is possible to adapt designs. A low cupboard can be heightened so its use is changed from kitchen storage to clothes hanging. A design with parts in solid boards can be altered to paneled parts. Variations in this way were practiced by early craftsmen. Many methods of construction can be seen following through a variety of furniture pieces. Once these techniques have been mastered, special designs can be made, and there's a fair chance that someone in the past would have made something similar.

The furniture in this book is described mainly as authentic reproductions. Some amateur furniture makers might decide not to strive for absolute authenticity. This is particularly so in broad panels, such as backs of cabinets. The modern treatment would be to use plywood, instead of to build up from many thin boards. The choice is yours.

The designs used are all either identical with existing old pieces of furniture or based on a type in which there were variations. When furniture was made singly, there were many changes to suit needs or the available wood, so there is scope for individual treatment and minor changes to design without spoiling the work as a reproduction.

In most cases, there is no specific wood quoted. Some pieces of furniture were made to the same design in different places with different woods, and the same could be done today. There is general guidance to the woods that were available and probably chosen in particular areas.

All measurements given are in inches. The lists of material are given for guidance and are generally accurate, but wood was often used in the size it happened to be, since there was no power saw to rip it down, and avoiding too much physical labor was obviously desirable. Wood of odd sizes can be used. If two parts which would be power-sawn to the same size today are made slightly different without affecting appearance or use, the work is likely to be more like the original. If the insides of old furniture is examined, uneven and rough edges where they do not matter are quite common.

No instructions are given for finishing the furniture. Please refer to the *Do-It-Yourselfer's Guide to Furniture Repair and Refinishing—2nd Edition* (TAB #2994), also part of the TAB Furniture Woodshop Series.

Visiting museums or collections of old furniture will provide ideas for many other items of furniture to copy. Comparing old furniture seen with examples in this book will show what variations are possible.

I believe that Colonial and Early American furniture offers very satisfying designs to be used by the modern amateur to exercise his growing skill. Probably in no other way can he learn the traditional processes that are at the base of true woodworking craftsmanship.

Furniture Wood

MAN HAS ATTENDED to his creature comforts by making furniture almost from the earliest times. Some of it was very primitive, but as tools developed so did the quality of furniture. This applied all over the world, and the early residents of the American continent must have produced furniture of various sorts. Some of the lost civilizations of South America apparently progressed to a high standard of design and craftsmanship, but there is little evidence of much sophisticated furniture making by the early residents of North America.

Explorers from Europe must have introduced furniture from their homelands, but if the Vikings, Irish, and other early peoples who arrived on the American continent made furniture during their stays, we know little of it today, probably because their settlements did not last long. Wood does not last for centuries under everyday conditions, and such peoples as the Vikings did not produce records that included written and drawn matter. They relied on history passed on by word of mouth, and that is not a good way to record details of furniture construction.

Furniture worth reproducing did not appear until the arrival of peoples with a determination to settle. Columbus, Cabot, and others set immigration in motion at the end of the fifteenth century. Many European nations were in the exploration business, and their attempts to get a foothold in America brought differing ideas of furnishings as the settlers tried to reproduce things that they remembered from home. French and Spanish influence in the South brought designs markedly different from those used by English, Dutch, and other settlers of the North. The types of trees available for conversion to furniture also influenced furniture making The near-tropical hardwoods of the South happened to be more like those familiar to the French and Spanish, while the northern trees were of the hardy types suited to temperate climates.

The furniture of the northern states had the most lasting influence on the designs of the settled parts of North America, with the English influence having more effect than that of any other European settlers, because of their preponderance and greater numbers. Other cultures had effects, and these will be seen later in the book, but as designs developed and became American rather than ex-European, the many originals blended into a whole that was recognizable as something new, but that incorporated facets of the originals which were found to be suitable for the new conditions.

All this was an ongoing process and still is, without clearly marked breaks, but for convenience of description we need to define periods. *Colonial period* must mean that period from the first settlements, while the settlers were colonists of another nation, up to 1776 and independence from English rule. After that it is convenient to describe furniture as *Early American* for the period when most work was done with hand tools—up to the beginning of the Industrial Revolution in the middle of the nineteenth century.

With the advent of factory facilities, furniture could be produced by mass-production methods and a craftsman did not see a job through from start to finish, but he exercised what skill he had doing only a part of the work. This did not mean the end of the individual craftsman, but mass-produced furniture was cheaper and the choice of the majority of people, so individual craftsmanship was available only to the more wealthy. Mass production of furniture continues today, but methods of a century in wood techniques have had to give way to plastics and manufactured boards since the end of World War II.

The Industrial Revolution caused a recognizable break with furniture that had gone before, but there is no comparable obvious division between Colonial and Early American furniture. They have a family likeness, and differences are more the effects of natural evolution than abrupt alterations. Tools and equipment improved. With improvements in communications and transport, woods were imported or came from distant parts of the continent. Methods of seasoning improved. Better materials and improved tools, with some mechanization, produced better furniture.

In the earliest days of settlement in eastern America and again as man pushed west, furniture had to have an immediate practical use and little or no intentional aesthetic value. It was made from wood available locally and worked with the few tools available to a pioneer woodworker, many of which were primarily for much rougher carpentry. Such furniture is often described as *Primitive*. This might not exactly be a period, but it marked the early stages of furniture in particular areas as they were settled.

Northern settlers had to contend with a harsh climate and not very profitable activities, so wealth came slowly, if at all. Much of their furniture making was by their own hands. A farmer tackled most things and made his own furniture, usually with the minimum of tools. Specialist craftsmen came later. The southern settlements, with better climate, farms with crops more easily turned into money, and quick development of towns around harbors, were able to import furniture and employ craftsmen to specialize in woodworking, so luxury was tied to utility in much of their furniture, with ornament and decoration being important.

DESIGN

Primitive is not necessarily a description of something makeshift for limited use. Fitness for purpose is often one of the most important features of good design. There is often a beauty in something that has been designed to do a job properly, without the need for added decoration. Good proportions can be all that are needed to make something look attractive. The Shaker religious philosophy of rejecting vanity is seen in their furniture, which is all severely plain, yet much of it is very attractive because it is functional and nicely proportioned.

Another type of furniture, usually of comparatively plain construction, is that of the Pennsylvania Dutch (more correctly *Deutsche*, meaning German), which is embellished with bright colors and patterns.

More advanced furniture showed influence of the great designers, particularly such names as Chippendale, Sheraton, and Hepplewhite. These men not only made fine furniture in England, but published books of designs, some of which found their way across the Atlantic to the New World. By then American furniture was finding traits of its own. While good designs have a following anywhere, local influences are bound to be important. Craftsmen and designers learn from experience—their own and that of others—and appreciate what is good in design and adapt it to their own ways. Such is progress.

When a hand craftsman makes things it is unlikely that any two items will be alike. This is one of the attractions of individual craftsmanship and was even more so in the days of early settlers, when furniture might have had to be designed to suit available pieces of wood. If a craftsman had in mind a piece of wood, say 3/4 inch thick and a piece was available 7/8 or 1 inch, he did not put in the considerable hand labor of planing it down, but used it as it was. If shelves were wanted 6 inches wide and a board 7 inches wide was available, that might be just as acceptable without cutting. On another occasion, a similar shelf might have been made with 5-inch boards to suit available stock.

This means that in considering reproducing furniture from the days of handwork, there is no virtue in carefully measuring to fine limits unless the work is intended as a museum specimen or an exact replica for historical reasons. If it is something that would had been made many times over, possibly by a great many craftsmen, it is safe to assume that variations in sizes would have been considerable, and any modern reproduction using similar woods and methods of construction would be as good a copy as one made to within 1/16 inch of the measurements of a particular specimen.

The original craftsman's ideas of design probably were on the lines of ''If it looks right, it probably is right.'' He gained a feeling for good proportions, probably without being able to analyze his reasons. If something is to be made in the style of an old piece of furniture without having an actual specimen or drawing to follow, there are a few rules that will provide guidance.

Having measurements the same in two or more directions does not usually produce a good-looking shape. This means that a circle and a square (FIG. 1-1A AND B) are better avoided. An ellipse is generally more pleasing than a circle (FIG. 1-1C). Any rectangle should produce a better looking shape than a square, and various proportions are needed to suit what is being made, but there is a *golden proportion* that comes from way back into antiquity. Our Colonial craftsman might not have known of it, but by his feeling for a good shape, he often arrived at it. This golden rule says that the most pleasing rectangular shape has sides in the proportions $1:\sqrt{2}$. For practical purposes, this means that the rectangle is 1 1/2 times (or slightly less) in length than in width (FIG. 1-1D).

Another point to consider is never to make a design symmetrical on a vertical surface. If you put a pattern exactly in the center, it will appear to be below center (FIG. 1-1E). It is better, for the sake of appearances, to put it decidedly above center (FIG. 1-1F). This is more marked if the inner shape produces an even border. The bottom border will appear narrow (FIG. 1-1G). It is better to make the bottom border definitely wider (FIG. 1-1H). This concept is seen in paneled doors.

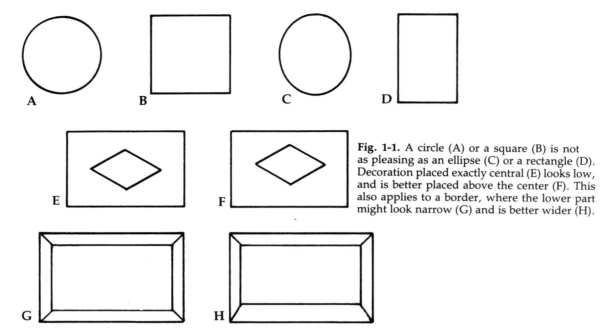

Fig. 1-1. A circle (A) or a square (B) is not as pleasing as an ellipse (C) or a rectangle (D). Decoration placed exactly central (E) looks low, and is better placed above the center (F). This also applies to a border, where the lower part might look narrow (G) and is better wider (H).

In framed pictures, the bottom of the picture mount is made wider than the sides and top.

This concept is seen in paneled doors. In framed pictures, the bottom of the picture mount is made wider than the sides and top.

With a three-dimensional piece of furniture, the various panels are better rectangular than square, although an occasional square will not matter. Such a piece of furniture will be more often viewed at an angle. Individual shapes must contribute to the whole. This means that the height and a diagonal measurement are better if not the same—legs could be higher or lower, or one of the horizontal measurements altered a little.

These rules are only guides to good design. It is safer to follow them than to ignore them, but design is not an exact science. Art is a feeling and we do not all feel the same. What looks good to one person might seem unsatisfactory to another. To a certain extent, taste can be trained. What seemed right to one generation might be unattractive to a later one. The Victorians were preoccupied with decoration and would not accept plain wood. Modern furniture design has gone the other way. If there is a moral to this, it is that we should please ourselves in selecting a design to reproduce, but we must always maintain the general style of that other day. For instance, a Colonial-style television cabinet should be unthinkable, but a nicely proportioned Early American side table should be just as useful today as it was to our forefathers, and just as attractive as a piece of decoration if properly made.

MATERIALS

Those early craftsmen worked in wood as it came from the tree. It might have been cut to get the best effect from grain markings, and it was seasoned by air drying for several years, but the cabinetmaker did his work in that wood, aided by glue, screws and nails. If he wanted a wide board and no tree would cut that width, he glued pieces edge to edge. If he wanted a piece for the bottom of a drawer, it was carefully cut thin from solid wood.

Today, we have a great many manufactured boards. The one that has had the most effect on furniture this century is plywood, but that only appeared after the Industrial Revolution. The makers of the furniture that interests us did not have it. Variations on plywood are blockboard and stripboard. Hardboard is made from wood and appears in some furniture. Particleboard or chipboard, made from pieces of wood embedded in resin, is veneered or covered with plastic to make much modern furniture. Most of these modern materials give us large panels of even character and density, with a regular thickness and mostly no tendency to warp or shrink. All this is fine and a mark of progress, but you must come back to wood, and wood only, if a reproduction is to have the mark of authenticity.

How true to the original a piece is to be depends on the maker. An enthusiast will not be satisfied with anything except a piece of craftsmanship made of exactly the same materials as the original. This means using the same woods and building them up to width where necessary. It also means choosing an animal glue instead of a modern synthetic one, and cutting any nails instead of buying machine-made ones. Another maker might decide to keep the general appearance correct, but for a back and a drawer bottom he chooses plywood. Is he doing wrong? If he is making something to please himself and to use in his own home, he is at liberty to make the item of any material he wishes. If he is commissioned to make a reproduction for display or sale, he is doing wrong, unless the other party agrees to the divergence from the original design.

The would-be reproducer of old furniture might come up against a problem of supply. It might not be possible to get a particular wood, or the wood might not be available in the sizes wanted. Fortunately, searching will usually produce what is wanted, even if the local lumberyard says it is impossible. Old and discarded furniture often will produce boards that can be used again. Although the piece of furniture that appeals to you might be made of a particular wood that now proves to be impossible to get, you might be able to use another wood without losing authenticity, if it is of a type that would have been available. Obviously, some exotic wood from Africa would not do, but another native wood should be acceptable. A carpenter in another part of the country or just a few miles away might have used a very different wood for a similar thing.

Akin to the choice of woods is the choice of tools. Tool details are given elsewhere, but there are some general considerations. How much mechanization did the original craftsman have? This depends on the date. When most settlers left Europe, some logs were converted to boards with pit saws, but there were frame saws powered by water wheels or horses. There were no planers and thicknessers. There might have been some rather crude drilling machines. There were certainly lathes producing good work, powered by water, treadle, or an assistant turning a wheel. At first, the American cabinetmaker only had the tools he brought with him. His methods had to revert to a century or so earlier than the methods being used in Europe. This meant splitting wood instead of cutting boards. Early conversion of wood was crude, but pits saws and water-powered frame saws were not long in coming into use.

A modern woodworker need not hesitate to use power to cut and plane wood, but he must then remove all signs of this preparatory work. Although craftsmen showed considerable skill in making furniture entirely by hand, there could not be the machinelike precision possible with modern equipment. In any case, a board might not have come up to size all over, and an inaccurate part might have been arranged where it was usually hidden. This means that reproduction work is better for not being perfect, particularly in things like regular thickness or the perfection of a surface that is now fairly easy with power planing and sanding, but might not have been attained with the original hand methods.

This impreciseness does not apply to things like dovetail joints. The old-time craftsman took a pride in his joints. He aimed at perfection there, and usually achieved it, even if wood flatness and thickness showed variations.

WOOD CONVERSION

There are several ways of converting a log to useful pieces of wood in the form of boards, whether the cutting is done with a pit saw by handwork, with a saw frame powered by water, horses, or steam, or in a modern sawmill. The simplest cuts are parallel and described as plain sawing or *through and through*. There might be flat surfaces cut top and bottom for ease in controlling the log, but otherwise the log is cut into a number of parallel slabs (FIG. 1-2A). The pattern of grain across the boards varies according to their distance from the center of the log, and affects both appearance and stability of the cut wood.

With wood that gets its beauty from the pattern of the grain, the boards farther from the center can be expected to have a better surface appearance. Against that is the risk of warping and twisting. Sap in the tree must be dried out by seasoning. The wood will shrink during this process, but not uniformly. Shrinking is more in the direction of the lines of grain in end view than across them in side view. This means that a board cut radially will become a little thinner, but is unlikely to distort (FIG. 1-2B). A board farther out shows grain lines becoming increasingly near parallel to a surface. A convenient way to consider the effect of shrinkage in this case is to think of the grain lines trying to straighten (FIG. 1-2C). In some woods that have been carefully seasoned, the amount of distortion is slight and can be corrected by planing, but in other cases the warping might be enough to make the board useless for anything except narrow strips.

Grain in the length of a log is not parallel even if the log is a fairly uniform cylinder. A new layer of grain is formed with each year of growth and this is affected by weather conditions, swaying of the tree, and soil conditions. This lack of mechanical uniformity provides much of the beauty of wood, but it means that its characteristics can vary along a board, so different degrees of shrinkage can cause warping and twisting.

Some woods are most attractive when they show what is often described as *figuring*, or *silver grain*. This marking comes from medullary rays, which radiate from the center of the tree. The rays occur in all trees, but they are not usually visible to the unaided eye. In some woods they appear as attractive markings across the normal grain lines if a board is cut parallel with them. This is called *quarter sawing*. To get exact radial cuts, you would be wasteful (FIG. 1-2D). Fortunately, the silver grain will still show in boards that are not truly radial, so it is possible to cut more economically and still get a majority of boards that show some silver grain.

One way is to first cut the log into 90-degree quadrants (FIG. 1-2E) and cut boards from this with only the center cut truly radial (FIG. 1-2F). Many of the wide boards will then show silver grain. Another way is to take a quarter log and make cuts parallel with one side (FIG. 1-2G). This will produce a few boards with silver grain. Other boards might still have interesting normal grain markings, but no visible silver grain. A way of getting more boards with silver grain is to cut a few boards parallel with the side of a quadrant, then turn what is left to make a few more cuts parallel with the other side (FIG. 1-2H). These boards will be narrower, but should have silver grain markings on their surfaces.

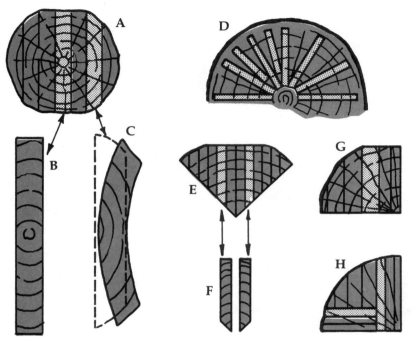

Fig. 1-2. A log cut across (A) produces boards that keep their shape (B) if cut from the center. These boards might warp if cut farther out (C). Cutting the boards radially (D) avoids warping, but is wasteful. Alternative ways (E-H) give many boards cut near the radius.

Even with woods that do not show silver grain, quarter sawing will produce boards with less risk of warping.

When buying wood for reproduction furniture, you might need to take the wood as it comes from the lumberyard. It is unlikely that you will be able to specify quarter-sawn boards for most woods, but if you examine the yard stock, the lines of grain on the end of a board will show which part of the log section it came from. Even when parallel boards are cut across a log, the ones near the center are the equivalent of quarter-sawn. If you can find pieces where the end grain lines are approximately at right angles to the board surfaces, you will have wood that is unlikely to warp; if it is a type where silver grain can be expected, this is your best chance of seeing it.

If you have the means for power sawing and machine planing, it is often a good policy to obtain wood in larger sections than you need for a particular project; then you can take into account grain direction when you reduce it to the size you want.

SEASONING

The life blood of a tree is its sap, which can be regarded as unwanted moisture in the wood. There is more sap present in the summer and less in the winter. Getting rid of most of the moisture is done by a process called *seasoning*. Trees felled in the winter need less drying, so that is the traditional felling season. The aim of seasoning is to reduce the moisture content to an acceptable level—around 15 percent.

Modern methods of seasoning treat the wood in several ways, but the effect is to remove the excess moisture in quite a short time. Our ancestors used *air drying*, or natural seasoning. If wood is left long enough it will eventually dry, and that is all there is to the process. The length of time necessary is considerable and can run into a great many years. Despite this fact, air drying is still used. Many craftsmen consider the quality of air-dried wood markedly superior to that which has been seasoned by any of the quick methods. Although waiting many years to use wood might seem difficult, once the initial period has been given, the wood can be replenished as some of the first is drawn off for use, and seasoning that way might not be regarded as delay.

A rule of thumb for air drying is "one year for each inch of thickness," but this time must be varied according to experience with particular woods. Most air drying is done in flat stacks with the cut boards separated by battens so air can circulate. There might be a roof to keep off rain and snow, but air must be free to enter all around.

Lumber from a reputable yard can be expected to have been properly seasoned, but it is good policy to buy wood some time ahead of using it, then store it to complete seasoning in the shop atmosphere or in conditions where the finished piece of furniture will be. Furniture used in a centrally heated room tends to dry out to less than the usual seasoned moisture content. This means that, if made as received, there is a risk of shrinking or warping, with possible splits after it has been in use for some time. If the wood is allowed to settle in an equivalent atmosphere before being made into furniture, it should remain more stable in the finished product.

FLAWS

Wood is a natural material. As a tree grows, many things happen to it that affect the boards eventually cut from it. Branches spread from the trunk. At the junction of every branch there is a knot in a board cut past that point. If a tree is growing alone, branches are likely to grow from quite low on the trunk, and knots can be expected at any point. In a forest, all trees aim to climb upward ahead of competitors to get the maximum benefit from the sun. This means a forest tree can be expected to have a longer and straighter trunk, and branches will only occur much higher. Some of the greater forest trees yield boards that are knot-free for considerable lengths. In any case, the tendency to grow branches and therefore produce knots varies between different species of trees.

Knots are not necessarily a bad thing. If the knot is a sound "bound" one that forms a definite part of the wood structure, it can be regarded as a decorative feature. A loose "dead" knot can be identified in most woods by a black outline, even if it is not already free to move. This obviously does not contribute any strength, and boards with dead knots might have a use in an out of the way place, or the knots can be cut around to make smaller parts.

Checks, *splits*, and *shakes* are names given to various cracks in wood. Some cannot be avoided. Checks may open along the grain at the ends of boards during seasoning. Ends often need to be sawn off or narrower pieces cut to avoid the checks, as for boards stored in the shop. Sometimes if you cut across a board, slight checking might start from the new end, but not usually enough to matter.

Shakes occur in the growing tree and usually cannot be detected until it is felled. They are splits resulting from the twisting and bending of the tree. A shake might follow the curve of the grain or radiate from the center. Nothing can be done about it, except to cut around it. Damage to a tree from handling after it is felled can cause a split. Less common are splits because of frost.

Coniferous trees might have *pitch pockets*, which are like shakes, but full of resin. They do not show until the wood is cut into boards. They do not have a significant effect on strength, but there is no satisfactory way of obscuring a resin pocket on a finished surface.

In a section of a tree, the *heartwood* near the center is better, stronger and more durable that the *sapwood* around the outside. In some woods, the difference is very marked, both in appearance and in durability. Using the wrong part of the tree for an external construction could mean rot in a few years instead of a reasonably long life. Not all woods are affected in this way. In some of the slower growing hardwoods, there is nothing to choose in characteristics between heartwood and sapwood, so any part of the tree section can be used.

Outside the wood is the bark, which has no furniture use. Any boards with a *waney edge* still holding bark or showing its outline should be trimmed far enough in to remove the obviously weak part immediately under the bark. However, it is interesting to make use of wood that shows uneven outlines or contains flaws. In modern lumber production, boards with shakes, loose knots, and other flaws are discarded. If you can obtain this wood and cut around the problem areas in the way our forefathers did, you can get pieces that might have more interesting grain than the straightforward parts of the tree.

WOOD SPECIES

Wood is available all over the world. Compared with many other things used by man, it is easy to extract from its source and convert to use. It is one of the natural products we use that replenishes itself in a comparatively short time. Things like fossil fuels do not regenerate with a speed to be of use to modern man, with his prolific consumption of these materials, but trees can grow to be of use in a few generations.

The wide distribution of trees in all kinds of situations and climates means that the types available run into thousands worldwide. Even in a comparatively small country like England, the supply and variety of woods was considerable, so woodworkers were able to ply their craft with wood that they did not have to go far to find. Elsewhere in Europe, forests were larger and the available woods were plentiful.

Some of these woods found their way into other countries. Around the time of the first settlements in America, European craftsmen were becoming familiar with woods other than those grown nearby. During Colonial times, exploration was going on in other parts of the world. Commerce was established and there was trade in new woods, particularly from the tropics and Africa. This meant that furniture was beginning to be made from woods previously unknown. Much of this wood was used for the furniture of the great master cabinetmakers.

The immigrant craftsman arrived in America to find trees in great variety and profusion. He could recognize some as being of the same species as those he knew at home, but there were a great many others, which he had to learn and find uses for. England took away large numbers of trees for the masts of her fighting sailing ships, but there seemed an unlimited supply, and there were many species other than those that would make masts. Wood was there, suitable for furniture, implements, house construction, and all the needs of a people setting up a new civilization. It did not take long to discover the woods most suitable for particular purposes, both utilitarian and decorative.

Woods have scientific classifications, and these names are needed for positive identification when two woods seem almost the same. For general identification, however, there are common names, although they vary among communities and users. The pioneer woodworkers who produced the furniture that interests us sometimes used names that were based on woods they had known at home, but were not in fact the same. In some cases the name has stuck—for instance, there are American oaks that would not be recognized as such elsewhere.

Wood is broadly divided into softwoods and hardwoods, which seem clear definitions, except they do not really define relative hardness or softness. Some hardwoods are softer than some softwoods. The names actually indicate the type of tree. Coniferous trees with needles produce softwoods. Hardwoods come from the broad-leafed trees. Most softwood trees are evergreens. Hardwood trees lose their leaves in the winter.

Hardwood and softwood trees can grow in many climates, but the softwoods used for woodworking grow mostly in the northern parts of North America, Europe, and Asia. Hardwoods have a wide distribution. Some of the more attractive ones for cabinetwork are tropical.

Nearly all wood will float in water, but there are exceptions. Lignum vitae and greenheart are very hard and heavy woods that will not float. Even harder is black ironwood (*Krugiodendron ferreum*), which grows in southern Florida and Central America. At the other extreme, another Central American wood is balsa (*Ochroma lagopus*), which is technically a hardwood, but is softer and lighter than most softwoods.

Early settlers in most parts of the country found a variety of hardwoods, and they were mostly used for furniture. Softwoods, however, generally offered easier working conditions, particularly when a man's muscles were the only source of power for his tools, so softwoods were used for many things, particularly when quick results, rather than durability, were important.

Softwoods

White pine. White pine grew plentifully and was used much. The trees grew high, with long straight trunks, so boards of sound wood in long lengths were possible. Such things as benches and tables could be made without waste or the need to cut around flaws. Much of this softwood was used quite thick to compensate for its lesser strength.

Cedar. Cedar, usually described as red, was another plentiful softwood. Types varied according to locality, with Carolina being considered superior to Virginia, which was supposed to be better than New England. Much cedar furniture was made from the New England version of the wood, however, and shipped to other parts of settled America. The aromatic oil that exudes, particularly from the knots, was valued as a moth deterrent in clothes chests.

Pines, firs, and larches. Other softwoods, variously described as pines, firs, and larches, were used when available. Some of them have characteristics and appearances similar to white pine. In reproduction work you might need to accept a softwood that might not be exactly the same as originally used. Swamp cypress (*Taxodium distichum*) with its greasy feel and sour smell has uses where a resistance to heat and moisture is valuable, but not in normal furniture. Douglas fir, sometimes called Columbian pine, Douglas pine, or Oregon pine (*Pseudotsuga taxifolia*) has modern uses in plywood, but its long, straight grain made it more suitable for large structures than for furniture. Scots pine (*Pinus sylvestris*), with many other names, was an alternative to white pine. Spruce (*Picea*) was considered inferior and only of use for rougher work.

Hardwoods

For more durable furniture, the choice had to be a hardwood. The uses of some of the native hardwoods became more specialized than in some furniture made in the Old World, where the tendency was to make a piece of furniture from the same species of wood throughout. In America, woods were chosen for their characteristics, and there might be three or four different woods in one piece of furniture.

The woods available governed what was used in the first instance, but there began to be an interchange of woods overland, and even more from sea transport. As life became more settled and the demand was for better and more fashionable furniture, ships that traded with the West Indies or South America returned with tropical hardwoods that could be made into furniture comparable with some of the best then being made in Europe. The country carpenter and furniture maker was mostly dependent on what grew around him, however, and this varied according to his region, although there was some overlap and some trees grew outside the specified regions.

Northern Region. Ash, aspen, basswood, yellow birch, butternut, cherry, elm, hickory, locust, hard maple, oak, walnut.

Central Region. White ash, basswood, beech, buckeye, chestnut, cottonwood, American elm, hackberry, shagbark hickory, sycamore, yellow poplar, American walnut.

Appalachian Region. Ash, beech, red oak, hard maple, white oak.

Southern Region. Ash, basswood, beech, birch, cottonwood, elm, hackberry, hickory, locust, maple, red oak and cherry-bark oak, pecan, sweet and red gum, sycamore, tupelo gum, black willow.

Some of the woods that were used for Colonial and Early American furniture follow. These are samples only, and those early woodworkers used whatever came to hand.

Ash (*Fraxinus exeelsior*). This is a white/grey wood with a rather coarse straight grain and little tendency to warp. It is tough and fibrous, with a springiness that made if favored for cart shafts and handles of tools like hammers. It could be steamed for bending and used in this way for curved parts of chairs. Common ash is not very durable in exposed conditions, but the species called white ash is better at resisting decay.

Basswood, or linden (*Tilia americana*). A near-white wood from the tulip tree. The softwood shows little grain marking and has few knots. Wide boards were used for chests. It is easily worked and was used for carving. Large boards could be shaped into chair seats.

Beech (*Fagus sylvatica*). This wood is close-grained, stable, and easily worked. It was much used for planes and similar tools. Its color varies between reddish brown and white. It turns well on a lathe and can be steam bent.

Birch (*Betula*). This wood tends to be brittle and can crack; this brown wood makes furniture and its wide boards were used as panels. With a suitable stain it matches mahogany. Does not bend and can split if nailed without predrilling.

Butternut, or white walnut (*Juglans cinerea*). Not a very strong wood, but it is used in furniture, being easily worked.

Cherry (*Prunus*). This fruit wood could not be obtained in very wide boards, but its deep reddish heartwood and pinker sapwood gave it an attractive appearance for making furniture. Age enhances the appearance. Frequent tool sharpening was necessary to get a good finish.

Chestnut (*Castanea sativa*). This is the wood of the sweet chestnut, not the horse chestnut. It looks similar to English oak, but does not have any obvious silver grain when quarter-sawn. Its main use was for structural parts of drawers and cabinets.

Elm (*Ulmus*). Common elm has a confused brown grain with a resistance to splitting. Large trees produced wide boards, many of which were used for chair seats. In addition to furniture, it has uses in wagon building and boat building. Rock elm (*Ulmus thomasi*) and wych elm (*Ulmus glabra*) are straighter grained, hard, strong, and suitable for steam bending.

Hickory (*Carya*). This is a very hard wood suitable for steam bending and used for the bows at the backs of chairs and similar applications. It is a springy wood with very similar characteristics to ash, but with closer, harder and more attractive grain. Hickory had many applications in wagon building, and this demand caused a shortage.

Locust. Another chair seat wood, this very hard wood dries from a tan to a grey/yellow color and is very durable, although it does not take nails readily.

Mahogany. This is a name covering a range of woods not native to Northern America, but it was a popular furniture wood in Europe and supplies came into America by the beginning of the seventeenth century. Spanish or Cuban mahogany (*Swietenia mahogani*) was a rich brown and the well-known furniture wood. Honduras mahogany, or baywood (*Swietenia macrophyela*) was lighter in weight and color, but otherwise similar.

Maple (*Aceraceae*). Varieties are known as rock maple, hard maple, and sugar maple. This is strong and hard with a great many uses in woodworking as well as in many parts of furniture. Some of the twists in a tree produced special grain formations, such as bird's-eye maple, which was used in veneers.

Oak (*Quercus*). The dark brown, open-grained English oak was famous for building fighting sailing ships, also much medieval furniture. It is the oak most suitable for quarter sawing to show silver grain. This, and other oaks, can be cleft or split, so it allowed cleaving with a froe or axe as an alternative to sawing in the length. Red oak (*Quercus rubra*) has similar characteristics, but with a reddish tinge in the color. White oak is another variety. All parts and kinds of furniture have been made of oak. Quarter-sawn oak may be described as *wainscot oak*, from its use in the paneling around a room, or from an earlier German word for a wagon side.

Poplar, or tulip tree (*Liriodendron tulipifera*). This is an even close-grained yellow/white wood, similar to basswood, with which it is sometimes confused.

Sycamore (*Platamus occidentalis*). The white/yellow hardwood is close-grained with ripples often apparent in the grain. It has a clean look and has been used for equipment and furniture associated with food, because of its hygienic appearance. It turns well. "Fiddle-back" markings make it suitable for veneers.

Walnut (*Juglans nigra*). It is a brown/purple close-grained wood that finishes to an attractive surface. This stable wood is easy to work. Outside of America this is "American black walnut" to distinguish it from the lighter colored European walnut.

2

Tools and Techniques

THE MODERN WOODWORKING SHOP, whether its user is amateur or professional, is becoming increasingly mechanized. Electric power is convenient and lends itself to the use of tools that have their own motors. While some tools are fixed, others are portable and take their built-in small motors with them. The overall effect is to take much of the drudgery out of routine tasks and make the performing of accurate and often intricate work comparatively easy. Of course, there is nothing wrong with this and it is a welcome sign of progress in technique, but it leads to a dependence on power. Many modern craftsmen turn to power tools for even the simplest task, so their attitude toward their work is very different from the days when the workman had to provide power with his muscles to make any tool work.

The makers of Colonial and Early American furniture did their work almost entirely by hand. The logs were converted to boards, which were then seasoned before being supplied to the man at the bench. From there on, it was his problem to take a rough-surfaced piece of wood, that might have warped or split, and convert it into furniture by using his hand tools. He had to scheme the best way to cut the parts he needed to avoid flaws and benefit from the way of the grain. He would also be considering how to do this with economy of effort. He was close to the wood he was using and developed an affinity and feel for the different species of wood. He knew from the choice of wood and how it behaved under the first strokes of the plane what its characteristics were and what sort of finish he could expect to get.

Much of this feeling for wood is lacking in modern methods. Someone else has converted the wood and it has been artificially seasoned. Any part with flaws has been discarded long before the wood comes into the hands of the cabinetmaker. So far as it is possible, wood supplied is a substance of uniform size and quality bought by the length. The opportunity to take a piece of wood in its early stages and make use of twisted grain, adapt designs to suit, and arrange construction to feature unusual grain markings is no longer ours. Wood for making furniture is almost as much a factory product as cloth sold by the yard. This is a pity if you want to make reproduction furniture, but it is still possible to produce worthwhile results. If you have an opportunity to obtain wood from an earlier stage in its conversion, getting authentic appearances is that much easier and more interesting.

If you wish, you can go back to those hand methods. This might give you much satisfaction, but what you produce might look no different from a similar thing made by another craftsman who takes advantage of modern power tools, as well as hand tools. The skill comes in using power tools without this being discernable in the finished piece of furniture. Therefore, finishing stages should be by hand. Power tools might lessen the labor of early stages and get parts close to finished sizes, but there should be enough wood left for hand tool work to completely obliterate any evidence of power tools.

POWER TOOLS

It is reasonable in modern furniture making to use a power planer and thicknesser to get wood to size and smooth surfaces, then follow with power sanding. You do not need to have a great experience of examining furniture to see from the wood when it was treated this way. A power planer leaves a good surface, but it is different from the surface left by hand planing. The rotating cutters hitting the surface leave ridges across the wood. With hasty work, they might be very obvious, but with sharp cutters and slowly fed wood, the effect is much smoother, although the discerning eye can detect the method used. Power sanding might obliterate the machine plane marks, but it suffers from being too good for period furniture. The surface is very uniformly smooth, in a way that would be almost impossible to achieve by handwork. Obviously, evidence of these modern methods in a reproduction of a 200-year-old piece of furniture would destroy some of its authenticity and diminish the satisfaction to be got from it by its maker and owner.

If you must bring the available wood to size to suit the cutting list for the furniture being made, you can use a table or other power saw and a power plane to smooth the surfaces, but leave a little for completion by hand planing. In effect, hand planing gets the wood to the stage that the old-time craftsman did with his jack plane, although accuracy is likely to be much greater.

The hand tool to use is a smoothing plane. It need not be a traditional wooden one; a modern metal plane, such as the Stanley 4 or 4 1/2, is suitable. Its purpose is to remove enough of the surface to destroy any evidence of machine planing. If in the process it slightly destroys some of the perfection of machine planing, that is not a fault for this type of work. If you place a straightedge or square across an original article, it is possible to detect how the craftsman was aiming at precision but did not quite make it. This is a feature of work done exclusively by hand— accuracy to a stage that was adequate for the intended purpose was all that was needed. If a surface, such as a quality tabletop, had to be flat to look right, time was spent getting it accurate, but if such quality was not vital in something of less importance, the standard worked to was not as high.

Machine work can get something close to perfection with little effort on the part of the operator. While this is a desirable attribute in much modern cabinetmaking, there are parts of older furniture that did not have such exactness of finish, and perfection in a part of a reproduction that would not have had it in an original could be too obvious evidence of machine work.

You can use various types of power saws. Originally, general sawing was with handsaws, and a backsaw was the general-purpose saw for cutting on the bench. Most woodworkers have a backsaw, but it would be advisable to make more use of it in reproduction work. It is possible to make some of the traditional types of joints with power tools, but the marks left on the wood by a circular saw or a band saw are different from those left by handsawing. In most cases, the sawn edge will get further treatment or be hidden, but if you want to avoid the evidence of the use of power saws, get into the habit of making more use of a backsaw.

HANDWORK

When woodwork was all done by hand, it was customary to plane one surface and one edge at right angles to it and mark them as the *face side* and *face edge*, respectively, with a traditional pencil marking (FIG. 2-1A). Other marking and measuring used these surfaces as data. A try square was always used against one of these faces. If there was to be a saw cut across the grain, the fibers were first severed with a knife (FIG. 2-1B). The knife line was "squared around" all four faces for a cut right through.

Fig. 2-1. The face side and edge are traditionally marked (A). Lines at right angles are marked with a try square and knife (B).

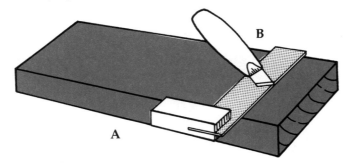

With power tools, this sort of working is not so important, but when working on reproduction furniture, adoption of these methods helps in getting accuracy with the greater use of hand tools, as well as influences your attitude to the work, so you get more of a feeling akin to that of the original craftsman.

Many woods do not yield as smooth a surface as might be required from planing. A power sander might do all that is necessary to finish this smoothly on modern furniture, but the handworking craftsman followed planing by scraping, particularly on parts of hardwood with grain that tore up whichever way it was planed. Quite often, this was an interesting feature included for the sake of appearance. There are hooked scrapers available today and others with the scraper blade-mounted in a body like a plane or spokeshave. Earlier workers had similar tools, but they usually depended on a scraper that was just a rectangular piece of tool steel of the type used in saw blades.

Mastery of such a scraper is a big help in finishing period furniture. The method of sharpening this and the blades mounted in bodies is unusual, but not difficult. The edge of the scraper should be straight and at right angles to the sides (FIG. 2-2A). You can file it but you should rub it smooth on a flat oilstone (FIG. 2-2B). The next step is rubbing with a hard piece of steel, such as a round burnisher (FIG. 2-2C), or with an ordinary gouge or chisel. The object is to turn over the edge, by angling the rubbing a little one way and then the other (FIG. 2-2D). The amount turned over might be quite slight, and felt rather than seen.

To use the scraper, push or pull it over the wood surface at an angle that causes the turned edge to cut (FIG. 2-2E). It is usual to bend the sheet steel scraper slightly so the cutting edge meets the wood at a slight curve. If you push the scraper, hold it at the sides with the thumbs pushing the center forward to a curve (FIG. 2-2F).

You can scrape diagonally to the grain or in any direction that gets good results. Angle the scraper so it removes very thin shavings. If the waste comes away as dust and the angle is right, that is a sign that the edge is blunt. You can restore the edge several times by first rubbing the burr straight, using the burnisher on the flat surfaces (FIG. 2-2G), then turning it over again (FIG. 2-2D). When this no longer works, start sharpening from the beginning again.

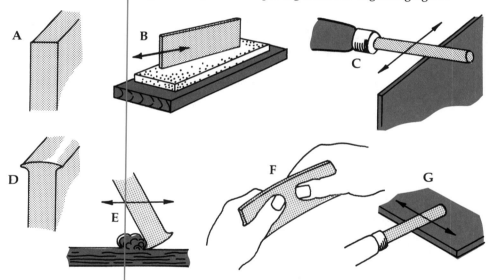

Fig. 2-2. A steel scraper starts with a square edge (A) rubbed on an oilstone (B), then a hard steel burnisher (C) turns over the edges (D) to give a cutting action (E). This is helped by curving the scraper (F). When worn, the edge is rubbed flat with the burnisher (G) and sharpening started again.

SHAPING

Shaped outlines can be cut with a saber saw or a band saw. Originally these shapes were cut with a framed bow saw, keyhole saw, or other narrow handsaw. Because you likely will treat the surface by further tool work, it is improbable that any of the regular and distinctive power sawing surface will remain.

Hand craftsmen smoothed nearly all these outlines with a spokeshave, but this was the wooden type with a low-angled cutter (FIG. 2-3A) and not the higher angled cutter more like a plane in a metal body (FIG. 2-3B). The older type is nicer to use and gives a good finish. Obtain one or more, if possible.

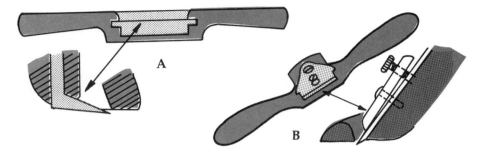

Fig. 2-3. A traditional wooden spokeshave has a low cutting angle (A). A modern one has a higher angle (B), like a plane.

Modern hand shaping is more likely to be done with a filing action, using either a woodworking rasp or a Surform tool. These are acceptable on reproduction work, but be careful to follow with enough sanding to remove all marks they make.

Very little filing of wood was done by hand craftsmen, partly because the craftsman considered wood should be cut and not just rubbed away. Also, the only files and rasps available were rather inefficient tools.

Colonial and Early American furniture requires more chisel work in shaping and making joints than does modern furniture. Modern chisels and gouges cut in the same way as those of 200 years ago, so there is nothing wrong with using them and leaving surfaces from them. You might need more chisels than for modern work, since traditional joints must be cut and cleaned up, with the different constructions involved. Extra chisels worth having are long, thin paring types, preferably with beveled edges, and one or two stout mortise chisels.

A problem comes in the production of grooves, dadoes, and rabbets. Most of us have power tools that make these cuts easily and accurately. If it is a side of a joint into which that part will fit and the method of cutting is not obvious, there is nothing wrong with using a power tool for this work, but if it is something that will be visible, like a rabbet forming part of a decorative edge, the power part of the work should only remove the bulk of the waste. You should finish the job with a rabbet plane, or do scraping and sanding in the recess enough to remove evidence of power cutting.

One of the biggest differences between the tool kit of the Colonial carpenter and the modern woodworker is in the means of making holes. Right up to the Industrial Revolution, the quality and efficiency of hole-making equipment was not as high as the tools available for other woodworking processes. It needed engineering thought and factory methods to produce drills and the means of driving them to make good, clean holes of many sizes and depths. As a result, the smooth cylindrical hole with no flaws that can be produced with an electric drill might be regarded as very desirable in modern furniture production, but if the piece of furniture is supposed to emulate the work of those early immigrant craftsmen, it is too good.

If holes are part of the construction, making part of a joint or being filled with a screw, you need a modern, exact hole. If the hole will be part of the finished work and open to view, do something to roughen and make it slightly inaccurate. Drilling with a center bit in a brace might give a better look than using a rapidly rotating bit in an electric drill. Hand drilling from one side until the point shows through, then turning over and drilling back into it should produce a more authentic appearance.

FINAL APPEARANCE

Abrasives play a large part in modern woodworking. Power sanders of various types do useful work. There were abrasives in the early days, but they were neither plentiful nor good. There was also a different attitude to woodworking craftsmanship. There was a pride in getting a finish from the tools. The surface left from a sharp plane or chisel might be followed by scraping, but in much furniture that was all. Some old furniture that has survived might now have a smooth, mellow sheen, but that is more likely to be the effect of long use and some later owner's application of polish than any original treatment.

Any reproduction should have a good tool finish and any sanding should be by hand and kept to a minimum. Power sanding is best avoided. Early sanding was with sand, and the name has survived, although modern abrasives are many things, but not sand. Powdered glass was also used. There were sheets of abrasive paper with the sand or glass spread on glue, but abrasive powders were also used on a cloth pad, sometimes wet.

Modern hand sanding is best done with abrasive paper wrapped around a block. Traditionally, this was a block of cork, but it can be wood, preferably faced with a piece of stiff rubber or other material with a slightly greater resiliance than wood. Sand *with* the grain, to avoid marks that may show through any finish. Slight rounding of corners is acceptable. Any sanding of end grain should be thorough, but not such that it gives the appearance of power sanding.

It is necessary to decide what final appearance is required. When the things we are considering were first made, the cabinetmaker aimed to give the work as good an appearance as possible. If it has been in use for a century or more, it will have acquired the patina of age; it will show signs of use; it might have evidence of damage; it will have that well-worn appearance we expect.

What do we expect of a reproduction? Do we want to make something comparable to the work as first produced, or do we want to make something that looks old? Only the maker and user can decide. It seems a form of mild cheating to pass off something made now as being old. It is very unlikely to pass scrutiny and be accepted as an old piece of work. Trying to pass a reproduction as a genuine antique could bring trouble with the law.

Nevertheless, many people find furniture with an old appearance attractive, although they know it is of recent construction. Others prefer a reproduction that looks like the original probably did when new. This latter attitude seems to be the preferable one for the maker to adopt.

GLUES, SCREWS, AND NAILS

Coupled with tool work are fastenings and fittings, findings or hardware. The only glue used in the original work was produced from animal bones, hoofs, and sometimes fish. This glue was melted in a two-part glue pot, with water in the outer container and the glue in the inner one, so the glue was never overheated. It was a foul-smelling mixture. If obtained from another supplier and not made by the carpenter, it came in resinlike slabs to be broken up and melted. The glue had a reasonable strength under dry conditions, but would lose its hold when wet. There is, however, much furniture from times earlier than Colonial days still sound and with elaborate veneer decorations undamaged, all secured with this sort of glue.

Such glue is not obsolete, but very nearly so, and getting any might be difficult. There are more recent glues that are basically the same, but more refined so the smell is less objectionable and application is easier. Some can be used direct from the can, but the better ones need moderate heating in hot water. If you wish to make glued joints as near as possible in the same way as the original workers, you will find these glues suitable.

Most modern glues are synthetic and mostly stronger than those earlier types. Some are either water resistant or fully waterproof. These are obviously desirable features, but not consistent with the characteristics that the original craftsman had in his adhesive. In most constructions, however, the glue is not obvious when the work is finished, and the use of a modern glue should not detract from the appearance and effectiveness of the article of furniture. It should produce greater strength. There are some experts who can identify the adhesive from an exposed glue line, so if the work is to pass any scrutiny, it might be better to use a traditional glue in a place like an exposed dovetail corner joint, where fairly extensive glue lines are visible.

Lack of trust in glue and a reluctance to use it can be seen in the way some furniture was designed and assembled so that joints interlocked. Joints were sometimes made with one piece of wood passing through another and then spread by wedging so even without glue the mechanical layout resisted separation. These and other joints are described in the next chapter.

Screws were known, but early ones were without points, and the threads were not as clean as modern ones. They were probably not very plentiful. Consequently, much early woodwork was without screws. Fortunately, the surface appearance was much the same as today, so if you use modern slotted screws (not Phillips heads), they should look right. Steel screws should look sufficiently like the early iron ones. Modern brass screws are yellower than early ones. Bronze screws look more like older brass.

Nails are more of a problem, although it is only the heads that show. Round wire nail have been in use for a long time, but they do not go back further than the Industrial Revolution. Earlier iron nails were individually forged or cut from sheet metal. On the surface, the appearance was a plain rectangle, without any of the pattern seen on some machine-made nails. Such nails are still available from specialist suppliers, but it might be possible to file the heads of other nails to give an acceptable appearance on the surface.

It was only in less important work that nail heads were left on the surface. Otherwise, they were punched below the surface and the hole filled with a stopping. As a result, you can use almost any nail in that reproduction, but a rectangular head punched in leaves a rectangular hole at the surface—not a round one—so it is worthwhile filing a piece of iron to make a punch with a rectangular end to give an authentic look after driving in the nail.

In some cases, nails were forged with decorative heads, which were left standing on the furniture. It is possible to buy reproduction nails for this purpose, but an alternative is to make the joint with any nail, then punch and cover it with a head filed to shape on a short stub and held in with epoxy glue.

Much hardware was wrought iron, made by a local smith. Some copies can be bought. It would be unwise to spoil the work by using modern hardware. Early hinges were rather crude. Most extended over the surface to provide a grip, and often were given decorative outlines. Modern butt hinges to mount in the thickness of the wood came later. Metal handles mostly had flat brass plates filed to a pleasing shape, with wire bails fixed to bolts or other simple arrangements. More elaborate handles were imported.

To avoid metalwork, many handles were of wood, either bars or turned knobs. Examine pictures of period furniture to see the styles made.

There were no mass-production fittings. Where handles or other items of hardware bolted through, nuts were individually made, and not the hexagonal or square patterns standardized today. Shapes were usually only roughly squared.

3

Joints

IT IS IN THE WAY parts of an assembly are joined that cabinetwork made by hand differs most from things made with the help of power tools. Much modern work has quite satisfactory methods of assembly that have been developed to suit techniques appropriate to machines of various sorts. Even today there are different methods of construction between furniture made in factories and that made by individual workers. Factories have large and expensive machines, while the individual craftsman has portable power tools and less advanced shop tools. Even the most basic modern woodworking shop has equipment that the carpenter of 200 years ago would regard as so advanced and sophisticated that he could not comprehend much of it.

Therefore, if you want to make reproductions of early furniture, you should do some rethinking. The original craftsman joined his wooden parts in ways that were suited to his hand tools. Many of the joints also took into account the fact that they had to provide strength and security without such a dependence on glue as is possible today. Dowels were not unknown, but they were made individually and there was no ready supply of quantity-produced ones, so doweling did not play as big a part in construction as it does today. Other joints were cut in the solid wood to serve the same purpose, and the mortise-and-tenon joint was the most common in many situations where a modern assembly would be with dowels.

You might be able to use dowels or power tool joints in some reproduction furniture in places where they would not be apparent, but for most articles of period furniture, choose traditional joints. The original craftsman had to do quite a lot of heavy chopping with chisels and mallet. You can lessen the labor by removing waste with a power drill or other tool, but you will usually need to finish the joint by hand. You can use a circular saw to cut tenons and a band saw to cut the sides of dovetails, then use a router to remove waste from a groove or dado, but what is important is that the finished joint has the same form as it would have done when made entirely by hand.

If you are unfamiliar with traditional handmade joints, you might find it worthwhile to spend some time practicing joints on scrap pieces of wood, before making furniture using these methods. If you make a specimen joint completely by hand, you will appreciate the problems of the original worker. You will also be able to think of ways of using any available power tools to ease the labor of cutting the multiplicity of joints there might be in the cabinetwork being planned.

There is really no virtue in reverting to solely hand methods if a modern power aid can make the work easier and often more accurate. Obviously, it would be wrong to go so far as to alter the visible joints to suit power and get an incorrect appearance. There are some modern versions of older joints that have been adapted to suit power, and the appearance is no longer the same, as will be seen in some examples later.

EDGE JOINTS

One problem in the days before manufactured boards of reasonable width was the making up of narrower pieces to get the size required for such things as tabletops and the backs of cabinets. The width of available boards depends on the size of the tree. Wide boards were probably more generally available 200 years ago than they are now. Care was taken in conversion to keep a board as wide as possible, where today it is more likely to be ripped down to a standard width. Even with the widest boards, edge joints were essential in many cases. Some woods, such as some choice varieties from fruit trees, were no more than 6 inches wide in any case, so widths had to be made up for many pieces of furniture.

The simplest edge-to-edge joint is a glued one. Both edges must be perfect right angles if the surfaces are to finish in the same plane (FIG. 3-1A). The hand worker used a *shooting*, or *shuting*, board to hold the wood and to slide his long trying or shuting plane on (FIG. 3-1B).

If a power planer is available, you can plane edges true with little trouble, but there are some points to watch. A machine-planed surface does not take glue as well as a hand-planed one. Glue gets a grip by entering the pores of the wood, and power planing tends to close many of them. It is advisable to follow power planing of edges to be glued with a skim over of a hand plane.

There is a tendency for edge joints to open at the ends, if they weaken at all. As a guard against this problem, plane edges very slightly hollow, then arrange a bar clamp centrally to press the ends of the joint together (FIG. 3-1C). Other useful devices are *pinch dogs* (FIG. 3-1D), which were used by early carpenters and are still available. Driving one into each end of a joint uses a wedge action to press the boards together (FIG. 3-1E).

So far as possible, arrange boards so they compensate for each other's tendency to warp. If grain lines are through the thickness, there is unlikely to be much movement, but with the curves of grain about the same way as the surfaces of the boards, arranging pieces opposite ways will make any overall warping minimal (FIG. 3-1F).

Although a simple glued joint should have adequate strength for many purposes, there are ways of further stiffening it. You can arrange dowels between the parts (FIG. 3-1G). Groove the dowels to let air and surplus glue ooze out, and make the holes slightly deeper than needed so the dowels do not hit the bottoms before the surfaces are tight.

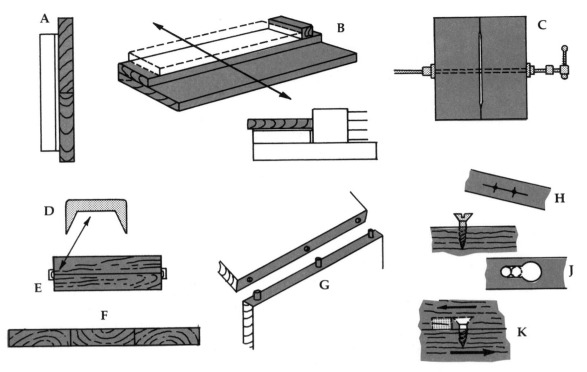

Fig. 3-1. Boards joined to make up width should assemble flat (A). A shuting board (B) helps to guide the plane to get the edges square. Planing edges hollow (C, exaggerated) gets joint ends tight. Dogs (D) are alternatives to clamps to pull joints together (E). Any risk of warping is minimized if grain directions are alternated (F). Dowels strengthen joints (G). Secret slot screwing (H-K) is another way of strengthening and closing joints.

An interesting version of doweling used in early construction was *secret slot screwing*, and this is just as useful today. Drive stout screws at intervals into one edge, until the heads are 1/4 to 3/8 inch above the surface. Mark their positions on the other piece, with additional centers about 1/2 inch away (FIG. 3-1H). Drill holes large enough to clear the heads at these positions, and make a slot from each to the other positions, starting it by drilling a series of holes of a size to clear the neck of each screw (FIG. 3-1J). Make a trial assembly by inserting the screw heads in their mating clearance holes, then drive one board along the other. The screw heads will cut their way along as their necks pass along the slots (FIG. 3-1K). Knock the boards back and dismantle them. Give each screw a tightening quarter turn. Apply glue and knock the joint together again. Tightening the screws will have put on just that little more clamping thrust.

Joints are made today with splines in plowed grooves (FIG. 3-2A). The spline is quite often plywood. If this is used, it would not do for the plywood to be visible in furniture copied from something belonging to the days before plywood. There could be a cross-grained piece of solid wood at each exposed end of the plywood joint.

Similar to this is a tongue-and-groove joint (FIG. 3-2B). Matching planes were used for Early American furniture. Such a joint was glued to make a solid joint, but a variation of it was used to allow for expansion and contraction when many boards had to be used to make a back for something broad, like a hutch. The joints were left without glue, but the ends of the boards were nailed or screwed. The exposed side of the joint was made less severe by working a bead on the edge of one piece and a matching bevel on the other (FIG. 3-2C). The joint could then open and close appreciably and still look attractive.

A

Fig. 3-2. Tongued-and-grooved joints can be close and glued (A,B), or they can be beaded for decoration and assembled dry to allow for expansion and contraction (C).

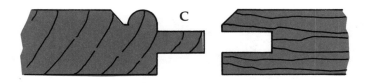

C

B

Matching planes are no longer made, although they might sometimes be found among old tools, but you can make the parts of these joints with power tools. This type of backing to open shelving is necessary and preferable to any sort of more recent flat sheet material if the result is to look authentic.

HALVING JOINTS

When two pieces of wood cross each other at or near the same level, they must be notched into each other in a *halving*, or *half-lap*, joint. The crossing does not need to be at right angles; an example of a diagonal crossing comes in some bottom rails of a rectangular table. The crossing does not need to be within the length of both pieces of wood, but can be at the end of one or at a corner between the two, although there are usually better joints for these situations.

The simplest half-lap joint has two pieces of similar size crossing (FIG. 3-3A), either flat or on edge (FIG. 3-3B) in a *cross lap*. If one meets the other in a T-shape, it is a *middle lap* (FIG. 3-3C). At a corner, it is an *end lap* (FIG. 3-3D). If the pieces are of different thicknesses, a stronger joint will result if you do not cut much from the thinner part (FIG. 3-3E). If there might be a pull on the center part of a middle-lap joint, you can give it a dovetail shape on either one (FIG. 3-3F) or both sides (FIG. 3-3G) to resist the load.

To use the traditional hand-cutting method, prepare the two parts and mark the face surfaces. Mark the width of each piece on the other, using the actual pieces of wood instead of measuring with a rule. Square these lines around the wood with a pencil. Set a marking gauge to half the thickness and use it to mark both sides of both pieces, with its stock against the face side each time. Mark what is to be cut out of each piece (FIG. 3-4A). Where the saw cuts are to come, sever the fibers by going over the pencil lines with a knife. Use a fine backsaw, keeping it on the waste side of the line. For small work, this can usually be done by eye, but for larger work use a chisel to cut a guiding groove inside the knife line (FIG. 3-4B).

After sawing down the side of each groove, remove the waste with a wide chisel, working upward in turn from each side, to get down to the gauge lines (FIG. 3-4C). Then make cuts straight across (FIG. 3-4D).

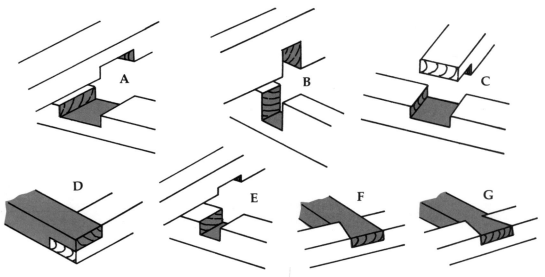

Fig. 3-3. There are many variations on the cross-lap joint in traditional furniture. Basically, half is cut from each crossing piece (A,B), but the joint may come at the end of one piece (C) or at a corner (D). For different sizes (E), the cut is uneven. Dovetail shapes (F,G) will resist pull.

Fig. 3-4. For hand-cutting cross-lap joints, mark the parts (A). Make a chisel slice inside the line (B) to guide the saw. Chisel waste from both sides (C,D). Saw an end (E-H) in stages. A table saw will cut accurately (J).

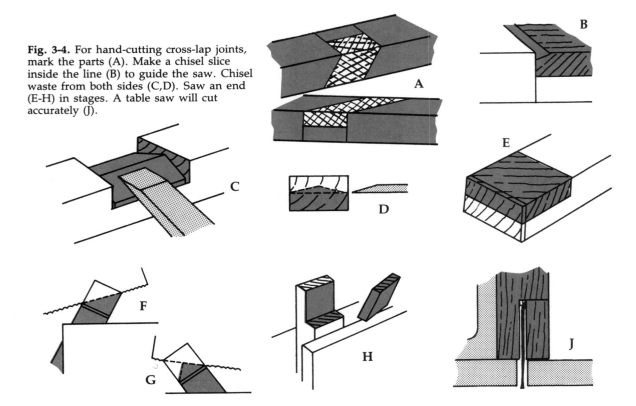

Even when power tools are available, it is probably wisest to mark out in the same way and saw across the grain with a handsaw, but you can use a router to remove the waste. The best joint is a drive fit that finishes level on the face sides. It is better to make the cutout parts very slightly hollow than to have the centers high.

With other cross laps, you can adapt marking out to suit a diagonal crossing or thick and thin pieces, but the method of working is almost the same. With a middle lap, one part has an open end, and with an end lap both parts are open. You can cut both parts completely by sawing. Leave the open-ended piece a little too long and gauge it around the end, as well as on the sides (FIG. 3-4E). Make a cut across at the shoulder. Use three cuts for hand-sawing the other way to ensure you keep to the gauged lines. The first cut is diagonal into one side and the end (FIG. 3-4F). The second cut is diagonal the other way (FIG. 3-4G), and the third one straight through, so the waste piece falls out (FIG. 3-4H).

With a table saw it is possible to make the end grain cut with one pass, using the fence and height adjustment (FIG. 3-4J). If there is a small amount of excess length on the end, you can plane it level after the joint has been glued.

MORTISE-AND-TENON JOINTS

The type of joint having a tongue of one piece projecting into a cavity in another piece has a wider use in traditional furniture than any other joint. The tenon is the projecting piece, and the hole it fits into is a mortise. Some of the applications of the joint have been taken over in modern furniture with dowels, mainly because dowel joints are more adaptable to mechanical production methods.

When there was no good reason for doing otherwise, the mortise in a straightforward joint was made one-third the width of the wood or to the width of the mortise chisel nearest this amount.

In the basic *full* mortise-and-tenon joint between pieces of wood of the same thickness, the tenon goes right through (FIG. 3-5A). If the tenon does not go through, it is a *stub* mortise-and-tenon joint (FIG. 3-5B). If the tenoned part is thinner, it is a *bare-faced* mortise-and-tenon joint (FIG. 3-5C).

If the two pieces meet at a corner and the joint is open, it is more likely to be called a *bridle joint*. Neither this nor the end-lap joint have much place in good-quality cabinetwork. Instead, a *haunched* mortise-and-tenon joint is used. This can be worked in two ways. You can cut the tenon back so a short stub goes into a groove and is visible in the finished joint (FIG. 3-5D). You can use this method when the frame is grooved to take a panel, but otherwise it is better to taper the haunch (FIG. 3-5E).

A full mortise-and-tenon joint might be merely glued, but there are examples where they were wedged. Bevel the ends of the mortise outward slightly. You can use wedges in one of three ways. You can drive them outside the tenon (FIG. 3-5F); you can make saw cuts in the tenon before it is driven, then drive wedges into these cuts (FIG. 3-5G); or if the tenon is near square, you can drive a single wedge into a diagonal saw cut (FIG. 3-5H). In all cases, cut off the ends of the wedges and tenon and plane them level.

To tighten a stub tenon, use *fox-tail wedging*. Make saw cuts in the ends of the tenon and insert wedges (FIG. 3-5J), so as the joint is driven they spread the end of the tenon against the bottom of the mortise (FIG. 3-5K).

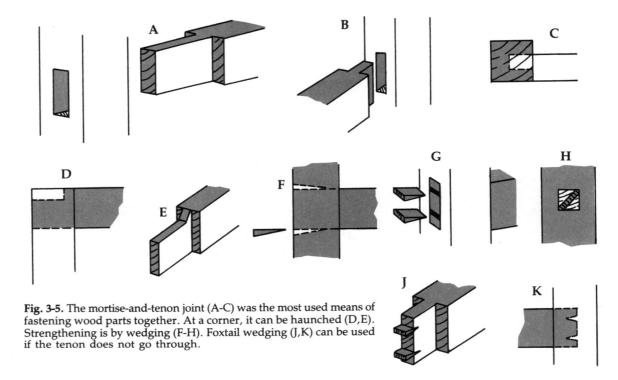

Fig. 3-5. The mortise-and-tenon joint (A-C) was the most used means of fastening wood parts together. At a corner, it can be haunched (D,E). Strengthening is by wedging (F-H). Foxtail wedging (J,K) can be used if the tenon does not go through.

You can adapt mortise-and-tenon joints in many ways. If a wide board is to be tenoned, as with the rail under a tabletop into a leg, you can use two or more full-length tenons, with a short piece between (FIG. 3-6A). If this is not done, so much will be cut from the leg for a wide tenon that it will be weakened. If the rail is thick, rather than wide, two or more tenons alongside each other (FIG. 3-6B) are stronger than one thick one. *Tusk tenons* that go right through and are locked with a key, peg, or wedge (FIG. 3-6C) go back to medieval days and were more

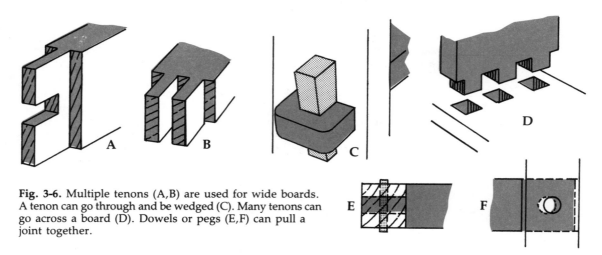

Fig. 3-6. Multiple tenons (A,B) are used for wide boards. A tenon can go through and be wedged (C). Many tenons can go across a board (D). Dowels or pegs (E,F) can pull a joint together.

common in some middle European countries than in Britain, but they are found in some Colonial furniture. If a wide board joins another wide board, one way of joining them is with a series of mortise-and-tenon joints (FIG. 3-6D).

Clamps were not very plentiful nor efficient, and any joint that would pull itself tight without outside aid was welcomed. This is seen in the pinned mortise and tenon, which was used in house construction, as well as furniture. As well as the pin through the joint locking it (FIG. 3-6E), the holes were drilled so the pin pulled the joint tight as it was driven. The wooden pin (*treenail* or *trunnel*) was made overlong and its end tapered. The hole in the tenon was drilled a little nearer the shoulder of that piece than the hole through the mortise (FIG. 3-6F). As the tapered end of the pin entered the inner hole, it pulled the tenon farther into the mortise.

Mark both parts of any mortise-and-tenon joint out from the face sides. A mortise gauge had two pins adjustable in relation to each other, so both lines could be marked in one pass. You can use an ordinary gauge with two settings if a mortise gauge is unavailable. You can allow a little extra length on the end of a full tenon, but you must mark and cut a stub tenon the correct length. Take all marks around both pieces (FIG. 3-7A).

You can cut tenons in the same way as described for the open-ended parts of lap joints, but you will need to make cuts by handsawing on both sides. To ensure accuracy, make lengthwise cuts diagonally before cutting through. You might need to do some paring with a chisel, but be careful not to take off too much. Pay particular attention to the angles between the cross-grain and end-grain cuts—any particles of waste wood there would prevent the joint from closing properly.

You can cut tenons conveniently with a table saw in a similar way to that described for lap joints, but in two passes.

Mortises were chopped out with a thick mortise chisel and a mallet. It is more convenient today to drill out much of the waste and leave chisel work to the final cuts. The drill should be slightly smaller in diameter than the width of the mortise. Drill as many holes as can conveniently be fitted in the length (FIG. 3-7B). Drill from both sides of a through mortise to minimize the risk of splintering or breaking out. Leave some wood to be removed by chisel at the end-grain parts of the mortise.

Remove waste wood with a chisel no wider than the mortise, chopping between the holes and levering chips out, but be careful not to damage the wood that will show outside the joint. Work from both sides of a through mortise. If necessary, use a wider chisel to trim the sides of the opening. Do not trim the ends of the mortise until all other parts are finished, then pare vertically to remove the final waste (FIG. 3-7C).

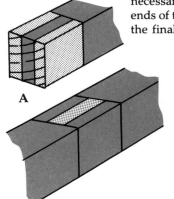

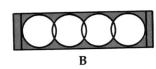

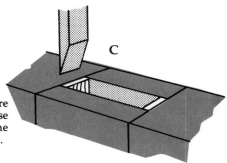

Fig. 3-7. The mortise and tenon are marked to match (A). Some mortise waste can be drilled (B), then the shape finished with a chisel (C).

The traditional craftsman always made a point of not making a trial assembly. He argued that this would wear the joint loose. He preferred to trust his skill in getting it right first time. He had a point, but if you have less experience, you can test a joint at least partway before applying glue and driving it together.

Haunches are a simple matter of sawing, but if a mortise is to be made near the end of a piece of wood, it is advisable to leave a few inches of spare wood there until after cutting out, to prevent the risk of the short grain breaking through during drilling and chopping with a chisel. Wide tenons might need careful paring with a chisel. The tool particularly intended for this is the low-angled rabbet plane, called a *shoulder plane* from its use in trimming the shoulders of tenons.

SHELF JOINTS

In the simplest construction, the end of a shelf rested on a strip of wood glue, nailed or screwed to the upright part. This might be satisfactory in the reproduction of a primitive block of shelves. For better construction the shelf was grooved into the upright, in what is now usually called a *dado joint*, but the original craftsman probably called it by the English name of *housing joint*.

In its simplest form, a dado joint features a groove across the upright as wide as the thickness of the shelf and deep enough to support it without weakening the other part (FIG. 3-8A). For extra strength, there can be a strip of wood underneath (FIG. 3-8B). Where fastenings through the end will spoil appearances, drive nails or screws diagonally from below (FIG. 3-8C). This *through dado*, or housing, *joint* might not be considered pleasing at the front. For a better appearance, use a *stopped dado* (FIG. 3-8D), with just a short width of the shelf notched around the end of the dado. Another way to improve appearance is to have the shelf wider than the upright (FIG. 3-8E). If both sides of the joint would be visible, you can use a stop dado at the back as well.

A normal dado joint does not offer any resistance to a pull. You can rectify this situation by using a dovetail form. For thick wood, there can be beveling top and bottom (FIG. 3-8F), but for most constructions it will only be on one side, usually the bottom (FIG. 3-8G). A further refinement, needing greater skill but providing maximum tightening, has the dovetail part tapered, so the joint tightens as the shelf is driven in from the back (FIG. 3-8H).

For hand cutting, mark the dado out in a similar way to that described for a half lap, with a chiseled bevel inside the cut lines as a guide for the backsaw, then remove the bulk of the waste with a chisel (FIG. 3-9A). For handsawing a stopped dado, you need to cut away the far end with chisels before sawing. This is done for about 1 inch, carefully paring out to the full width, but leaving a small pad at the end (FIG. 3-9B) to take the inevitable knocks from the end of the saw. This cutaway part enables you to saw the sides of the dado with a limited movement, then chisel the waste out, and trim that pad to size last of all.

Although it is possible to get the bottom of a housing joint flat with a chisel, it is helpful to use a router. This may be the modern power tool of that name, which might cut the dado completely without sawing, if you use guides. The name *router* is, however, also applied to a hand tool, with a projecting cutter to level the bottom of the groove. Metal versions are available, but it is interesting to make what those early cabinetmakers called an *old woman's tooth plane*. It is just a piece of wood with a hole to take a chisel held by a wedge (FIG. 3-9C). It can be used in a dovetail dado by turning to cut at an angle under the overhang.

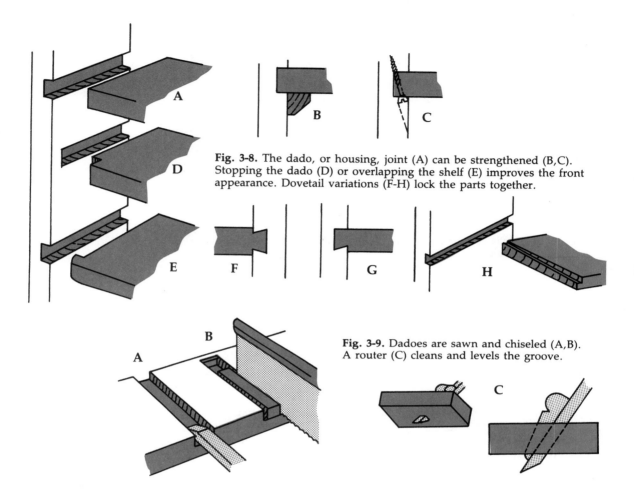

Fig. 3-8. The dado, or housing, joint (A) can be strengthened (B,C). Stopping the dado (D) or overlapping the shelf (E) improves the front appearance. Dovetail variations (F-H) lock the parts together.

Fig. 3-9. Dadoes are sawn and chiseled (A,B). A router (C) cleans and levels the groove.

DOVETAIL JOINTS

Handmade dovetail joints were the pride of the old-time cabinetmaker, from before the days of settlement in America. The ability to make neat and accurate dovetails indicated mastery of the cabinetmaking craft. Sometimes the joints were made unnecessarily complicated and difficult, probably to show off skill. Exposed dovetail joints have become a feature of some types of furniture. In others, they can still be seen, although not on the more exposed surfaces. Others were completely hidden in the finished work, but the craftsman who took a pride in his work put them there knowing they were the strongest way to make the joint, although only he knew at the end that they were there.

In a simple through dovetail joint, the *tail* is the part that is shaped and the projections each side of the sockets are *pins*. In the simplest form, two strips are joined with a single dovetail at a corner (FIG. 3-10A). The angle of the side of a dovetail was probably found by experience, but the angle of old work is about 1 in 8 (FIG. 3-10B) in hardwood and broadened to about 1 in 6 maximum for softwood (FIG. 3-10C).

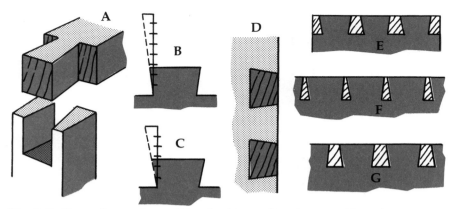

Fig. 3-10. Dovetails are the traditional cabinetmaking joints, with angles to suit the wood (A-C). Mechanical dovetails have the pins and tails the same size (D), but hand-cut dovetails have narrow pins (E-G).

Glue strength is poor on end grain and very much better on side grain. The only places where side grain meets side grain are between the sides of the tails and pins, so they are where the greatest strength is. This means that in joining wide boards, a joint made with a large number of dovetails will have more side glue area and be stronger than one with fewer. Obviously there are practical considerations, but if old work is seen with a great many dovetails on something like a drawer side, they were there for strength and not just to show the skill of the cabinetmaker.

Dovetails were cut entirely by hand. There is no modern way that you can make similar dovetails throughout with power tools. It is possible to make dovetails by machine and there is a device that can be powered by an electric drill. These are perfectly satisfactory dovetails for modern work, but unfortunately they have one feature that would make them look wrong in reproduction work. Machine-made dovetail joints have the pins and tails the same width (FIG. 3-10D). A hand craftsman does not make them that way and never did. The pins are always narrower than the tails (FIG. 3-10E). How much narrower depends on the particular worker, but there was a phase when dovetail joints in the higher class work were made with pins that had sides almost meeting at a point (FIG. 3-10F). There seemed no good reason for this and the joints were difficult to cut, so they only showed off skill. They could not have been as strong as slightly wider pins. In reproduction work, then, it is better to have moderately narrow pins, perhaps about one-quarter the width of the tails (FIG. 3-10G), unless the original in one had minimal width pins and truth in the copy is desired.

If you join wide boards with dovetails, it is usual to keep the tails and pins a uniform size, which means experimenting to get sizes that will divide into the width (FIG. 3-11A), but some work has narrower tails toward the edges of the boards (FIG. 3-11B), a tail of a special width to accept a groove (FIG. 3-11C), or a half tail at a bottom to hide an insert (FIG. 3-11D).

In many parts of furniture, the joint has to be a *stopped*, or *half-blind*, dovetail, in which the ends of the tails are hidden. It can be thought of as a through dovetail with a flap extension. It is a common joint on a drawer front (FIG. 3-11E). Pulling out a drawer of an old piece of furniture will usually show stopped dovetails at the front and through dovetails at the back. Half tails will usually be found to cover where the drawer bottom is fitted.

The other cabinetmaking dovetail joint is a *blind*, or miter, joint. Externally the joint shows a miter, with no pins or tails visible since the dovetailed part is enclosed by extensions that meet each other when the joint closes (FIG. 3-11F). This is a difficult joint to cut because there is not much scope for sawing and most of the shaping must be done by careful work with chisels.

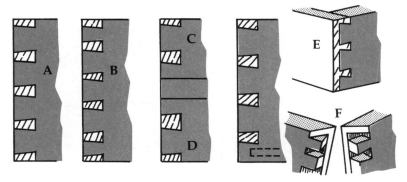

Fig. 3-11. Dovetails can be even (A), narrow at the edges (B), or spaced to suit other joints (C,D). Special dovetails can be hidden one (E) or both ways (F).

To make a simple through dovetail joint with a few pins, mark the parts to length, but cut them with a little waste left on the ends. This should not be much or it might make cutting difficult, but if you leave less than 1/16 inch, you can plane the ends level after you assemble the joint. You can mark the angles of the dovetails with an adjustable bevel, or make a piece of sheet metal into a template (FIG. 3-12A). You also can make a wooden template with plywood (FIG. 3-12B). Mark the width of each piece on the other and square these marks around (FIG. 3-12C). Divide the dovetail part suitably and mark all the dovetails. It might be helpful to pencil on the parts that need to be cut away (FIG. 3-12D).

Fig. 3-12. Templates help with making dovetail angles (A,B). The dovetails can be marked before the pins (C,D), the waste sawn and chiseled out (E,F), then the pins marked (G), and some waste sawn (H).

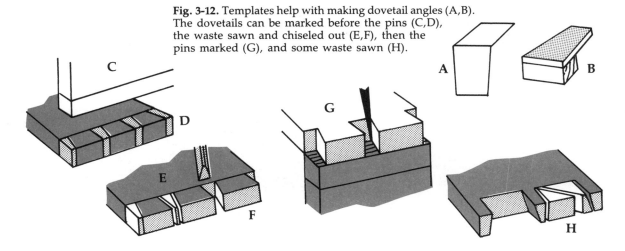

Saw down the sides of the tails, keeping the saw kerf on the waste side of the line. You can do this step by hand with the wood held in a vise, or you can use a band saw. You can remove some of the waste by other cuts (FIG. 3-12E), but you must chop out the rest of the waste with a bevel-edge chisel. Chop out a little at a time from each side, getting both sides cut almost back to the line before hand-paring with the chisel just to the line (FIG. 3-12F). Be careful not to leave the center of the wood higher than the outside. Also remember not to cut into the tapers of the pins.

Put the dovetail part in position over the other piece. Use the lines marking the insides of the joint as guides. With a finely sharpened pencil or a scratch awl, mark each side of the dovetails (FIG. 3-12G). Square these marks down the sides of the wood. Pencil on the waste parts and saw by hand on the waste sides of the lines.

You can remove some of the waste by sawing, but if you use a band saw, have the wood with the narrow sides of the openings upward to reduce the risk of cutting into the pins (FIG. 3-12H).

Some cabinetmakers prefer to work the other way around and mark the dovetail shapes on the end of the piece that will have the pins. They saw and chisel this piece, then use it to mark the dovetail piece. Working this way gives wider openings to mark through and would be advisable if the work has extremely narrow pins, but for most work it is probably better to cut dovetails first.

A skilled man trusts his craftsmanship and does not make a trial assembly, but applies glue and drives the joint together, preferably with a strip of wood to spread the pressure of mallet or clamp.

If several joints must be the same, as they would at the four corners of a chest, it is possible to get them all the same by marking out on one piece only at first. Mark lengths and thicknesses of wood for all corners, but you can hold two pieces together and cut the sides of the dovetails using the markings on the front piece only. If you turn the second piece end for end and put the other end behind the first, you can saw its dovetails by using the saw through the first cuts. You can do the same with the fourth corner. Do further work on each joint separately.

For a stopped dovetail joint, make the part with the dovetails first. In this case, cut it to exact length. Mark on it the amount it overlaps the other piece (FIG. 3-13A). You can leave a slight extra piece of waste on that piece to be planed level later. Mark the shapes of the dovetails on it and square them down the surface, penciling on with waste parts (FIG. 3-13B). It is possible to saw only a small amount (FIG. 3-13C). Be careful not to saw too far on either surface. You can remove some of the waste with a chisel used at the same angle as the sawing (FIG. 3-13D).

You must cut out further waste with chisels, first across the grain to sever the fibers, then along the grain and at the sides of the pins. You need a narrow chisel to tilt for the cross-grain cuts beside the pins, so as not to cut too far into the bottom of the recess.

It is important to remove all waste from the internal angles of the joint. You can bevel the inner edges of the dovetails slightly to reduce the risk of them fouling the bottoms of the cutouts and preventing tight assembly.

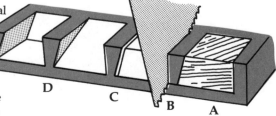

Fig. 3-13. For a partially stopped dado (A), you can mark the area (B), partially saw it (C), then finish with a chisel (D).

OTHER JOINTS

A great many other handmade joints will be found in early furniture, but many of them are adaptions of those just described, and their cutting is obvious.

Nailed joints might not be quite as obvious since they appear on the surface. They were often driven at alternate angles to give a dovetail effect for greater strength (FIG. 3-14A). If a screw head was to be hidden, it was more likely to be counterbored and covered with a wooden plug than to be merely deeply countersunk and covered with stopping because there probably was no satisfactory stopping available. There were no plug cutters for making round wood plugs from similar wood to that being plugged. There might have been hand-cut round plugs, although sometimes the plug was square or diamond shaped in a chiseled hole (FIG. 3-14B).

If several boards were used to make up a width of something to be used in kitchen or wash house, the effects of damp had to be allowed for. Stout battens were put across the underside to prevent warping. To allow for expansion and contraction, however, only the middle screw was through a round hole. All the others were slots (FIG. 3-14C) of increasing length as they got farther from the center on a broad assembly.

For a more important assembly in less damp conditions, the batten was tapered across and driven into a tapered dado slot and its ends trimmed after maximum tightening (FIG. 3-14D). For an even stronger assembly without nails or screws, the batten had a dovetail section (FIG. 3-14E).

Not all assemblies could have battens. One method of resisting warping was a variation of the tongue-and-groove joint (sometimes called a breadboard joint), with the tongue in the end grain of the wide piece mating with a groove in the narrow piece with its grain across (FIG. 3-14F). This joint might be used in a table or cabinet top with a molded edge worked all round.

One corner joint that is fairly common today, but has no place in reproductions of old furniture, is the *combed joint*, with projections from each part fitting between those of the other part, something like straight-sided dovetails. This is a joint for machine production.

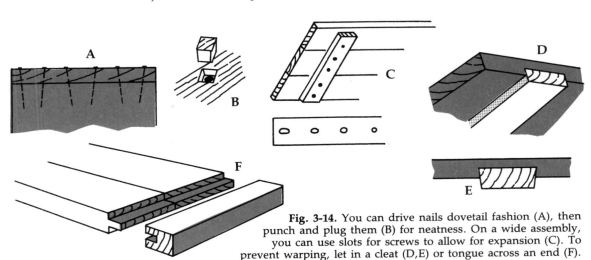

Fig. 3-14. You can drive nails dovetail fashion (A), then punch and plug them (B) for neatness. On a wide assembly, you can use slots for screws to allow for expansion (C). To prevent warping, let in a cleat (D,E) or tongue across an end (F).

Although hinges produced in the earliest Colonial days were crude and usually fitted on the surface, as designs progressed to better quality furniture, the usual hinges were then *butt hinges*. The better ones were solid brass made by extrusion. Cheaper ones were of sheet metal wrapped around the pin. Cabinetmakers had special ways of letting butt hinges into the edges of cabinet doors. Sometimes the parts were let equally and squarely into the door and post (FIG. 3-15A), but more often the two parts were set at an angle. The important consideration, in any case, is the position of the pivot point through the pin. The door must swing clear about this point as it is opened. With the door flush or set back from the post, the hinge was let in at an angle, so the pivot was over the edge of the door and not the post (FIG. 3-15B). The same sort of angled mounting was used when the door overlapped the cabinet side (FIG. 3-15C).

With nothing like plywood and other manufactured boards available, panels had to be solid wood, so designs had to be arranged to allow for panels of reasonable size by building framed structures to enclose them. This produced an attractive appearance, but a solid wood panel of perhaps 12 inches in width might be expected to expand and contract up to 1/4 inch, and this had to be allowed for. With most woods, movement in the length of the grain was negligible, so joints in that direction could be tight. Joints in the width were grooves, made deeper than the panel was expected to go, to permit movement (FIG. 3-15D). No glue was used and the panel edge formed a push fit.

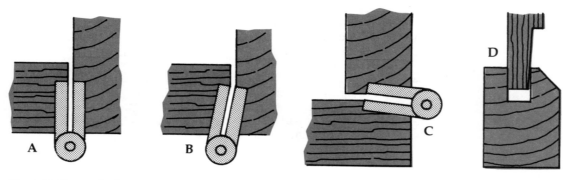

Fig. 3-15. You can let hinges in evenly (A), but many old cabinetmakers angled them (B,C). Panels should not reach the bottoms of plowed grooves so there is space for expansion (D).

4

Special Processes

ALTHOUGH A WOULD-BE maker of reproduction furniture might have a good general knowledge of woodworking using hand and power tools, there are special techniques appropriate to some older furniture that are not so widely practiced today and therefore might not be so well known. This chapter is intended to provide some general instructions as guidance to anyone with a modest woodworking capability. If you need more detailed instructions, there are many complete books on each of the subjects.

The woodworker of a century or more ago, working without the mechanical aids available today, used his general skill to make properly jointed and designed pieces of furniture, which were often sufficient in themselves. He also had some skills and facilities that allowed him to decorate and embellish his work, in ways that were probably ahead of the general woodworking of which he was capable. These techniques were used to show his skill and the fact that he was up to date in his design and thinking. The results are characteristically attractive examples of the work of the period.

Some of these special processes are veneering, carving, turning, and molding. None of them are essential constructionally, but they improve the appearance of the furniture on which they are worked. In a few cases, the process is carried to excess and the thing becomes over ornate by modern standards. In general, however, the added work has been applied with restraint.

VENEERING

A *veneer* is a very thin slice of wood, which has to be glued to a solid backing. Veneers have been cut in many ways. Some cut by saw were comparatively thick—as much as 1/8 inch. Others cut by knife are much thinner—1/25 inch or 1 millimeter. Some veneers are cut on a sort of lathe, with a broad knife slicing off a layer around the circumference of a log. It is this type that has made the production of plywood possible. Examination of the surface of a piece of plywood will show a grain pattern that comes from the wood being cut that way. Other knife-cut veneers are cut across the wood, so the width of the veneer is limited by the width of the board. It is this last type that was, and still is, used mainly for applying to furniture.

Veneers can be cut from woods that are also used in solid form, but they are also cut from woods with attractive grain markings that would be unsuitable for solid construction. Veneers also make possible the cutting through many times of a decorative curl or other feature of the grain, so it can be applied many times to furniture, where it could only be featured once if the wood had been used solid.

Veneering as sometimes practiced today differs in several ways from the traditional methods, which should be used on reproduction furniture. The ground is often plywood. For modern work, this is a good choice, but it would be inappropriate in a copy of piece of Colonial furniture, except possibly in a situation where there would be no evidence in the finished work that plywood had been used.

There is also the choice of glue. Much modern work is done with impact adhesive, which was not available for the original furniture and is considered to have some drawbacks by experts.

Traditional veneering is now sometimes described as *hammer veneering* because the principal tool used is called a *veneer hammer*, although it is not a hammer of the type that is swung. Some veneer hammers look like ordinary hammers with a wooden handle and a round head at one side, which is actually used as a second handle, and a very broad cross peen at the other side. This cross peen is thin and rounded, and can be up to 4 inches wide (FIG. 4-1A). It is more usual to have a veneer hammer made of wood with a brass or aluminum face, which is about 1/8 inch thick and up to 4 inches long, set in a hardwood stock with a handle wedged to it (FIG. 4-1B). This is preferable to the iron hammer because iron will react with the tannic acid in some woods and cause staining. In any case, the lower edge should be straight and smoothly rounded, with any sharpness at the ends taken off.

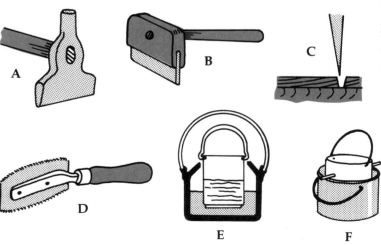

Fig. 4-1. A veneer hammer (A,B) is used to press veneer down. A knife leaves an angled edge (C), but a veneer saw (D) cuts squarely. Hot glue is prepared in a double container (E,F).

Veneer can be cut with a knife, and for many purposes this is the tool to use, drawn along a steel straightedge for straight cuts. However, even with a thin razorlike section to the knife, the edge left on the veneer will be slightly beveled (FIG. 4-1C). In some cases this does not matter, but if you want an upright cut, it is better to use a saw. This is made in several versions, but the important part is a thin saw blade about 3 inches long, with very fine teeth without set. Usually the edge is curved in its length. The saw may be double-edged. One convenient version has a handle attached to a cranked tang, so you can keep your hand from any guiding board and can reverse the tool (FIG. 4-1D). Some of these saws are made with the edge thinned to a knife edge, which defeats the object of having a saw and leaves beveled edges. That type is best avoided.

There are no other special tools. Use a low-angle block plane for trimming off excess veneer at edges, and a hand scraper to finish surfaces, particularly to remove glue or paper there.

Used animal or fish glue, sometimes described as *hide glue*. Suitable glue is available in sheets, which have to be broken into small pieces with a hammer, or in pearls, which are small grains or balls ready for melting.

Since the glue is all-important in veneering, care is needed in its preparation and use. Soften new glue by soaking in water. Then pour off the excess water and put the glue into the inner container of a double glue pot.

There are double glue pots with electrical heaters thermostatically controlled. Other simpler types stand over a gas flame, or even a fire (FIG. 4-1E). It is even possible to do a limited amount of work with an arrangement of two cans of different sizes, with wire handles (FIG. 4-1F). The important thing is to keep the inner container surrounded by water so the glue itself does not boil or burn.

When the glue is melted, you might need to add water. You can stir the mixture with a piece of wood. The right consistency is found by experience. It should flow from a brush, but not like water—more like honey or syrup. The consistency will vary during prolonged use and heating, so do not assume that if it is right on one occasion, it will still be the same an hour later. Long heating causes evaporation of the water, so you might need to add more.

If possible, use a brush for the glue that does not have any metal in the mounting of the bristles, then you won't risk staining some woods.

Like other glued work, it is the edges that are most likely to come away. Veneers, as supplied, tend to curl if they are not kept in a press or under weights. If you glue veneer in place with its concave side downward, its natural tendency to curl will help to keep the edges pressed down. If the new dry veneer is remaining flat, you can moisten both sides to see which way it tries to curl.

Some veneered work is arranged as a pattern. This was called *marquetry* and much of it was geometric in form, with beauty coming from the use of grain patterns to get effects. The name now seems to be applied more to the use of veneers to build up a picture, using the color and grain of different woods for pictorial effects. Much of either form of marquetry can call for a considerable amount of patience in fitting the parts closely. Practice work for furniture should be in covering surfaces and edges with single pieces or very simple patterns. This is what was done, in any case, on much veneered Colonial and Early American furniture.

Although veneering is normally done on surfaces first, with edges following, the technique is best understood by dealing with an edge. Cut a strip of veneer slightly wider than the edge to be covered. Do not make it very much wider, or the excess glue exposed to the air will dry quicker and might cause the veneer to curl away. Cut the strip with a knife along a steel straightedge, or use the veneer saw with a piece of wood as a guide.

Hot glue is not very sticky, but as it cools its stickiness increases, until it sets when it is cold. The greatest strength takes about 24 hours to build up. You need to work fast while the glue is still liquid. It is possible to soften the glue again with heat, if necessary. With an edge, however, reheating should not be necessary.

Apply glue to the edge first. Some workers then put the strip of veneer on the edge face side down, quickly apply glue to the surface, turn it over quickly, and press down with the hammer. The advantage claimed is that the glue picked up helps the hammer slide easily. The alternative is to put the strip face down on some paper and apply glue there, so the face side remains dry. Hold the hammer with its rounded edge straight down and draw it along with good pressure to squeeze the glued surfaces together and force out any air bubbles or excess glue (FIG. 4-2A). A straight pull with the pressure from one hand is probably all that is needed on an edge. Some workers prefer to push, but so long as the pressure is there, the direction does not matter.

If the glue gets too cold before the veneer is positioned, you can apply heat with an electric domestic iron. Ideally, you should keep an old one for the purpose or try to find an old flat iron, to be heated over a flame or on a hotplate. Rub the iron over the veneer to transfer heat and quickly follow with the veneer hammer.

You can remove some of the excess veneer and glue from the edge with a knife. Be careful not to use the knife in a way that would lift unsupported veneer. Dipping the knife in hot water helps it clear excess glue without becoming coated with glue. Leave trimming to exact size until the job has stood for 24 hours, then treat the edge with a sharp block plane, angled so cuts are toward the solid wood (FIg. 4-2B) to reduce the risk of grain breaking out.

If you are veneering plywood, it is advisable to let veneer grain and top ply grain cross at an angle (FIG. 4-2C). The crossing need not be at right angles. If you are veneering particleboard, there is no grain, so any direction is possible. Veneer laid with the grain in the same direction as plywood might develop cracks later. If the ground is solid wood, it is better to lay the veneer with its grain in the same direction as that below it (FIG. 4-2D). Expansion and contraction of the two layers are then likely to match. If the ground wood is thick, it should resist any tendency to warp caused by adding the veneer. If it is thin and unsupported over a large area, you should veneer the opposite side as well, so any stresses set up by gluing are balanced and the wood will not pull out of shape.

Veneering a surface follows the same sequence as described for an edge. Moisten the veneer and coat both the ground and it with glue. Position the veneer by laying it with a curving action from one end (FIG. 4-2E). Use the hammer with a zigzag action and plenty of pressure near the center (FIG. 4-2F). The way the veneer is laid will reduce trapped air to a minimum, but the first work is to get any air out at the edges by working from the middle. Keep the hammer close to a right angle to the grain at all times.

Not much can be rubbed down with the hammer before the glue gets too cool. Iron over a part to soften the glue, then work over the same part with the veneer hammer and plenty of weight. Reheat an adjoining part and move on to that. Let heated and worked parts overlap and progress toward the edges. Air and excess glue might be persuaded to progress to and escape from the edges.

If the veneer is not wide enough to cover the ground in one piece or there is to be a pattern made up of adjoining parts, it is best to cut the meeting edges in position. Lay one piece then the other with about a 1/2-inch overlap (FIG.4-2G). Cut the two pieces through together. Tilt the saw and its guide board slightly to allow for the amount of wood removed by the thickness of the saw (FIG. 4-2H). If necessary, reheat the work so you can remove the waste piece on top, then lift the top veneer to remove the waste piece underneath. More reheating and work with the hammer should make the pieces lay down with a very close joint. It might help to put a strip of paper along the joint until the glue has set. Use the ordinary glue, or a piece of self-adhesive masking tape to stick down the paper. You can remove paper and excess glue by scraping.

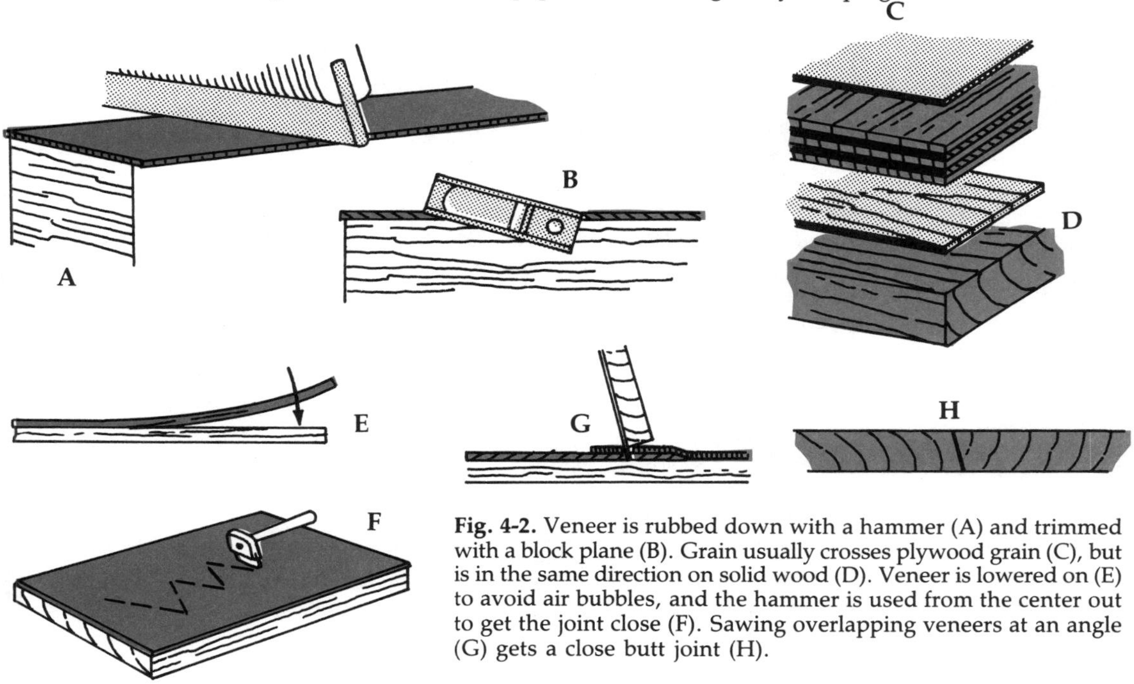

Fig. 4-2. Veneer is rubbed down with a hammer (A) and trimmed with a block plane (B). Grain usually crosses plywood grain (C), but is in the same direction on solid wood (D). Veneer is lowered on (E) to avoid air bubbles, and the hammer is used from the center out to get the joint close (F). Sawing overlapping veneers at an angle (G) gets a close butt joint (H).

Some of the more attractive grain in a veneer has a considerable tendency to twist and curl. Getting this sort of veneer to lay flat might be difficult with the hammer only. You might need to put the veneer under pressure until the glue has had a day to set. If it can be clamped, put stout paper over the surface, with a stiff board above, and clamp that. The alternative is to put weights over the board.

If you have finished the work and found an area where the glue is not holding, reheat it and use the hammer over the affected part. If there is an air bubble and you cannot persuade it to come out through the pores of the wood, a short cut along the grain will let the air out and not show after the veneer has been stuck down.

If you intend to veneer a board on the surface as well as its edges, do the surface completely first, including leaving it to harden and trimming the edges. Follow by veneering the edges as a separate operation.

Veneering is sometimes done with the grain the narrow way. Examples will be seen where the edges have the grain lines across. A surface might have the central panel surrounded by a frame with the grain directed toward the center and mitered corners. The method of laying and trimming adjoining pieces is as described, but care is needed in the use of the hammer, which should be as near as possible to a right angle to the grain it is covering for most of its work, otherwise the fibers might be stretched across the grain. If the veneer does not crack during laying, it might open later as a result of the cross-grain stresses.

CARVING

Carving as a means of decoration or artistic expression in wood is a craft that goes back a long way. The work can range from a few cuts in an otherwise plain piece of work to intricate figures, foliage, and three-dimensional work in which the carving is more important than the structure it is a part of. Many Early American furniture makers used carving to add style and decoration to things that were otherwise purely functional. If they had artistic ability, they were able to cut representations of animals, leaves, and similar things in lifelike form, but in most cases the practical ability was there, but the craftsman was not an artist. In that case, he followed an existing pattern by someone else or, more often, used formalized and geometric designs. Properly applied, these can be quite effective.

In the Old World, wood carving and wood turning were specialized crafts, with enough work available to keep men occupied exercising their particular skills on furniture that was otherwise made and completed by a cabinetmaker. The cabinetmaker usually had some knowledge and facility for carving and turning, but it was not until he emigrated that he was called on to see production right through with his own hands. This meant that the earlier American furniture makers might have been feeling their way with carving, which was limited by the few special tools available. Wood-carving tools are mostly gouges and chisels, but their variety ran into hundreds, particularly in Victorian times, when many pieces of furniture were expected to be carved all over.

Much of the carving by early cabinetmakers was done with the tools used for cutting joints and other general woodworking. This usually meant a few chisels of various widths, very few gouges, and maybe a few knives. Because the tools were mostly bigger than the usual carving tools, carved work was either bold or limited to simple cuts.

Some of the simple cuts were in patterns now often called *chip carving*. This is based on triangles, which can be made entirely with a chisel, aided by a pointed knife. In the basic cuts, a triangle is penciled and the chisel pressed in two sides, angled toward the corner where they meet (FIG. 4-3A). The chisel is pared from the other side to the point (FIG. 4-3B). The corner must be a right angle for the usual square-ended chisel to be used; otherwise, the chisel end can be sharpened askew or the final cut made with a knife, if the angle is more acute than a right angle. In any case, the point of a knife might be needed to clear the corner. These triangles are built into a pattern in many ways. A series in alternate directions makes a border (FIG. 4-3C), where the effect comes from shadows cast by diagonal light.

A further step is to let three triangles meet, sinking to a point at the meeting corners. The shape is drawn and a knife used to cut along the lines from the center outward (FIG. 4-3D). A chisel pares each triangle toward the center, progressively getting deeper (FIG. 4-3E).

The shapes do not have to be all straight lines. You can build up a simple pattern from straight-sided meeting triangles (FIG. 4-3F), then curve the outside edges to a fan pattern (FIG. 4-3G) or with a concave curve at corner (FIG. 4-3H). Old furniture will show a variety of patterns that were cut in this way, with only simple tools.

It is unnecessary to obtain an elaborate collection of carving tools to work on most reproduction furniture. Only later examples that were based on European originals at the time of great popularity of carving, would call for a profusion of carving tools to make properly. Modern makers of carving tools have limited their range considerably, so if you want to buy new tools, you can obtain only the most popular shapes.

Carving tools are made like common firmer gouges and chisels, but rather lighter. Wooden handles with metal ferrules are preferred to plastic. The tool has a tang into the handle and a bolster to press against and resist hitting with a mallet (FIG. 4-4A). Gouges are sharpened with a bevel on the outside, without any break between the ground and honed angles. It is usual to sharpen inside so there is a light angle there as well (FIG. 4-4B), unlike tools for general use, where such an angle is avoided and the inside kept absolutely straight.

Carving gouges come in widths from 1/16 to 1 inch in twelve steps, but within each width were as many as nine different *sweeps*, meaning curves, from nearly flat to deep U shapes (FIG. 4-4C). Only a very limited number, mostly around the middle sizes and average shapes, are now available. In addition to straight patterns, there are gouges curved in the length (FIG. 4-4D). For getting into awkward places, there are spoon-bit gouges (FIG. 4-4E).

A deep, narrow gouge is worth having. It was called a *veining tool*, from its use in outlining veins of leaves, but it is a good tool for cutting in any outlines. Another tool for similar work is a V-*tool*, or *parting tool*, with a V section, sharpened on the outside like a double chisel (FIG. 4-4F). They were made in widths from 1/16 to 1 inch and in at least three angles of about 40, 60, and 90 degrees. One parting tool of average size should do all that is required of it today.

Carving chisels are used much less than gouges, and most work can be done with general-purpose chisels. Carving chisels are thinner and in widths from 1/2 to 1 inch. They might have the second bevel similar to a gouge and might be given skew ends (FIG. 4-4G). Chisels are made curved in the length and in spoon and other bit types for getting into awkward places.

Much carving is done with hand pressure only, but for harder woods and heavier cuts, a mallet must be used. Any mallet already available can be used, but a carver prefers one with a round head (FIG. 4-4H).

An expert carver took pride in his cut backgrounds and generally preferred not to use punches to decorate the background. Early American furniture makers who did their own carving often punched backgrounds to show up the work done on raised parts. If you examine original backgrounds, you will see that homemade punches were used. They were merely iron rods filed across the end (FIG. 4-4J).

Carving is mostly done with two hands on the tool. The hand gripping the handle provides direction and thrust. The other hand over the blade provides pressure and is ready to restrict when a cut reaches its intended limit or shows signs of going too far. Because you are using gouges, always keep their points above the surface of the wood; otherwise grain will break out. Make deeper cuts in stages. So far as possible, make cuts diagonally across the grain (FIG. 4-5A). A cut straight along the grain might generate a split.

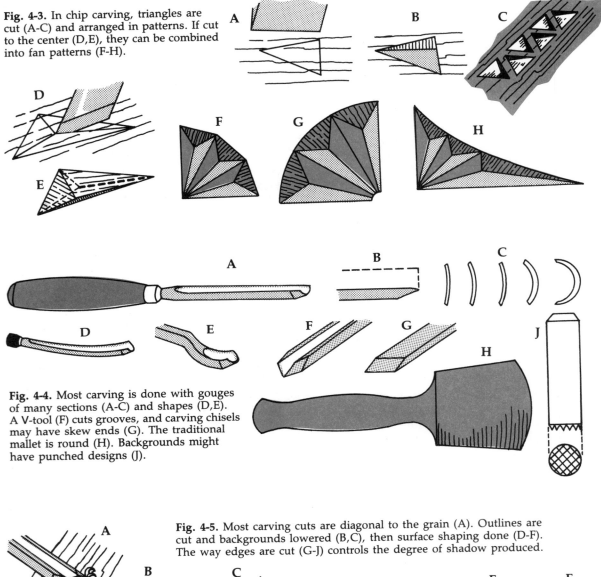

Fig. 4-3. In chip carving, triangles are cut (A-C) and arranged in patterns. If cut to the center (D,E), they can be combined into fan patterns (F-H).

Fig. 4-4. Most carving is done with gouges of many sections (A-C) and shapes (D,E). A V-tool (F) cuts grooves, and carving chisels may have skew ends (G). The traditional mallet is round (H). Backgrounds might have punched designs (J).

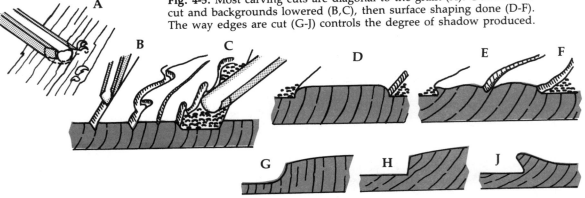

Fig. 4-5. Most carving cuts are diagonal to the grain (A). Outlines are cut and backgrounds lowered (B,C), then surface shaping done (D-F). The way edges are cut (G-J) controls the degree of shadow produced.

Much of the carved work on period furniture is comparatively low relief and worked on surfaces. After drawing the main outlines, it is usually best to cut down the background. First outline the background with a veiner or parting tool (FIG. 4-5B), then cut the waste away with a fairly broad gouge of shallow sweep (FIG. 4-5C). If there is much wood to be removed, you can use a power router, but do not take it to the full depth. Finish with hand tool work. Be careful that router cutter marks do not show around the outline, and avoid leaving the background so uniformly level that it has obviously been done by machine.

The raised part of relief carving should show an overall carved appearance. It would look wrong if parts of it remained flat and level with the surrounding uncarved parts. This means that you should make any curved section complete and not leave it with a flat top (FIG. 4-5D). Give leaves and similar things an undulating section (FIG. 4-5E). Outlined and carefully curve veins so adjoining parts curve and blend in (FIG. 4-5F).

Outlines are strongest if they curve into the background (FIG. 4-5G). They are more distinct if cut at an angle or upright (FIG. 4-5H). If the carved part is intended to stand out, you can undercut it. An upward curving edge of a leaf might appear to be much higher above the background than it is, if undercut (FIG. 4-5J). Of course, undercutting might leave a weak edge, only do it when you are using a strong wood or the grain is across the cut. Undercutting along the grain, leaving lengthwise fibers in a thin section, might cause crumbling or breaking some time after the work has been completed.

Keep carving tools sharp so they produce a good surface. It is usual to leave carving untouched by abrasives. You occasionally might need to use a file or rasp. Little files on narrow extending shafts that serve as handles and are called *rifflers* are the carver's tools for getting into difficult places, but they would have had little use on Colonial furniture and are unlikely to have been in the cabinetmaker's tool kit. Smooth surfaces by careful paring; do not sand. If tool marks show, that does not matter and are characteristic of carved work.

Most carved decoration on early furniture is simple. The steps in its working can usually be visualized, so a reproduction can be tackled in the same way. It will be necessary to decide at what stage carving is to be done. Obviously, it would be unwise to have comparatively delicate carving knocking about the bench on a piece of wood requiring other work on it. Usually, it would also be unwise to wait until assembly had been completed, when it might be difficult to support the wood being worked on or manipulate tools properly because of other parts of the assembly.

With most pieces of furniture, it is advisable to cut all joints and have the parts that are to be carved ready for assembly, so nothing more than perhaps a light cut with a smoothing plan will follow, then do the carving. Usually, it is possible to temporarily clamp the wood on the bench top. This method is better than putting it in the vise because the solid bench top below the wood gives good support for cuts made with the aid of a mallet.

Details of carving patterns are given with particular pieces of furniture later in the book, but if you are not used to carving, try working a few practice patterns on scrap wood of the type to be used. Although softwood might be easy to cut, it does not permit very fine or complicated work because parts of the pattern must have some substance if grain is not to break out. Hardwoods are more usual for detailing carving. Open-grained hardwood, such as oak, has a long history of very fine ecclesiastical carving, but it is not so easy to carve delicately as a more closely grained hardwood, such as beech.

TURNING

A wood-turning lathe does not need to be a very complicated machine, and it will still function adequately if it lacks precision in much of its construction. This is seen in some of the quite crude lathes still used by some peoples, such as Asians, who produce well-made things for the tourist trade. Lathes have been known for a very long time. At the time of the early American settlements, European lathes were operated by treadle or by helpers turning a large wheel. Not long before that time, the usual type was a pole lathe, where a rope from a springy bow was passed around the work and taken down to a treadle. A push with the foot revolved the work and the bow provided a return stroke. Cutting could only be done on the down stroke. It is probable that much of the first American turning was done on improvised lathes of this type.

There is no need for you to revert to such a basic lathe, but the fact that wood was turned in this way means that it was all comparatively simple. It would be wrong to include very fine detail in wood turning intended to reproduce work of the earliest Colonial type. Nearly all the turned work in early furniture is what is often called *spindle turning*. This means parts are long, rather than thick. Early turners did not have the facilities to make things of large diameter in relation to their length, like bowls and very bulbous feet. Instead, their products were table and chair legs or decorative spindles—all of which have diameters much less than their lengths.

Such work can be done on the simplest lathe. Small work can be turned on a lathe powered by an electric drill. Larger pieces can be made on a simple lathe, preferably with a capacity up to 30 inches between centers, so it will accommodate the usual length of table leg.

A lathe takes its power at a *headstock*, usually with a belt drive from a treadle or electric motor. The spindle extends and carries a *driving center*, which is an arrangement with a central spike and teeth to engage with the wood being turned (FIG. 4-6A). This is mounted on a *bed*, which can be in several forms, but usually must parallel parts of metal or wood. On this slides a *tailstock*, the main purpose of which is to support a plain center in line with the headstock center. The plain center provides the bearing on which the other end of the wood revolves. The tailstock can be locked at any position on the bed to accommodate various lengths of wood (FIG. 4-6B). The Colonial turner probably called the headstock a *fixed poppet* and the tailstock a *sliding poppet*.

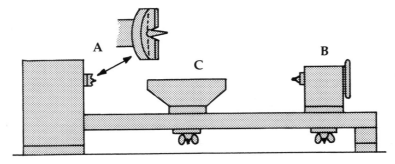
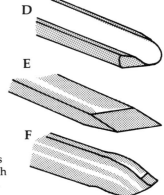

Fig. 4-6. A lathe revolves the work with a driving center (A). The other end is supported by a tailstock (B) and work is done on a tool rest (C). First shaping is with a gouge (D); smoothing is with a chisel (E). A parting tool (F) cuts straight in.

The only other essential is a *tool rest*, which can be fixed at any position on the bed and usually has a T-shaped top that can be adjustable in height (FIG. 4-6C).

Wood turning is done with gouges and chisels. It is not a case of gouges for curved work and chisels for straight work. In general, gouges are the roughing tools and chisels are the finishing ones. There can be considerable leverage on a tool when it cuts into the work and turning tools are longer than their bench equivalents. As the tool is never hit, it tangs into its handle without a bolster. The tool blade may be about 10 inches long and the handle extends a like amount. Fortunately, you do not need a large variety of turning tools.

Gouges are from about 1/4 inch up to as much as 1 1/2 inches, but most roughing can be done with a 3/4-inch gouge; then a 1/4-inch one can supplement it for closer curves. Chisels are in similar sizes, but almost everything can be done with just a 1/2-inch one, although an additional narrower one is useful.

The end of a turning gouge is beveled on the outside and given a curved outline, and is called *spindle nosed* or *fingernail ended* (FIG. 4-4D,E). An expert might have other outlines, but this type serves for all spindle turning. The end of a chisel is angled and sharpened on both sides equally (FIG. 4-4G). The amount it is cut on the skew is not important.

It helps to have a *parting tool* (different from the tool of the same name used for carving). This is a sort of narrow chisel, deeper than it is wide and narrowed behind the cutting edge (FIG. 4-6D). Its use is to push straight into the revolving wood to cut down a recess or part the wood right through.

To make something like a stool leg, choose square wood 1 inch or so over length. Find the center of each end and make a dent with a center punch. It might help to make a shallow saw cut across the dent for the teeth of the driving center to engage (FIG. 4-7A). In most power-driven lathes, you can mount the square wood in the lathe and turn it immediately, but if the power is not great or there is a fear of wood breaking out during the first cuts, you can plane off corners to make the wood approximately octagonal (FIG. 4-7B). In any case, press the wood on to the driving center and bring the tailstock up tightly, with a spot of lubricant on its center. Adjust the tool rest to be reasonably close to the work and with its top edge slightly below center height.

The first job is to make the wood round, without bothering about the final shape. This is done with a gouge. Have one hand pressing down on the tool over the tool rest. The other hand should be at the end of the handle and usually near your side for steadiness. It will probably be best for the hand over the tool rest to grip with the fist on top, at first, but later there will be occasions when it is more convenient to only have the thumb on top.

Advance the gouge to the work. At first have it almost horizontal, but as it begins to cut, tilt it so it is giving more of a slice (FIG. 4-7C). Do this at several places along the wood. You do not need to withdraw the gouge at each position; you can slide it along the tool rest. Practice will soon show how heavy to make a cut and what rate of progress to use along the work. The wood will apparently be round, but if you stop the lathe, you will probably find there are still flats on it. Continue to turn until the wood is round. It helps to get the tailstock end down to a full circle and use that as a guide while turning the rest of the wood.

You can now get the shape very roughly formed with the gouge, leaving enough for finishing. You will need to use calipers for checking diameters. They can be the precision spring-bow type, but many turners use simple ones with friction joints (FIG. 4-7D). Inside calipers are rarely needed.

Have a drawing of the intended leg or spindle available. If it is a leg, it is usually convenient to have its foot at the tailstock end. Allow a little waste there, then mark other key positions by holding a pencil on the tool rest (FIG. 4-7E). Use the gouge to get the wood close to size, checking with the calipers and remarking with pencil if necessary.

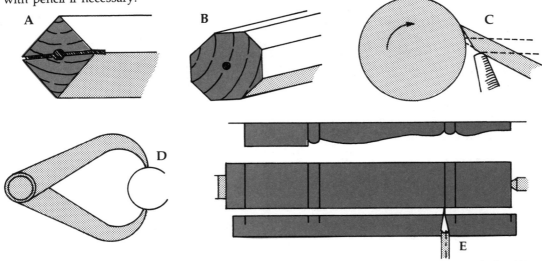

Fig. 4-7. The driving end of wood to be turned is prepared with a saw cut and center punch dot (A). Corners can be planed off (B). The work revolves toward the tool, which tilts up to cut properly (C). Calipers are useful for checking sizes (D). A marked strip of wood can be used with a pencil to mark the wood (E) for shaping.

Mark positions with a chisel held on edge with its longer point downward and thrust straight into the revolving wood (FIG. 4-8A). Grasp with both hands in the same way as for a gouge to cut into the wood. The surface left from a gouge is quite rough. It is made smooth by a slicing action with a chisel. It should not scrape, but waste wood should come away in definite shavings.

Hold the chisel firmly with both hands and slope it toward the direction it is to cut, with the lower corner leading. Adjust its position so one bevel is in contact with the revolving wood. Aim to cut with the center of the edge. The long point must be kept clear of the wood at all times. If the short point enters the wood, it is not as serious. Tilt the tool slightly in the direction it is to go and it will start cutting. As it does, slice along by moving the tool, still at the same angle, along the tool rest (FIG. 4-8B). Stop the lathe and examine the wood. Where the gouge leaves a surface comparable to a saw, the chisel leaves a surface more like a plane.

Use the chisel in the same way on curved surfaces, but always cut from high to low—from thick parts to thin parts. On a convex curve, you cut from the outside into the hollows (FIG. 4-8C). On a concave part, you work into the hollow (FIG. 4-8D).

Much turning includes *beads*, either alone or in series (FIG. 4-8E). They are worked with the chisel. Outline them by cutting straight in with the long corner of the chisel. Now treat each side of a bead in the same way as described for turning any curved surface. Have the short corner in the direction you wish to cut, but with the usual small bead you do not need to slide the chisel along the tool rest, but merely roll it (FIG. 4-8F). In a series of beads, make all the cuts on one direction, then turn the tool over and cut the other sides.

With parts of varying diameter, it is sometimes convenient to cut in with the parting tool where an angle comes in the outline. This shows where the limits of each size are. The parting tool does not leave a very good surface on the exposed cross grain. You can smooth this surface with the chisel point downward, but angled so one of the sharpening bevels is pointing straight in (FIG. 4-8G).

The finish from the tools should be quite good, but you might need to do some sanding. Bring the tool rest out of the way, so abrasive paper cannot catch on it. Hold the paper underneath the revolving work. Keep it moving, so as to get different parts of the paper in contact, as well as to cover different parts of the wood; otherwise heat is built up and might cause scorching marks.

You can cut a turned part to length with the parting tool. At the tailstock end, you can turn a stool or table leg slightly hollow by angling the tool as it enters. At the other end, it might be necessary to part in so far and use a chisel to smooth the end before parting further and cutting off.

Turned work must be joined to other parts of the furniture. Table legs often have square tops for mortise-and-tenon joints to be made. This calls for careful centering so the leg does not run out of true and produce an eccentric turned part. It also calls for careful cutting where the square part blends into the round; otherwise corners might break out. Angle the gouge to cut from what will remain square toward the rounded part, and do any work with the chisel in the same way.

In some cases, a dowel is turned on the end of a spindle to mate with a hole in a flat part of the furniture (FIG. 4-9A). If this can come at the end toward the tailstock, it is possible to drill a hole in a scrap piece of wood and use that as a gauge to test the dowel for size (FIG. 4-9B). If dowels come at both ends of the work, you can test the one at the other end with calipers (FIG. 4-9C), but it is always better to use a hole when possible. Cut a slight bevel on the end as the final work on a dowel (FIG. 4-9D) to help it enter its hole.

MOLDING

In nearly every way, we are better equipped than those woodworkers of over 200 years ago. We can do most of the same work with much less effort and with a much greater degree of accuracy. However, there is one aspect of woodworking in which earlier woodworkers were better equipped than we are today: the hand-cutting of moldings. It is possible to make molding with suitable cutters on a spindle, but not everyone has those facilities. Some combination planes are still made with a range of molding cutters, but they are expensive. The old-time cabinetmaker had a number of molding planes. They are no longer made and it is difficult to find used versions in working condition.

It is possible to form many moldings by working in steps and using several planes. Fortunately, most of the moldings to be reproduced are fairly simple. The pioneer cabinetmakers did not have the tools nor the inclination to use complication for complication's sake when something simpler would be just as effective.

Molding planes were made of wood, with a cutting iron narrowed to a stem held with a wedge in a slot. The sole of the plane and the edge of the iron were shaped to produce the molding shape required. In many cases, the tool was used at an angle on the edge of a board and the intended angle was marked on the end (FIG. 4-10A). Plane soles were reinforced with harder wood or metal, particularly where a narrow part had to be provided.

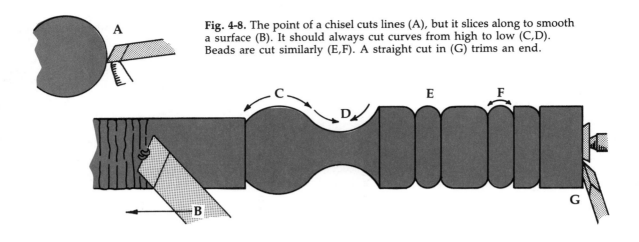

Fig. 4-8. The point of a chisel cuts lines (A), but it slices along to smooth a surface (B). It should always cut curves from high to low (C,D). Beads are cut similarly (E,F). A straight cut in (G) trims an end.

Fig. 4-9. Turned parts assemble with doweled ends (A). A hole in scrap wood acts as a gauge (B) at an end. Elsewhere the dowel must be measured (C). Tapering the end helps assembly (D).

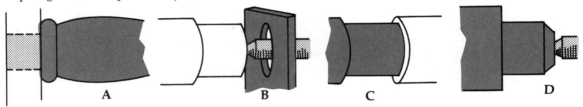

Fig. 4-10. Much early furniture had molded edges, hand cut (A), with beads (B-D) or more complex patterns (E-G).

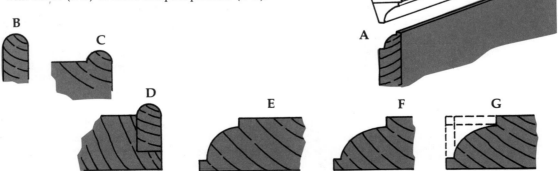

In addition to full molding planes, there were *hollows* and *rounds,* made in the same way. The names indicate the shape cut, so a plane with a rounded bottom is a hollow. You can do much of the work of a round with a flat-bottomed plane, but if you can obtain any hollows, they are useful tools in reproduction work.

One of the simplest moldings is a bead, which can be worked with an ordinary plane, followed by sanding, on the edge of a piece of wood (FIG. 4-10B). A *cocked bead* stands above the surface (FIG. 4-10C). It was sometimes worked separately and let into a rabbet (FIG. 4-10D). This would be the best method today.

An *ovolo molding* might be found around the edge of a tabletop. In its simplest form, it is part of a circle (FIG. 4-10E), or it may be elliptical (FIG. 4-10F). If you do not have a suitable molding plane, you can work an ovolo molding by cutting two rabbets and planing some of the corner off (FIG. 4-10G), followed by careful work with a rabbet plane and sanding.

The *ogee* is a much-used molding, appearing in many variations, but the important feature is the double-curvature section. There may be a common ogee (FIG. 4-11A) or a reversed ogee (FIG. 4-11B), and either can be combined with quirks and beads. With a suitable molding plane, any of these forms is easy to make; otherwise you must work the shape in stages. Draw a full-size section on paper and plan sequence of cuts. You can remove some of the waste with a simple chamfer (FIG. 4-11C). To shape a convex curve, use an ordinary plane. You can cut into the hollow with a plow or circular saw (FIG. 4-11D). Even if a suitable hollow plane is available, this serves as a guide to keep the cut straight. You can also tilt a rabbet plane in the cut and remove more waste, then use coarse abrasive paper around a shaped piece of wood to true the shape (FIG. 4-11E).

Fig. 4-11. Double curves (A,B) can be made by progressive planing and sanding (C-E).

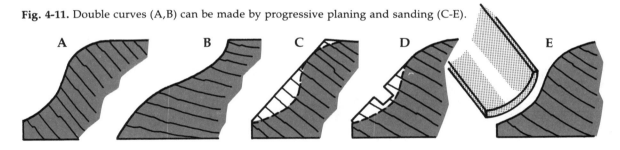

Fig. 4-12. Beads are made with progressive saw and plane cuts, whether on an edge (A-D) or a surface (E).

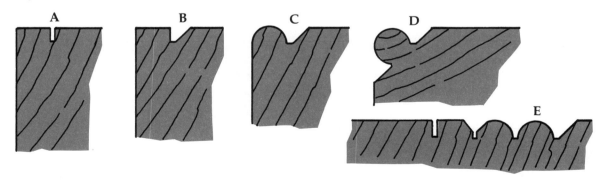

You can copy many other molding sections by similar sequences of cuts. If you must cut beads with narrow gaps alongside, it is often possible to cut in with a circular saw (FIG. 4-12A) or use a cutting gauge. Then use a rabbet plane to bevel the wood (FIG. 4-12B) to leave enough clearance for using the same plane to round the bead section (FIG. 4-12C). A further step is a bead worked on a corner section (FIG. 4-12D).

You can work a series of several beads, called *reeds* if away from an edge, in a similar way if no suitable plane is available. Cut narrow grooves, then take a little off each side of the cut with a rabbet plane progressively until you can shape each bead (FIG. 4-12E).

Moldings of a great many sections were used. The majority are based on classical forms, going back to Greek and Roman days, but some merely followed the particular craftsman's ideas. The most pleasing moldings have all or most curves based on parts of an ellipse, and not on sections of circles. For instance, you can make an ogee with one quarter-circle hollow blending into another quarter-circle round. This looks better if one part is to a very different radius from the other, but the whole thing looks even better if the two curves are parts of ellipses.

5

Boxes and Chests

THE BASIC CONTAINER for household goods is a box. Most of the early settlers arrived with their possessions in boxes and chests, made of heavy sectioned wood and stoutly constructed to stand up to the rigors of a sea voyage of those days. There were no equivalents of modern traveling cases. Those chests, with their lids, also served as seats, in the same way that medieval dwellers in Europe often used chests as almost the only pieces of furniture in simpler homes.

A chest has the advantage of fully enclosing the contents, and for things like bedding and spare clothing it will offer protection that is better than provided by most other storage furniture. In an early home, where dust and dirt could not be avoided, this sort of protection for treasured items of special clothing and other things that only came out rarely would have been important.

Chests and boxes varied in size and design, from larger ones, usually described as *blanket boxes* and often made of cedar because of its aromatic and clean preservative air, down to boxes for books, particularly the family Bible, candles, and trinkets. Chests developed so they became more suitable for secondary uses. A chest often had to stand on an earth floor, which might be damp, so ends or corners were extended to make legs so air could circulate under the bottom. If a chest was to be used as a seat, there was an advantage in adding a back, which might be of full height or a low one supported by the chest ends extended to form brackets.

A simple chest is more utilitarian than beautiful. A plain box with a lid might still have its uses and be worth making. Craftsmen favored chests for storing their tools, particularly in the days when a man might need to travel to a job in a cart having little springing over roads that were barely passable. A tool chest for storing equipment that does not have frequent enough use to justify fitting in racks behind the bench, yet needs to be kept in good condition, might be produced in an amateur craftsman's shop and stay there. There are some examples of old chests that are bare and well worn on the outside, but inside there are sliding compartments and drawers, and the underside of the lid is carefully veneered, usually with an elaborate marquetry design. This would have been a cabinetmaker's masterpiece. Toward the end of his apprenticeship, he was expected to make something to prove his skill in his trade, and his tool chest was often the chosen example. In later life, he was faced with a specimen of his best craftsmanship and a standard to live up to every time he opened the lid.

Some early examples of chests were quite plain in their construction, but they were decorated by carving and less frequently by veneering. Others were painted. Sometimes there was an overall treatment in one or two colors, but there are examples with skillfully painted designs, such as geometric or stylized leaves and flowers, and others with scenes on each face of the box. With this sort of decoration, it is better if the chest starts quite plain, but it should be made of a close-grained wood that can be given a smooth surface, and is able to take several coats of the base paint that serves as the ground on which the decorative painting is done.

The construction of most chests was quite simple. Corners were often nailed through simple overlaps. The hand-forged iron nails had much rougher surfaces than modern wire nails, so they gripped the fibers of the wood quite well. To make a modern reproduction secured by nailing, use reproduction nails and leave the heads level. If you use modern nails, buy fairly long ones and drive them dovetail fashion, rather closer together, then punch them below the surface and cover the heads with stopping. Bottoms were sometimes nailed on (FIG. 5-1A), but there was greater strength if the bottom was enclosed by the sides (FIG. 5-1B).

Not much sheet metal was available, but where it was, bottoms and corners were reinforced by bent straps nailed on. These straps were sometimes simple rectangles (FIG. 5-1C), but if a blacksmith made the hinges and these straps he sometimes shaped the parts to similar outlines to give a more pleasing effect (FIG. 5-1D). That type of construction was used on chests of earlier days than the first settlements, but memories of older furniture might have provided the ideas for this sort of construction.

Corners were often dovetailed. Wide dovetails and pins are easier to cut than narrow ones, and it is obvious in some early chests, particularly those made of softwood, that the easy way out was taken, either because of limited equipment available, little ability, or the need for quick results. Later chests made of better woods usually have narrower dovetails, and sometimes the pins between them are very narrow in the manner favored by cabinetmakers.

Resistance to pulling apart is provided in a dovetail joint by the shape of the dovetail. The joint cannot be separated in that direction without breaking the wood. In the other direction (which is the way the joint was assembled), strength depends on tightness or glue. You might think that the greatest probable strains in use would have been to pull chest sides off ends and not ends off sides, but it is interesting to see in many old chests that the dovetails are cut in the sides, so the ends have the greatest resistance to coming apart (FIG. 5-1E). It is only when the sides flare outward that dovetails are always found cut in the ends (FIG. 5-1F). This is probably because an angled dovetail joint is easier to lay out and cut that way, rather than because the maker thought the flared sides would have more tendency to pull apart than the ends. Well-cut dovetails with modern glue should have ample strength in both directions.

The various types of notching for corner joints made today with power tools and often used in wooden construction were not used 200 years ago and would be inappropriate in any reproduction unless they were hidden. In some boxes, the sides overlapped the ends. In that case, shallow grooves were cut in the sides to positively locate the ends, but the joint was still nailed from outside (FIG. 5-1G). The dado was quite shallow, to prevent it from weakening the side. In many such boxes, the extended sides were linked with crossbars to form handles, so strength was needed if heavy loads had to be lifted.

Hinges and fasteners were difficult to obtain and had to be made individually, if at all. As a result, the use of metal fittings often had to be avoided. The simplest way of dealing with a box lid was to make it lift off, so no metalwork was involved. The lid then had pieces attached to locate it within the box (FIG. 5-1H), or a rim all around to fit outside the box top (FIG. 5-1J). In both cases, the added parts had the advantage of reducing the risk of the top warping.

For the lid of a large chest, the hinges had to be substantial. There are chests with blacksmith-made strap hinged and extending across the top and down the back. An outside hinge strap above was not wanted if the top was to also serve as a seat. Another hinge had the top strap inside. The important consideration was having the hinge knuckle outside, so the lid swings free (FIG. 5-1K).

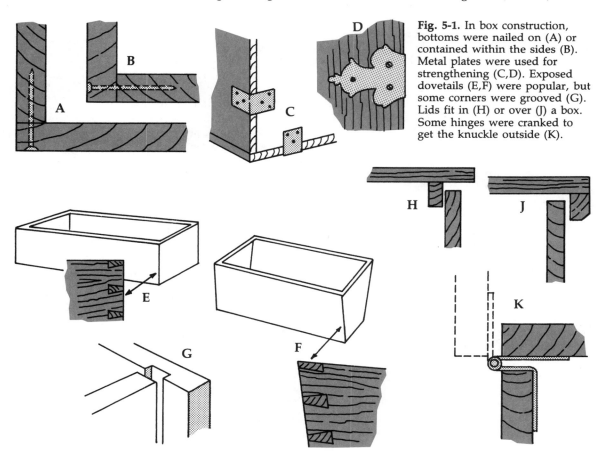

Fig. 5-1. In box construction, bottoms were nailed on (A) or contained within the sides (B). Metal plates were used for strengthening (C,D). Exposed dovetails (E,F) were popular, but some corners were grooved (G). Lids fit in (H) or over (J) a box. Some hinges were cranked to get the knuckle outside (K).

Construction of Chests 55

SIMPLE CHEST

The size of a chest was probably determined by the sizes of boards available, although the contents had to be considered, such as blankets folded a certain number of times. Construction might be the same whatever the size. The example shown in FIG. 5-2A is a suitable height for sitting, and the size should suit folded blankets and sheets. For that purpose, aromatic red cedar would be a good choice of wood, but for use elsewhere the wood could match other furniture. For shop use, it could be a strong hardwood.

If you must join boards to make up width, deal with these glued joints first. It is advisable to stagger joints so they do not meet at a corner (FIG. 5-2B). The overlapping corner joints then serve to clamp the board joints.

Care is needed in planing the wood true. Sight along to check for twists. Be careful that all angles are right angles. In any construction with little embellishment, slight variations from true become very obvious. Cut the two ends to length and plane their cross-grain true, checking with a try square from the face edges and trying one end against the other. Mark the lengths of the sides, but let them remain slightly overlong until after nailing to the ends, and then plane them level (FIG. 5-2C). It is the top corners where you can expect most strain to come, so nails there can be closer and might be longer (FIG. 5-2D).

If the chest is to stand with its bottom on the floor, it will be better to enclose the bottom wood within the sides and ends. Nail one side to both ends and use that assembly as a guide for the size of the bottom. Get one end of the bottom planed to a right angle to its side, then pull the three-part assembly to this and mark the other end and width. Fit the bottom into the one side and two ends before adding the second side (FIG. 5-2E).

You can give the chest a *plinth*, which is a border around the bottom. In addition to improving appearance, it allows the bottom to be nailed on instead of let in. This is a simpler method because you can leave the bottom oversize and plane it to match after fitting. The plinth then projects below the bottom and strengthens it with nails, while keeping it off the floor (FIG. 5-2F).

Another way of raising the bottom off the floor is to extend the ends to form legs. Although this could be done with the grain of the ends across, it is stronger for the legs, if the grain is upright. The ends need only project a few inches, then cut a V in them to form feet (FIG. 5-2G).

Much depends on the intended use of the chest. The box part could be shallower and the leg extensions longer. A very shallow box with a lid is then more of a stool than a chest.

You could splay the ends outward. Draw a side view of at least half the chest full size, with the end splayed to come under the end of the top and with the outline of the intended shaped edges of the sides. Also draw a view of the end, with the amount of splay. Mark out the two ends, using the full-size drawing as a guide to sizes. Cut the angles across with a jigsaw or coping saw. Clean up the shapes with a chisel or rasp and finish by sanding. You also need to bevel the sides.

In any case, if the chest is to form a comfortable seat, it should have its top between 14 and 16 inches from the floor. With the grain upright, it will be necessary to put cleat strips across the top to prevent warping (FIG. 5-2H). They can come outside and have the lid extended over them, or be inside for a closer lid. Having these cleats outside lets them serve as handles.

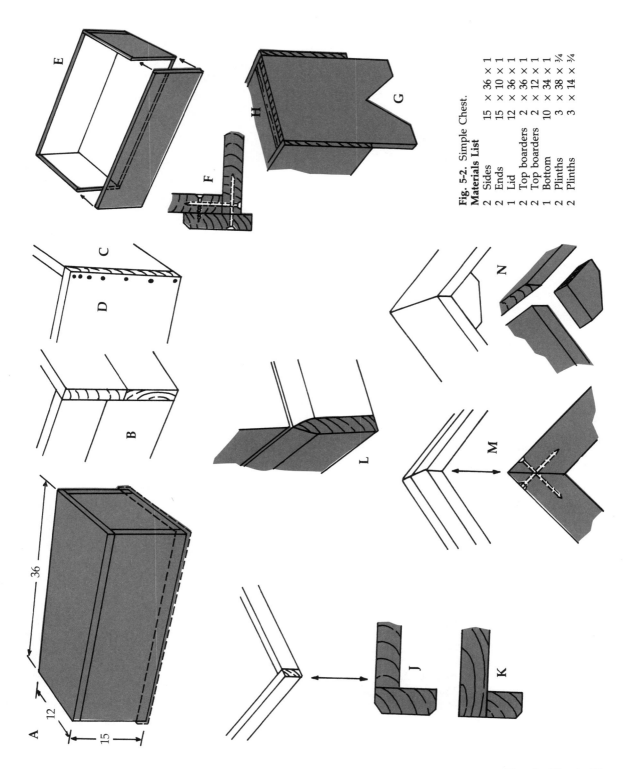

Fig. 5-2. Simple Chest.
Materials List

2	Sides	15	×	36	×	1	
2	Ends	15	×	10	×	1	
1	Lid	12	×	36	×	1	
2	Top boarders	2	×	36	×	1	
2	Top boarders	2	×	12	×	1	
1	Bottom	10	×	34	×	1	
2	Plinths	3	×	38	×	¾	
2	Plinths	3	×	14	×	¾	

The simplest lid is a single board that lifts off. Cleats across near the ends can locate the lid by fitting inside the box (FIG. 5-1H). Make them deeper than they are wide to give stiffness and resist any tendency of the lid to warp. Another type of lift-off lid has a border around it. Many early chests have the border pieces fixed around the outside of the lid (FIG. 5-2J), but a stronger assembly is made by having them below the lid (FIG. 5-2K). The only advantage of the first method is that it allows you to use a slightly smaller board.

Overlap and nail the corners of the lid border and the parts making up a plinth, then cut the overlapped parts to the same profile as the parts they join (FIG. 5-2L). A neater joint is a miter, but under the lid strengthen the joint with a nail each way (FIG. 5-2-M). Under the plinth add a reinforcing block, which also functions as a foot (FIG. 5-2N).

If the lid is to be hinged, there should be no border at the back, as it would interfere with the lid lifting. Otherwise construction is the same as for a loose lid.

CHEST WITH TRAYS

In some communities, particularly the Pennsylvania Dutch, there were bride's chests, or hope chests, in which a girl put the things she had made in anticipation of marriage. Similar chests were used for general storage. Smaller boxes made in the same way could be used on a table for jewelry. Painted decoration was used by the Pennsylvania Dutch, but other chests were made of good-quality wood and finished by polishing. The stark outline of a rectangular box was broken by shaped feet and some molded edges.

The specimen in FIG. 5-3A is of moderate size, but originals were in all sizes, from those to be carried in one hand to blanket boxes. You could nail corners and hide the holes with stopping, but dovetails are better. Enclose the bottom within the sides and ends. You can use plywood or other manufactured board for the bottom since its edges are covered and it would not be easily identified. Thinner material might have supporting battens underneath (FIG. 5-3B).

A plinth goes around the bottom with a small overlap and with much of the lower edge cut away to leave supports at the corners. Miter corners and put blocks inside to strengthen the joints and provide extra bearing surfaces on the floor (FIG. 5-3C). You can mold the top edge of the plinth or fix a separate strip of molding around with glue and thin nails or pins (FIG. 5-3D).

The lid can be a single stout board, preferably cut with the end showing grain lines vertical, so there will be the minimum of risk of warping. Mold the edge and place strips around below it to provide a dust seal to the box; the whole top should have enough overlap on the carcass of the chest to allow for this (FIG. 5-3E). The rear edge of the top is not molded, but should finish level with the box back so it will swing up on its hinges.

Some of these chests had a single fixed compartment inside at one end. This did not interfere with reaching into the bottom of the box, but it provided a place for small items (FIG. 5-3F). In the best construction, the side and bottom of the compartment are let into the sides and end of the chest (FIG. 5-3G). You must make the grooves before you assemble the chest and put the compartment parts in before you fit the second side. The side of the compartment should have its top edge well rounded in cross section. You can hollow it at the center.

An alternative arrangement has a lift-out tray. In some chests this was full size, so it had to be lifted out to get at the lower part of the box (FIG. 5-3H). You can arrange compartments in this tray to suit the contents. If you can arrange

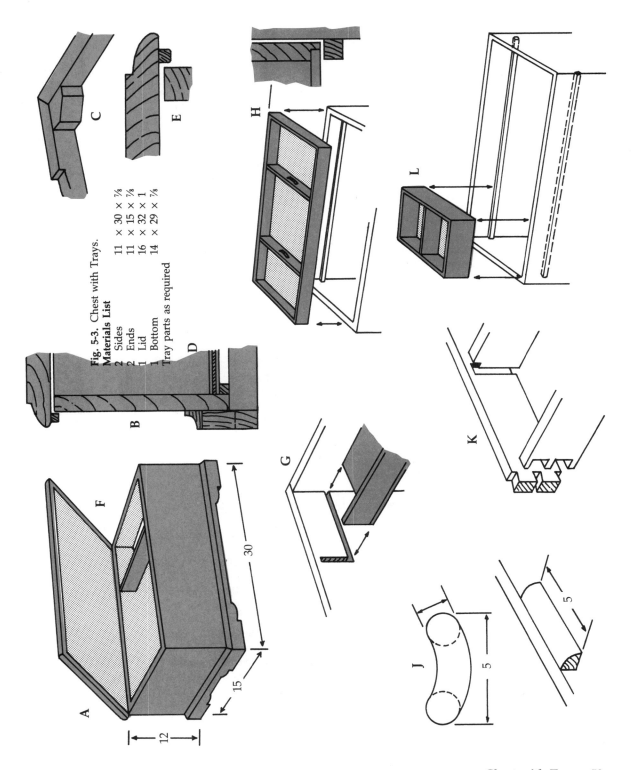

Fig. 5-3. Chest with Trays.

Materials List

2	Sides	11	×	30	×	⅞
2	Ends	11	×	15	×	⅞
1	Lid	16	×	32	×	1
1	Bottom	14	×	29	×	⅞
	Tray parts as required					

divisions conveniently, you can cut handholds in them for lifting (FIG. 5-3J); otherwise you should make in the ends of the tray or fix blocks there for lifting (FIG. 5-3K). The tray rests on strips of wood across the ends or the sides—there is no need to fit them all around.

Another arrangement has one or two trays resting on lengthwise strips, so a tray can slide along or be lifted out to aid access to the bottom of the box (FIG. 5-3L). In addition to household use, this was a common arrangement in tool chests. Dovetail the corners of trays if possible, and round the top edges of the trays and any dividers. Bottoms of trays would have been solid wood cut thin, but they could be plywood if they have their edges hidden by letting into rabbets. For jewelry or precision tools, you can line the bottoms of trays with cloth or rubber.

SMALL CHESTS

The chest method of construction was used for quite small boxes, which might have been for sugar or salt, or to hold trinkets or jewelry. Some of them were scaled-down versions of chests already described, but there were others. The smaller sizes allowed different uses of wood.

One box had the framing of the lid a continuation of the body of the box (FIG. 5-4A). This is a method frequently used today, but none of the earlier larger chests appear to have used the technique. The advantage of making a box this way is that the lid will always match the box.

To make this type of box, mark the joint line with a space to allow for the saw kerf and arrange dovetails each side of it (FIG. 5-4B). Cut joints and glue the sides and ends of the box together. Fix top and bottom—in this case with glue and nails. both can overlap slightly, to be planed off later. Plane the top of this box to a curve before fixing (FIG. 5-4C). Clean up the outside of the box all around, planing excess wood level and smoothing the surfaces, except for final sanding.

Next, cut off the lid. The original makers cut around between the lines with a handsaw, but if a table saw is available, it is a simple matter to set the fence and go around the four faces. Unless it is obvious from grain markings, you might want to mark the mating parts of lid and box so they are put back together the right way.

Plane the sawn edges level and clean away any surplus glue inside the box. Arrange two hinges at the back. There is no need for any sort of handle, but some of these boxes were given small turned knobs on the front of the lid and matching turned feet under the corners of the box (FIG. 5-4D).

You can make a variation on this box in the same way, except allow the top and bottom to project all around, then give them molded edges (FIG. 5-4E). You could cut the back level so the lid would open some way, but if the lid projected, you could arrange it to act as a stop when the lid was vertical (FIG. 5-4F). You can line either box with velvet to make a jewelry case.

One way of avoiding the use of hinges, while providing a secure lid instead of having it lift off, is to extend the ends of the box at least as high as the thickness of the lid. You can even make the ends high enough to be fretted to form decorative handles (FIG. 5-4G). The lid fits over the sides, but between the ends. Round the underside of its back edge and provide pivots by nails through the ends (FIG. 5-4H).

A sliding lid is another secure type. This was seen in school children's pencil boxes, but the idea was also used in boxes for other purposes. In the simplest form, the sides of the box were grooved and the lid shaped to slide in the grooves.

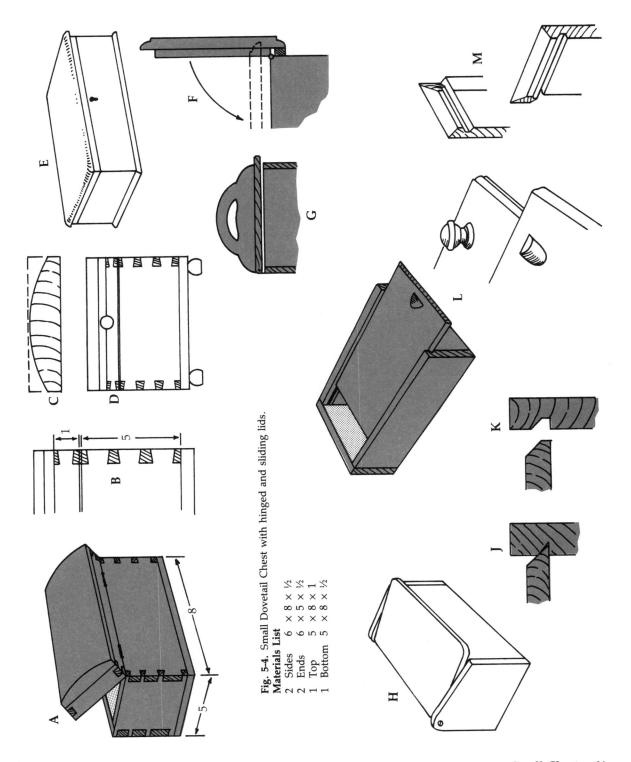

Fig. 5-4. Small Dovetail Chest with hinged and sliding lids.

Materials List

2 Sides	6 × 8 × ½
2 Ends	6 × 5 × ½
1 Top	5 × 8 × 1
1 Bottom	5 × 8 × ½

The simplest is a V-cut (FIG. 5-4J), but a stronger lid edge comes from plowing a groove and beveling its top edge (FIG. 5-4K). In a simple box, the end overlaps the sides and provides a stop for the lid, which passes over the other end and is either given a knob or a finger notch (FIG. 5-4L).

In a better box, the lid also enters a groove in the end. To avoid marring the surface where a groove in the overlapping parts ran through, miter the top corners for the depth of the grooves (FIG. 5-4M). This can be done whether the box has overlapped nailed corners or dovetail joints.

Small boxes became subjects for carving—probably as something that could be delt with in front of the fire during winter evenings. You can work panels of leaves or similar conventional carved forms on lid and sides. Some later boxes were veneered.

CHEST WITH EXTENDED SIDES

A large chest must be lifted by two persons. Handles of various sorts were provided on plain chests. The simplest handles were blocks of wood extending a few inches. Better wooden handles were hollowed underneath to provide a grip. Others were cut out so a hand could go through and the fingers wrap around. Seamen's chests usually had stout blocks of wood projecting with horizontal holes, so a loop of rope could pass through. The rope, which provided the actual grip, was often elaborately decorated with fancy knotting. Some early Colonial chests with rope handles might have belonged to sailors who had settled in the new country or to passengers who had seen such handles on the voyage to their new homes.

Another way of providing handles is to extend the sides and include a crossbar as a hand grip at each end. The crossbar could come near the top (FIG. 5-5A), where it might serve a secondary purpose as a rail for hanging towels or other cloths. If arranged lower down it allows a higher lift. For stability in carrying, the position should be above half the chest height (FIG. 5-5B). It would be unsatisfactory to depend only on nailed ends to the handle, and it should fit into the sides to transfer the load safely.

For a simple handle, use a square piece of wood, take off the corners, and tenon the ends into the sides (FIG. 5-5C). It is also possible, if you shape the sides suitably, to notch the handle through the sides (FIG. 5-5D), but do not cut much away at the handle ends and leave enough wood in the sides to take the load when the chest is lifted.

The handle has a more comfortable grip if it has a round section. It can be a parallel cylinder, made by hand planing and sanding, with its ends tenoned (FIG. 5-5E). If a lathe is available, you can decorate the handle and cut the ends as dowels to fit holes in the sides (FIG. 5-5F). The center, which has to be gripped, should be without much decoration and be about 1 1/4 inches in diameter for a good grip. The dowel ends can stop inside holes or pass right through and have their ends rounded where they project slightly.

The example of a large chest (FIG. 5-5G) could be varied in several ways, with different sizes or different arrangements of handles. Construction is generally similar to other chests, except for the extending sides. Cut the sides with some excess length and make the dado joints before doing any end shaping. The grooves should not be deeper than about one-third of the thickness of the wood. Use the ends as gauges for the width of the cuts, so the joints will be tight (FIG. 5-5H). Mark opposite sides together and check that the dadoes match when finished.

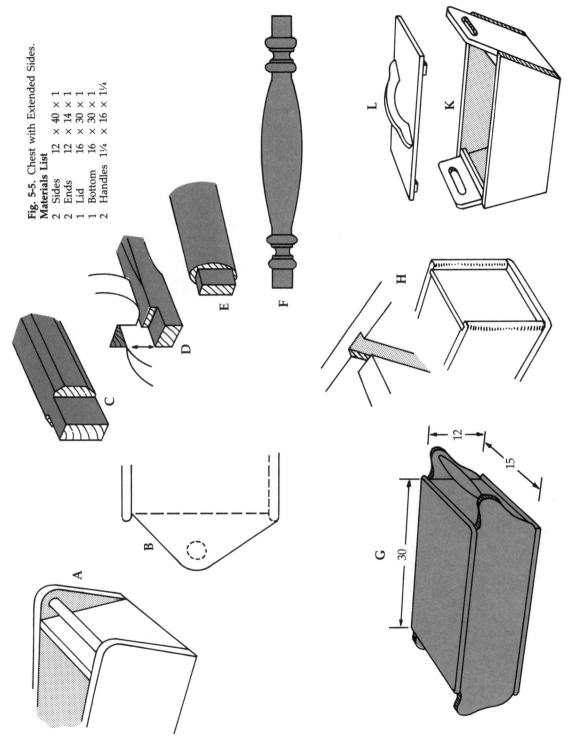

Fig. 5-5. Chest with Extended Sides.

Materials List

2	Sides	12	× 40	× 1	
2	Ends	12	× 14	× 1	
1	Lid	16	× 30	× 1	
1	Bottom	16	× 30	× 1	
2	Handles	1¼	× 16	× 1¼	

It is important for appearance that the end shapes be all the same. You can use a card or hardboard template, or lay out and cut one end, then use it to mark around the ends of the opposite side. When they are cut, you can use one of them to mark around the opposite end of the first side.

If you make the handles by hand, prepare them square and cut the tenons, then plane off the corners. You can leave the pieces with an octagonal section or plane off other corners and round the wood by sanding—first by pulling a strip of abrasive paper around the wood and finally by rubbing lengthwise. If the wood can be prepared in a lathe, it is simpler to turn dowel ends to fit drilled holes. In both cases, the distances between the shoulders must match the width between the sides when the chest is assembled. You should check this carefully by measuring or a trial assembly.

The handles must be fitted at the same time the chest is assembled. Fix the chest ends into one side and make and fit the bottom. Have the handles ready to glue in and fit them when the second side is added.

Chests can be made with the sides only extended enough to accommodate dado joints, but without handles between the sides. In some Colonial chests, the extending pieces are rounded. In others, the bottom also extends and is rounded (FIG. 5-5J), but it is a stronger construction to enclose the bottom between the sides.

Some small boxes, made like chests but intended for kitchen use, were given knobs on the ends so one person could hold and lift from both ends. This type of box might have the ends raised enough for handle slots to be cut (FIG. 5-5K). Lids usually were made to lift, although some were hinged. A wooden handle was usually provided and mounted diagonally, with fairly broad bearing surfaces on the lid, presumably to provide some resistance to any tendency of the lid to warp (FIG. 5-5L).

DOUGH TROUGH

After dough for bread was mixed and kneaded, it was left to raise before being formed into loaves and baked. A dough trough was a form of chest used for flour and for holding the raising dough. Sizes varied from those to be carried and put on a table, to others that were large enough to require a permanent place. A feature of all of them was flaring. The ends might be upright, but the sides opened outward to make the box wider at the top. In some examples, the sides were upright and the ends flared. In a few examples, there was flare both ways. To put the larger troughs at a convenient working height, they were given legs or arranged to mount on a stool or low table. Lids then became working tabletops.

Some small dough troughs were made in the same way as the boxes described earlier, but with flared sides. Handles or knobs were needed for lifting. Another type had the sides extended to provide four handles (FIG. 5-6A). There was a slight flare both ways and were simply nailed. Larger troughs were usually dovetailed, with vertical ends dovetailed into flared sides (FIG. 5-6B). After you prepare the boards, layout the ends first, and mark out lengths and angles together (FIG. 5-6C). Note that dovetail angles are arranged in relation to the length of the wood and not to the angled cuts, so the sides of the dovetail are at about 7 degrees to the sides of the wood (FIG. 5-6D) and not at 83 degrees to the edge (FIG. 5-6E). This arrangement gives greater strength. It might not be very different with a moderate flare, but when there is much of an angle, cutting dovetails in the second way results in too much weak "short" grain in each dovetail. Except for this step, layout and cut the joints in the same way as for a square corner—preferably with

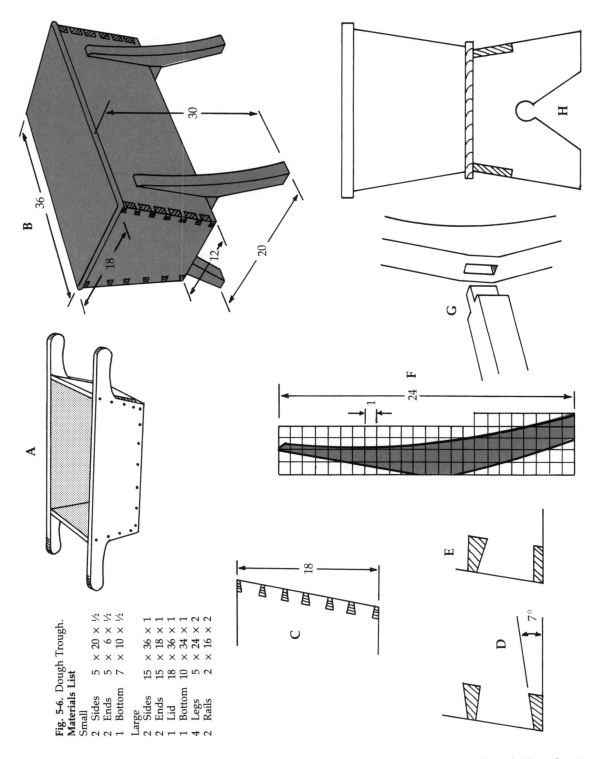

Fig. 5-6. Dough Trough.

Materials List

Small

2	Sides	5 × 20 × ½
2	Ends	5 × 6 × ½
1	Bottom	7 × 10 × ½

Large

2	Sides	15 × 36 × 1
2	Ends	15 × 18 × 1
1	Lid	18 × 36 × 1
1	Bottom	10 × 34 × 1
4	Legs	5 × 24 × 2
2	Rails	2 × 16 × 2

Dough Trough 65

the dovetail part first and the other marked from it.

Give the lid a slight overlap all round and position battens across the ends to locate the lid on the trough. If you are building in legs, they must stand wide enough to hold the trough steady for use as a working table. One type is cut from stout solid wood, extending up the sides (FIG. 5-6F). You can cut the shapes with a band saw. Chamfer the tops of the extensions and the outer edges.

Crossbars share the weight of the box, so tenon them into the legs. On each leg, arrange the part that will be mortised at right angles to the crossbar, to simplify marking and cutting the joint. Mortises might have gone right through in some early specimens, but if you are making a dough trough with a good finish to serve as a side table in modern surroundings, it might be better to have stub tenons finishing within the thickness of the leg (FIG. 5-6G).

Another way of supporting a trough to put the top at table height is to have a stool under it. This might be a separate item or you can make it so the bottom of the trough is also the top of the stool. It is important that the stool's feet stand wide enough to be steady under the wider top, so some flaring of the legs is required (FIG. 5-6H).

Instead of the stool construction, you can make the support more like a table (see Chapter 6). Although quite low if the trough is deep, this example can have table construction, but with the legs sloping outward to give a steady base.

Although there is no need for a dough trough, as such, in a modern home, the pattern makes a convenient table with storage space underneath. If you do not need the full depth of a traditional trough, there could be a shallowed bow with longer legs. It might be more convenient to hinge the lid than to arrange it to lift off. For use with dough, the troughs were bare wood and scrubbed after use, but for use in a living room there could be a stained and polished finish.

Another use for a trough is outdoors to contain plant pots, or soil and flowers planted directly in it. Of course, no lid is needed. You can vary the shape considerably to suit the position the trough is to take and how many pots it is to accommodate.

SEAT CHEST

Most early chests had to serve as seats. A plain chest put against a wall offered reasonable comfort, but if pulled away from the wall, as it might have been to bring the sitter nearer the fire, the lack of back support became noticeable after a short time. Chests developed into seats with backs and ends, eventually reaching heights sufficient to protect from draughts and become chairs with storage under the seat, rather than chests with seating accommodation.

Chests were given some seating comfort by extending the back and ends upward. The amount varied, but even 9 inches provided some back support, particularly if padded with a cushion or blanket. Continuing straight up too high led to problems of strengthening, and a high vertical back is uncomfortable, so further developments made more of a chair.

The chest shown in FIG. 5-7A is made into a settle or double seat. You could make it with one lifting top and the inside without a division, but dividing the inside and having two parts to the top allows one part to be opened without the other, and the support across the center prevents sag from developing in the seat. Although the seat could be sat on directly, it would become more comfortable and more attractive if provided with fitted cushions for the top and back. With each made in two sections, one side could be opened without disturbing the other.

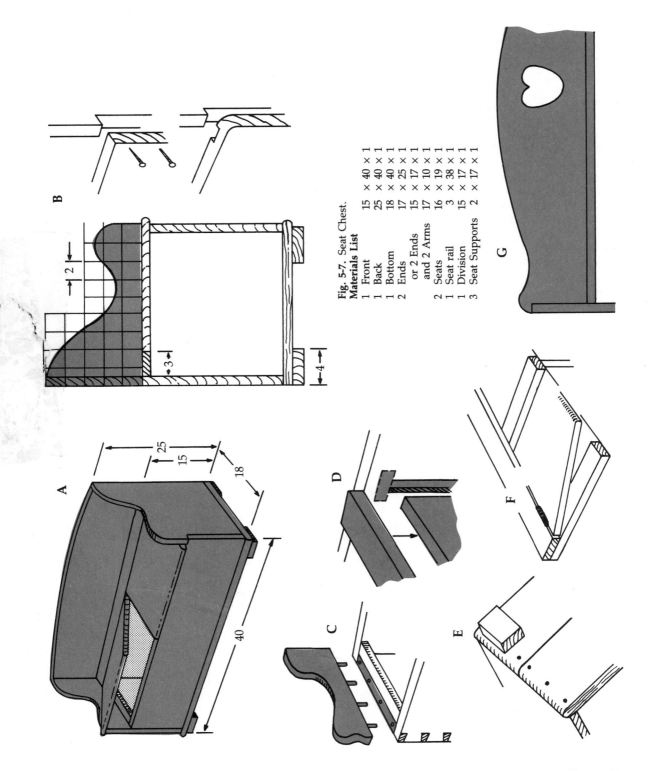

Fig. 5-7. Seat Chest.

Materials List

1	Front	15	× 40	× 1
1	Back	25	× 40	× 1
1	Bottom	18	× 40	× 1
2	Ends	17	× 25	× 1
	or 2 Ends	15	× 17	× 1
	and 2 Arms	17	× 10	× 1
2	Seats	16	× 19	× 1
1	Seat rail	3	× 38	× 1
1	Division	15	× 17	× 1
3	Seat Supports	2	× 17	× 1

The front has its grain lengthwise, but the ends will be stronger if their grain is vertical. If you shape the arms at the tops of the ends much, they will look better and be stronger if fairly thick—1 inch would be suitable—but if you only apply a simple rounding, they could be reduced to 3/4 inch. You can glue and nail both back and front in place or extend them enough to allow for dado joints (FIG. 5-7B). Dovetail joints are inappropriate since the vertical grain of the ends does not cut to make strong pins or dovetails. If you prefer dovetailed construction, you can make the ends cross grained, then make the arms separately and dowel them in place (FIG. 5-7C).

You can fit a central division into dado slots. It is kept low enough to take a broader top to provide support under the meeting lids (FIG. 5-7D). In the original construction, the division was probably nailed in directly without a dado.

The bottom shown was nailed underneath. Since this piece of furniture does not need to be carried about, maximum strength in the bottom is not as necessary. Bottoms were often made with the grain across the box and with many boards to make up the length (FIG. 5-7E). The projecting edges were rounded and blocks put under the corners to serve as feet. In a modern version you can make the main area of the bottom plywood, framing around with solid wood and rabbeting the plywood in, with the meeting edges covered by the box sides and ends.

The seat top is supported by battens across the ends at the same height as the center support. There is a rear strip full length at the back, nailed through the back and to the supports. The two seat parts that form lids rest on the supports and overhang the front slightly (FIG. 5-7F). To prevent warping, it is advisable to put battens across, far enough in to clear the supports. Hinge the lids to the rear strip.

You can leave the upper extension of the back straight, or you can shape it. If is to be hidden by cushions, it might as well remain straight. Too much shaping or carving should be avoided, in any case, as this could prove uncomfortable to lean against. A flowing curve to match the ends would be suitable (FIG. 5-7G). Some of these seats had cutout patterns in the back. Heart shapes were often used.

Round all exposed edges well. The type of chest extended to a seat was common to many settlers, so the finish can be anything from a plain polish to painting with symbolic or pictorial decoration.

PANELED CHEST

Early settlers were fortunate in finding trees of sufficient thickness to cut broad boards. The equipment they had for cutting was more appropriate to producing heavy stock, so most early chests are of quite stout construction, with parts often thicker than might really be justified if strength was the only consideration. The wood had to be prepared that way, however. As people became more established and towns were set up with more of the amenities of civilization, the plain and sometimes crude furniture was not wanted. Along with the demand for better furniture came better woodworking facilities. Sawmills were set up and wood of more delicate section could be provided. The cabinetmaker was able to equip his shop with more than the basic hand equipment, although for a very long time nearly all of the operations he performed depended on hand or foot power.

The newer furniture had to be lighter and better looking. Chests were still important in the home, and cedar in particular was valued for making chests to store blankets and clothing.

One type of chest that evolved had the sides and ends paneled. This was not new; medieval furniture had many examples of paneled construction. Without our modern plywood for wide panels, there was an everpresent problem of wide pieces of wood expanding and contracting with changes in moisture content resulting from atmospheric variations. Panels in a frame, however, could be arranged so expansion and contraction across the grain could take place without affecting appearance. Variations in the direction of the grain were so slight as to be negligible.

The making of paneled furniture by hand called for a considerable amount of skill and some hard work. With a modern table saw, much of the work can be done with greater precision and much less labor. Other power tools also have their uses in this type of work, but a modern hand plow plane will do much of the grooving better than the earlier tools could.

The chest shown in FIG. 5-8A has single panels at the ends, and sides made up of three similar panels. It would be possible to overlap assembled side panels

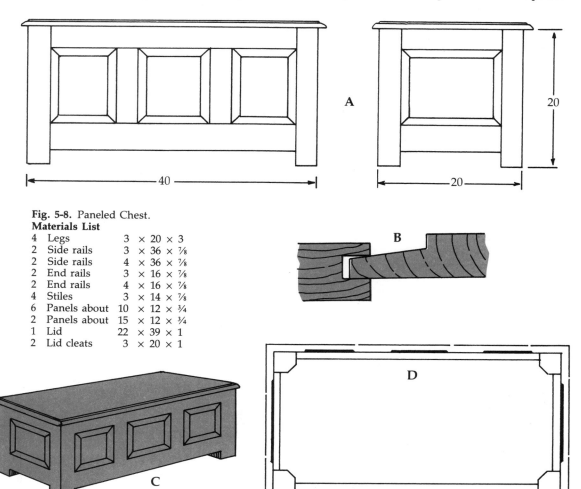

Fig. 5-8. Paneled Chest.
Materials List

4	Legs	3	× 20 × 3
2	Side rails	3	× 36 × ⅞
2	Side rails	4	× 36 × ⅞
2	End rails	3	× 16 × ⅞
2	End rails	4	× 16 × ⅞
4	Stiles	3	× 14 × ⅞
6	Panels about	10	× 12 × ¾
2	Panels about	15	× 12 × ¾
1	Lid	22	× 39 × 1
2	Lid cleats	3	× 20 × 1

on the ends in the same way as chests made from solid boards. Some chests were made this way, but this chest has corner legs. If you make variations, be sure that the faces of the legs, the upright stiles, and the top rails are all the same width on each side or end of the chest, and that the bottom rail is wider. If you make the bottom rail the same width as the other faces, an optical illusion will make it look narrower and spoil the appearance. There might need to be variations to suit the widths of wood available for panels. Having a center side panel wider than the two that border it looks good, but a narrower center panel between wider panels is not as attractive.

The panels have raised centers. Do not cut these until after you prepare the other parts. It is necessary, however, to examine the wood available and decide on sizes. The raised center of each panel is surrounded by what was called *fielding*. This slight taper is fit into a groove made deeper than needed for a close fit (FIG. 5-8B). As the wood expands or contracts, it moves in and out of the groove. If the panels are 3/4 inch thick, it should be satisfactory to settle on grooves 3/8 inch wide throughout the assembly.

The design is shown with all edges square. It is unwise to try to incorporate molding around the framing as this complicates the joints. All that is needed is for the sharpness (the *arrises*) to be sanded off just before assembly, particularly along those edges that will frame the panels.

The top is the only part that can have its appearance relieved by molding (FIG. 5-8C). The legs are square, but inside the chest it looks better if they have the inner angle taken off (FIG. 5-8D). You can cut this angle right through so the feet are the same shape, or stop at the bottom to leave the projecting feet square.

Like any other cabinetmaking project consisting of a great many parts, tackle the preparation systematically. It is advisable to collect the wood for all parts, then cut and plane at least the vital structural parts to width and thickness. There will be a few parts, like the bottom and panels, that you will not work to size until they can be fit into other parts, but you can prepare them to thickness.

The next work should be grooving. The legs, rails, and stiles have similar grooves, which all need to be at the same distance from the front (face) surfaces (FIG. 5-9A). Joints could be doweled, but the early cabinetmaker always used mortise-and-tenon joints. If you choose 3/8 inch for the width of groove, you can simplify the marking out and cutting of the joints by also using that measurement for the width of the mortise. The top rails go about 1 1/2 inches into the legs. Haunch them to fit the grooves (FIG. 5-9B). The joints for the bottom rails can be similar, although a 4-inch width is better arranged with two tenons (FIG. 5-9C). Where the stiles go into the rails, that tenon is the width between the bottoms of the grooves (FIG. 5-9D).

With grooves cut where needed, place parts requiring similar distances together and mark across them with a try square, so all distances that have to match will actually do so. Put the legs together. Mark across their length, but do not cut the ends close to the marks until after other work has been done. Use the ends of rails as guides to their widths and mark the positions of the mortises (FIG. 5-9E). You can use marks on the legs as guides for marking the stiles for their tenons—it is the distance between the shoulders that is important (FIG. 5-9F).

Mark the edges of the four lengthwise rails together and do the same with the four end rails. In all of these parts, it is the distances between shoulders that are important, and you should cut these around the wood with a knife. Slight variations in overall length affecting the tenons are not so important. Cut the

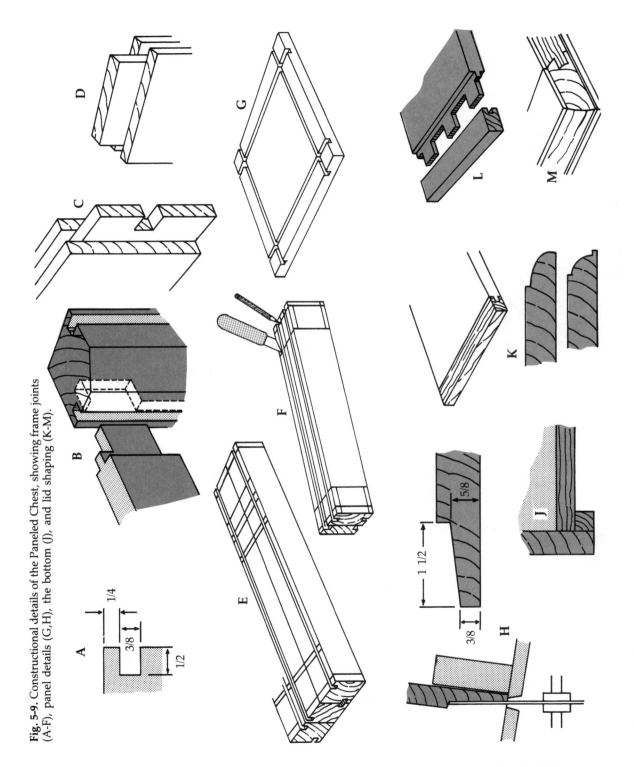

Fig. 5-9. Constructional details of the Paneled Chest, showing frame joints (A-F), panel details (G,H), the bottom (J), and lid shaping (K-M).

tenons by hand or with a table saw. Drill out some of the waste from the mortises and chop them to shape with a chisel. It is best to not make a complete trial assembly because this might cause wear in the joints, so they might not fit as closely in the final assembly.

Measurements from these parts will give the overall sizes of the panels. In the widths, allow for the panels to have approximately a 1/8-inch clearance above the bottoms of the grooves. Lengths can be similar, but as later variations along the grain will be slight, the wood can be a closer fit that way.

How to cut the fielding around the panels depends on the available equipment. The outline of the raised part of the panel is best cut around with a plowed groove (FIG. 5-9G). It might be necessary to cut deeply across the grain with a knife and make the groove on the waste side of this to avoid grain fibers breaking out. You can then cut the fielding with a table saw having a tilt arrangement (FIG. 5-9H). Leave a little to be removed by handwork with a shoulder plane, followed by sanding with abrasive paper wrapped around a wood block. You must remove machine marks, and uniformity of the four sections of fielding around a panel are important for appearance. Corners then will show neat miters between the bevels. These panels are the main decorative features of the chest, so they should be given as good a tool and sanded finish as possible.

If you will stain the chest, deal with the panels before assembly; otherwise shrinkage after assembly could show plain wood at the edges.

It is advisable to deal with assembly in two stages. Glue alone should be adequate, provided sufficient clamps are available. Some early chests had the joints secured with pegs or dowels. This can be done, particularly if it is necessary to move a clamp on after pulling a joint together. The dowel ends can be regarded as a design feature.

Put the panels and stiles between the lengthwise rails, then add the legs. With all these joints pulled close, check squareness by measuring diagonals before leaving the back and front for the glue to set. Sight along to check for twisted assembly. If you place the back over front in the relative positions they will eventually be, you can check them to match and hold them flat with boards and weights over them. Put newspaper between in case any glue oozes out and joins the two parts.

When the glue has set, clean off any surplus, particularly inside. If there is any unevenness inside, level the surfaces. It is easier to deal with inner surfaces at this stage than after the ends have been added. Put the end panels in place between their rails and assemble to the legs. Check the end assemblies for squareness. Have the chest standing so the four legs rest on a surface known to be flat. Measure diagonally across the tops of the legs to see that the chest is square in plain view. Stand well back and sight across the two ends and then the two sides to see there is no twist; then leave the assembly for the end glued parts to set.

The bottom fits inside. Solid wood was arranged with several boards having their grain across the box and resting on strips inside the bottom rails (FIG. 5-9J). If the rest of the chest is made of cedar for storing blankets or linen, it would be advisable to use thin cedar boards for the bottom, but for other purposes you can use plywood.

The lid could be a plain board, but it would need battens underneath to reduce warping, and this might be considered a rather crude and earlier method that would not match the more refined construction method of the rest of the chest. The better method is to tenon on cleats across the ends. A *cleat* is a strip of wood with its grain across the direction of the grain of the top (FIG. 5-9K).

A groove across the cleat has a matching tongue on the top, which extends in two or three places to deeper tenons (FIG. 5-9L). The number of tenons depends on the width, but in this case three should suit. To get a good fit, it is simplest to have the cleat too long and too thick; then you can work it to exact size after fitting. Molding around the top has to be carried around the cleat (FIG. 5-9M), which calls for care where lengthwise grain changes to end grain at the joints.

The lid should swing on three strong hinges, preferably of the strap type, bent to bring their knuckles outside. Although earlier chests rarely had locks or were fitted with staples, this later type might have a proper box lock let into the front to engage with a plate under the lid. This ties in with the more advanced cabinetmaking standard of this chest compared with the earlier ones.

6

Tables

CHESTS MIGHT HAVE SERVED AS SEATS before chairs were made, but the furniture next in importance were working surfaces at a convenient height for standing or sitting. The need was particularly acute in the home for preparing and then eating food. The simplest tables, in Colonial days and in earlier European days, were boards resting on any temporary support. The temporary supports became trestles or other folding devices, so when the table was not required, it and its supports could be put flat against a wall.

A later development was the takedown table, where the table and its supports made a fairly rigid and substantial structure, but they could be taken apart for storage and transport. This was an obvious advantage when a family expected to move westward from a temporary first home, and furniture that could be packed compactly had advantages.

There are surviving, very well made examples of takedown furniture, but there are others in which the features that were needed for folding are incorporated in tables with other parts that do not fold and prevent the first features from being taken apart. This seems a transitional idea where design was not properly understood.

The obvious table would seem to be one with four legs arranged upright at each corner (FIG. 6-1A). Such a table needs to have its legs braced. One way is to have broad rails at the top (FIG. 6-1B). Another way is to join them with rails lower down, and these provided scope for different arrangements and decoration (FIG. 6-1C). An alternative is to have fairly stout single pedestals at each end, broadening under the top and at the feet (FIG. 6-1D). Two pedestals or legs could be joined in this way (FIG. 6-1E).

There also could be a fairly broad board at each end, widening to form feet (FIG. 6-1F). This type is often called a trestle table, although it differs from the original trestle arrangement.

A different approach to legs is to have them in the form of a cross, often called a *sawbuck table*, from the similarity to an arrangement common for hand-sawing logs (FIG. 6-1G). This also lends itself to a folding arrangement, where the legs pivot on their joint and the top attached at one side can fold down (FIG. 6-1H).

Much thought was given to altering the sizes of tables, usually with drop flaps. In the common arrangement, a flap swung downward when not wanted. A bar through a slotted rail might hold it up (FIG. 6-1J), or there could be an extra leg to swing out (FIG. 6-1K). Variations on these methods are still used, as well as some more advanced ideas that were not available in earlier days.

A drawer under a tabletop makes a good place for cutlery and other things needed for a meal. Sewing tables had drawers for needlework items. For a normal fixed-top table, there could not be much depth of drawers or there would be interference with sitting, but some folding tables had deeper drawers, even to the extent of a nest of drawers, in the fixed supports. Seating was around the raised flaps.

As conditions became more settled and craftsmen became more specialized, some very ornate tables were produced. A distinctive style developed, related to design as used in Europe, but with special local characteristics. Tables, chairs, and other items became matched so design was a feature of a room as a whole and not just of one piece of furniture.

Fig. 6-1. Methods of table construction with legs (A-C), pedestals (D-F), sawbuck ends (G-H), and flap supports (J-K).

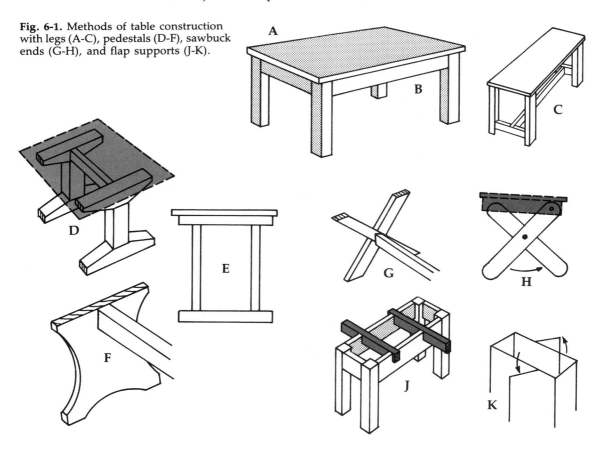

PLAIN TABLE

A simple four-legged table had many variations, and still has, and can be named according to its uses. A general purpose table might be a kitchen table, made with a softwood top and the legs and underframing of hardwood for strength. A smaller near-square table was usually a lamp table and stood at a strategic place for light at night. It would make a good side table. A similar table, rather smaller than a kitchen table, was often called a *tavern table*.

In the simplest table, the legs were square and parallel, but this design gives a rather heavy appearance and it was usual to taper them slightly. Many legs were turned, and the upper part left square for jointing. Usually the legs were stout enough to be rigid and hold their shape without rails, but some of these tables have lower rails and stretchers, which served as footrests.

If a table is to be used for purposes other than sitting to, it can be any size. A coffee table may be low, while one intended to carry a flower vase may be higher. The usual height for a table to be used with a normal chair has its top about 30 inches from the floor. There needs to be clearance under any rail of at least 24 inches so as not to impede the knees. Therefore, the thickness of the tabletop and the width of a rail under it should not exceed 6 inches, and would be better if rather less. These considerations led to many tables having rails lower down, to serve as bracing, when the joints between the top rails and the legs were considered unlikely to stand up to the loads on them. With modern glues and carefully cut joints, joint strength should be much better. The example shown is of tavern table size, but other sizes are made in the same way (FIG. 6-2A).

The legs (FIG. 6-2B) are square and parallel slightly deeper than the rail joint. Leave some excess length at the top. Mark out all four legs together and take the lines all round. You can mark tapers one way, but it is more convenient to cut the top joints before you shape the legs. The traditional way of joining the rails is with mortise-and-tenon joints, having two parts in the depth (FIG. 6-2C). It might be satisfactory to substitute dowels (FIG. 6-2D), but for a table expected to get heavy use, mortise-and-tenon joints are stronger. Mark the rail ends together.

Cut the joints before tapering the legs. With a suitable table saw it is possible to arrange a sliding fence to cut the tapers accurately so they only need light planing. Otherwise, mark the tapers on opposite faces and remove the waste by sawing and planing. Leave some excess length on tops and bottoms of the legs until after the framing is assembled.

Care is necessary to get all parts of a table assembled squarely. Lack of true in any direction becomes very apparent to a viewer.

Assembly should be in two stages. Make up opposite sets of legs and rails—usually the longer way. Put them together on a flat surface and check diagonals. Pull the joints tight with clamps. You can drive nails or dowels inside the legs to hold them and remove the clamps (FIG. 6-2E). Assemble the second side in the same way and put it over the first side. See that both assemblies rest level and match. If there are any discrepancies, put them right before the glue has started to set.

When the glue in those joints has set, add the rails the other way. At this stage, you must check diagonals at the ends, then diagonals across the top, while the legs are standing on a flat surface. Sight across the rails in both directions and see there is no twist, then leave the assembly for the glue to set (FIG. 6-2F).

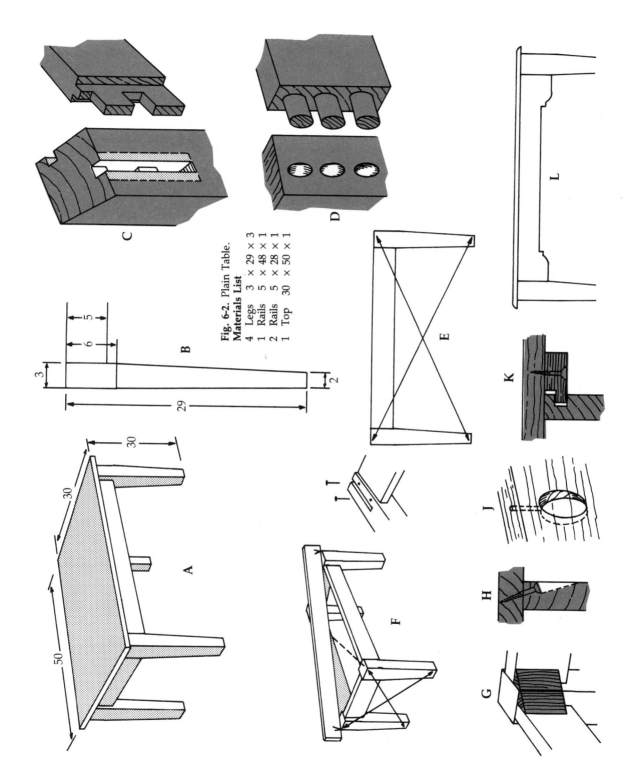

Fig. 6-2. Plain Table.
Materials List

4	Legs	3	× 29	× 3	
1	Rails	5	× 48	× 1	
2	Rails	5	× 28	× 1	
1	Top	30	× 50	× 1	

Further strength in the corners is provided by triangular fillets between the legs and rails (FIG. 6-2G). These are almost as deep as the rails, and glue alone should be sufficient, although you can drive pins to prevent slipping.

Level the tops of the legs with the rails. The whole surface should present a flat area to take the top. You can test it by inverting it on a flat piece of stout plywood or particleboard.

The top is made up of several boards glued together. Overhang was often more in the length than the width. You can cut edges square or round—or you could mold them. Elaborate molding would be inappropriate. Corners were well rounded for kitchen tables and even with side tables apparently square, the sharpness should be taken off.

The most basic table has the top nailed to the rails, possibly with the nails punched and stopped. It is better to fix from below so nothing shows on the top surface. *Pocket screwing* was used and this is still a good method. The screw goes diagonally upward through the rail into the top, and you must cut pockets with a gouge and chisel at intervals to let the screw head in (FIG. 6-2H). A simple way of cutting a pocket is to use a large-diameter bit in a brace and enter it at right angles to the line the screw will take (FIG. 6-2J).

Fixing a top rigidly makes no allowance for expansion and contraction of a fairly wide top. One way of dealing with this problem is to use pieces of wood under the top. They engage with grooves plowed in the rails before assembly. Screw in the buttons at intervals around the underside of the top. Their extensions free to move in the grooves (FIG. 6-2K).

You can remove some of the severity of appearance and provide better leg room by cutting away the undersides of the rails (FIG. 6-2L). This method allows for rather deeper joints for greater strength at the legs, but the cutaway parts should not be too close to the legs or there might be weakness caused by short grain breaking out.

TABLE WITH DRAWERS

If a table is to be used by people sitting on chairs and putting their legs underneath, any drawer must be shallow; otherwise its framing and the rails will come too low. Therefore, it is possible to make a kitchen table with a drawer with space enough for cutlery, with an internal depth of about 2 inches, but any more would be unsuitable. Many kitchen tables were made with these drawers at opposite ends and it is possible to frame up a table in this way, but cutting away end rails to admit drawers tends to weaken the structure. Therefore, good workmanship to make strong joints is essential.

If the table does not need to admit the knees of someone sitting on a chair, freedom of design is extended. Such tables can be for side use or as sewing tables. They might be lower as coffee tables today. A serving table in the dining room could have drawers deep enough to give useful capacity. If a table is made the same height as a dining table, it could serve to extend that when needed, although it would not be suitable for sitting with legs under.

This example is based on a Shaker original. The sizes would make a sewing or side table, with the top at a working height and a shallow drawer for cutlery or needles and thread, as well as a deeper one below. Depth in the assembly produces stiffness and strength. Although many of these tables were made in pine or other softwood, polished hardwood might be better for use alongside modern furniture.

Some comparable tables made by other colonial workers had molded edges to the top and shaped lower edges to the rails. The legs might have been turned below rail level.

There are many ways of making and supporting drawers. In much modern construction, there are plastic runners or the drawer side is grooved to run on a strip of wood. All early drawers ran on the bottom edges of the sides, over strips of wood called *runners*. As the drawer was withdrawn, it was prevented from dropping by a piece of wood above the side, called a *kicker* (FIG. 6-3A). If the actual assembly did not keep the drawer on its track in the width, there were guides on the runners (FIG. 6-3B). If reproduction furniture is to be authentic, you should use this method of controlling the movement of each drawer.

Drawer bottoms often were let into grooves plowed in the sides and front, but the back usually fit above the bottom (FIG. 6-3C). This design allowed the bottom to slide in from the back after the drawer joints had been glued and is satisfactory for light construction. If you examine larger and heavier drawers however, you will see a separate grooved piece inside the front and sides (FIG. 6-3D). This part gave an increased bearing area on the runner, so the possibility of wear was much less than when a comparatively thin edge had to take the weight.

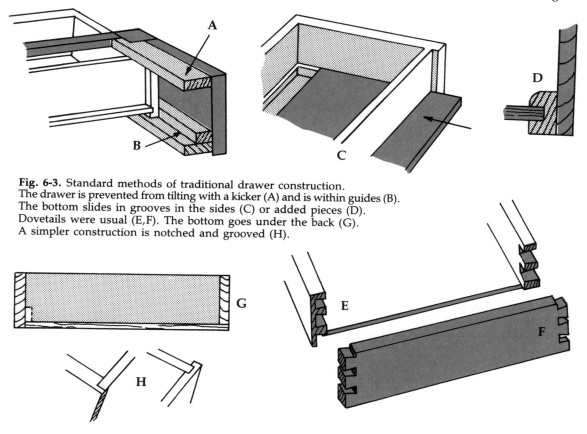

Fig. 6-3. Standard methods of traditional drawer construction.
The drawer is prevented from tilting with a kicker (A) and is within guides (B).
The bottom slides in grooves in the sides (C) or added pieces (D).
Dovetails were usual (E,F). The bottom goes under the back (G).
A simpler construction is notched and grooved (H).

The drawers in much modern furniture have their fronts projecting a little from the front of the structure or are made with a false front that overlaps the opening. This is a modern trend and simplifies construction because slight errors are not so apparent. The majority of traditional furniture, however, has the drawer fronts flush with the surrounding woodwork. This design requires more careful fitting, and drawers with equal narrow gaps all around were the mark of a good craftsman.

In reproduction furniture, you can compromise by making a drawer to stand out a short distance and rounding the outer edge. The gaps around are not then so obvious, and slight variations in their widths is not so important.

The best cabinetmakers always dovetailed drawers. If sides and front were grooved for the bottom a half dovetail at the bottom of a side enclosed the groove (FIG. 6-3E). The back of the drawer had through dovetails worked above the groove (FIG. 6-3F). If you follow this system in drawers for table or other types of furniture, the quality of the reproduction will be as good as the best by original craftsmen.

Not all early furniture makers were trained craftsmen. Sometimes they were not skilled enough to make dovetails. In the simplest construction, a drawer was no more than a nailed box, with its bottom nailed on from below. Such primitive construction is not really worth reproducing. Better examples had notched corner joints. The simplest drawer then had the sides notched into the front, but the back was lapped and nailed, with the bottom nailed to sides, back, and a strip inside the front (FIG. 6-3G). It is the bottom that bears on the runners, so nails had to be punched and the edges smoothed.

A better construction had the sides in notches or rabbets in the front, but the back was dadoed into the sides, above the bottom, as with dovetails. This is still a good alternative method of construction to dovetails, particularly if the bottom is grooved into the sides and front (FIG. 6-3H). Joints are made with glue, and either nails or screws sunk below the surface and stopped.

This table with two drawers is a good example of the type of construction where a cabinetmaker's *rod* is useful to ensure parts are uniform and the whole assembly is true. A rod is a means of transferring and comparing measurements without having to refer to frequently a ruler. In this case, the rod is used as a guide for all vertical measurements.

The sizes given make a table with a comfortable working height (FIG. 6-4A). As a first step, draw one leg with the outlines of the top, the drawers, and their rails (FIG. 6-4B). For the rails, use the sizes of the pieces of wood as they are and not what they should be, for drawing their locations. A wood width slightly more or less than the intended size will not matter if you allow for it when laying out parts to which it will be attached. Transfer all the vital measurements to a straight piece of scrap wood that will serve as a rod (FIG. 6-4C). From this point, mark rail positions and drawer depths from the rod, and not by using a rule.

Mark out all four legs together. Leave a little surplus length at the top until after you have cut the joints. The sides and back are best tenoned into the legs (FIG. 6-4D), in the way described for the Plain Table. Dowels are not so satisfactory for these deeper rails, although they can be used.

The place of a front rail is made up by the two drawers and the three narrow rails that accommodate them. Select straight-grained wood for the narrow drawer rails since warping after assembly could interfere with the action of the drawers. The rails can join the legs with barefaced tenons (FIG. 6-4E). With a table of the sizes given, there should be little risk of the rails warping, but if you have any

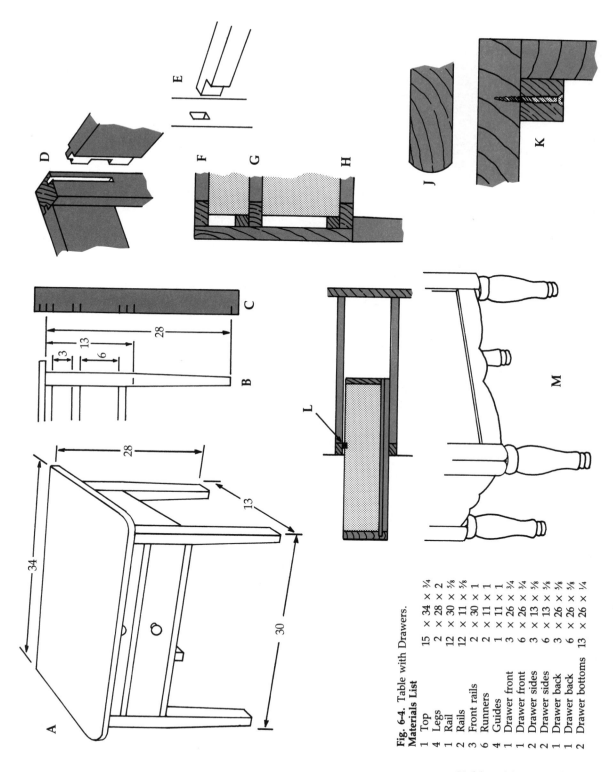

Fig. 6-4. Table with Drawers.

Materials List

1	Top	15	×	34	×	3/4
4	Legs	2	×	28	×	2
1	Rail	12	×	30	×	5/8
2	Rails	12	×	11	×	5/8
3	Front rails	2	×	30	×	1
6	Runners	2	×	11	×	1
4	Guides	1	×	11	×	1
1	Drawer front	3	×	26	×	3/4
1	Drawer front	6	×	26	×	3/4
2	Drawer sides	3	×	13	×	5/8
2	Drawer sides	6	×	13	×	5/8
1	Drawer back	3	×	26	×	5/8
1	Drawer back	6	×	26	×	5/8
2	Drawer bottoms	13	×	26	×	1/4

doubt or you increase the sizes, there can be pieces from front to back at the centers of the two lower rails. Keep their lower edges level with the undersides of the rails. The top edges should be level with or below the top sides of the rail, so they do not interfere with the drawer above.

Make up the table framework in the sequence described for the Plain Table, getting back and front right, before adding the ends and checking diagonals. You can prepare the top and try it in position, but do not fit it until after you do all the work associated with the drawers.

You can use the table assembly as a guide for first making the drawer fronts. Cut them to fit with just a little clearance in the two openings. Lightly pencil marks to show which way they go. Make a drawer side. It should be of such a length that it abuts the back rail when the drawer front is level with the framework, if that is the chosen design, or projects about 1/8 inch, if the front is to be rounded. Allow for the chosen method of construction. You can leave the rear end of each side slightly too long and adjust the finished drawer to get it at exactly the right projection and parallel at the front.

Assemble the drawers completely and try them in their openings. Make up kickers, guides, and runners to suit the drawers by testing them in position. Start at the top. There are plain kickers above the top drawer. Their thickness should be the same as the front rails. For the drawer, it is important that the lower surface be level with the underside of the top front rail. These kickers also will be used to take screws to secure the top, so the top surfaces should finish level with the tops of the side rails (FIG. 6-4F). The runners for the top drawer are also the kickers for the bottom drawer, so they should be the same thickness as the middle front rail, projecting far enough to give a good bearing to the drawer and with a strip added level with the inner surfaces of the legs to act as guides (FIG. 6-4G). The bottom runner is a similar piece (FIG. 6-4H), but accuracy of its bottom surface is not as important.

You might need to do a little adjusting of the drawers to get an easy action and a good fit. Back-to-front adjustment is by planing off the rear ends of the sides. If you are unlucky and a side is too short, you can glue on a piece of veneer or even paper. To adjust the width, plane the sides.

If the piece is to be authentic Shaker style, leave the top edges of the drawers square or give them a slight radius (FIG. 6-4J). If the table is to go against a wall, the rear of the top wood should be level with the legs.

To fix the drawers to the top, insert screws from below, through the kickers at the ends, and through each top drawer rail. There could be pocketed screws in the back rail, although another way is to have a strip inside the back rail and screw upward through that (FIG. 6-4K).

To prevent a drawer from being pulled out accidentally, attach small pieces of wood under the rail above the drawer to act as stops (FIG. 6-4L). If a stop is thin, it will bear against the back and stop the drawer, but if the front of the drawer is tilted up as the drawer is opened, the drawer can still be removed.

If you want a more decorative finish, you can turn the legs and give the rails shaped lower edges (FIG. 6-4M). You could mold the edges of the top or curve the outline.

There should be one or two knobs or handles on each drawer. Locate them slightly above half the depth of the front. For a Shaker design, they should be plain turned wood, but you can use ornamental metal (not plastic) handles with a more decorative table design.

DROP-LEAF TABLE

Some tables that can be adjusted in size are intended for sitting around, whether they are fully extended or in their reduced size. Another type is normally in its larger form for use, but the top can be reduced in size so the table occupies less space when not in use. There are several ways of arranging this, but usually part of the top is arranged to fold down. When it is hanging down, there is no space for a sitter's knees, so it is unsuitable for eating off when folded, although it can still serve for storage as a side table. The example shown in FIG. 6-5A is based on an Appalachian original, but the type was common to many early households.

Make the table framework in the same way as for the Plain Table. Legs could be square and tapered, but lathes came early and many legs were turned. The drawing is of an original type (FIG. 6-5B). A drawer at one end is useful and easily incorporated. The main construction is basically similar to that of the Table with Drawers.

Attach upper and lower drawer rails at one end, extending them for at least the distance the drawer is to go with runners and kickers. Make the guides level with the inner surfaces of the legs (FIG. 6-5C). Use small blocks of wood on the runners to stop the drawer at the right position (FIG. 6-5D). Delay fitting these until the drawer is made and put in position, then locate the blocks to come against the drawer. It helps in stiffening the table to make the lower drawer rail wide, with twin tenons (FIG. 6-5E). A large table may have a rail across the center, which this could also act as a drawer stop.

The main part of the top is a simple rectangle with a reasonable overhang at the ends, but only slightly wider than the distance across the tops of the legs. You can use brackets on hinges to hold up the drop leaves (FIG. 6-5F). The amount of overhang of the top should be enough to allow the leaves to hang with some clearance over the brackets when folded (FIG. 6-5G).

Make the brackets to a right angle you might theoretically expect them to hold the leaves level when swung out, but wear and slackness in the hinge knuckles, as well as the need for clearance to allow for moving the brackets, cause the leaves to sag slightly, unless something is done about it. Where a bracket comes under the leaf, fit a small wedge, longer and going deeper than you expect at first (FIG. 6-5H). The bracket swings on to this and can be moved as far as is necessary to level the top. There could be a stop on the wedge, but usually it is sufficient to continue the deep part of the wedge parallel for a short distance.

In the simplest arrangement, the leaves hang on hinges and have square edges (FIG. 6-5J). Locate three hinges so they do not come in the way of the brackets when the brackets are swung out.

Although square-edged boards might have been practical, the joint was not beautiful, and many cabinetmakers brought with them knowledge of what was usually called a *rule joint* as the normal way of dealing with boards in a drop-leaf tabletop. This was in use in Europe and extended hinges, called *back-flap hinges*, were used to give stronger joints. The name *rule joint* comes from a similarity of the section to the joint used in some two-fold rules (FIG. 6-6A).

For the traditional method of making the joint, there had to be hollow and round planes, but a modern way of forming the shapes could be with a spindle molder or suitable router cutters. When the tabletop is up, the edges should meet closely. The leaf should follow the curve as it swings down so there is little gap showing and the meeting surfaces have a molded look (FIG. 6-6B). A back-flap

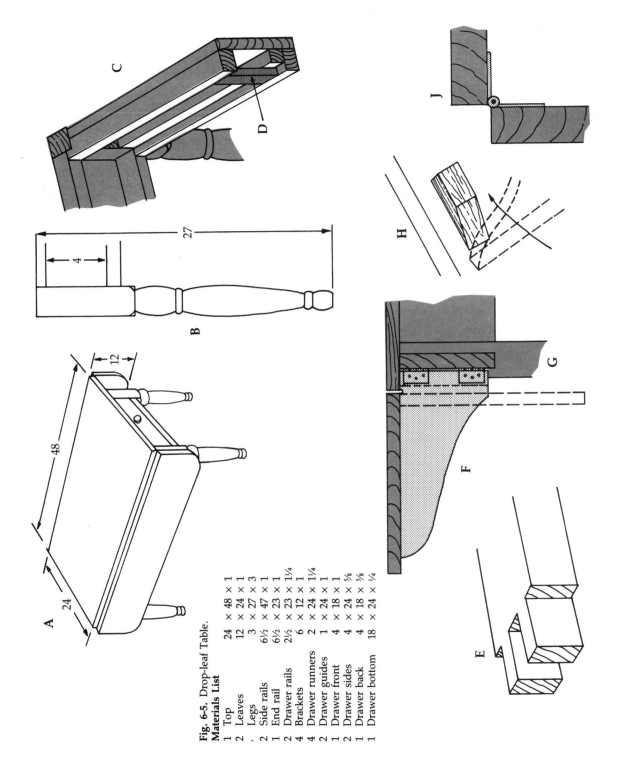

Fig. 6-5. Drop-leaf Table.
Materials List

1	Top	24 × 48 × 1
2	Leaves	12 × 24 × 1
4	Legs	3 × 27 × 3
2	Side rails	6½ × 47 × 1
1	End rail	6½ × 23 × 1
2	Drawer rails	2½ × 23 × 1¼
4	Brackets	6 × 12 × 1
4	Drawer runners	2 × 24 × 1¼
2	Drawer guides	1 × 24 × 1
1	Drawer front	4 × 18 × 1
2	Drawer sides	4 × 24 × ⅝
1	Drawer back	4 × 18 × ⅝
1	Drawer bottom	18 × 24 × ¼

Fig. 6-6. A glue joint for a drop flap, showing the relative positions of the parts.

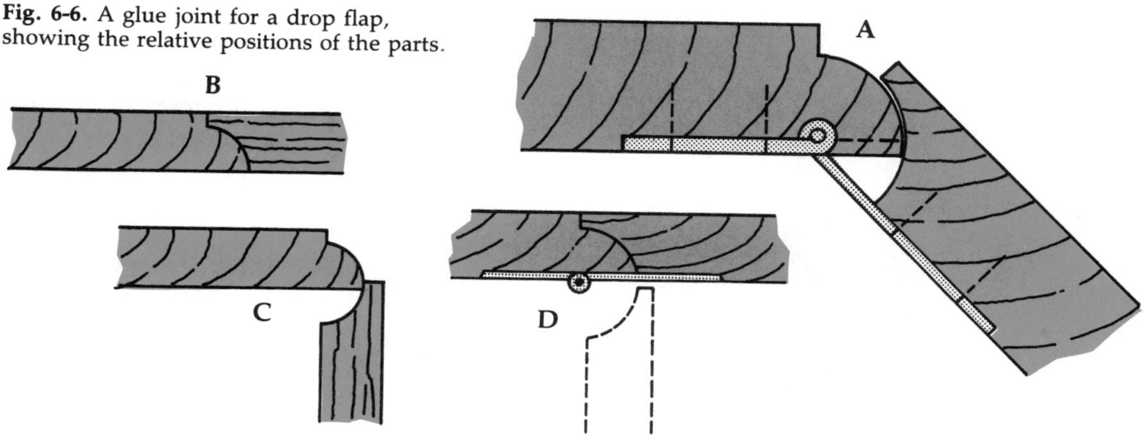

hinge is designed to be used with its knuckle upward and the two parts can swing back to a right angle, which is further than normal hinges will go. Notch the knuckle into the wood so it comes at the center of the curve molded on the edge (FIG. 6-6C). If you use an ordinary hinge, it will have to be arranged with the knuckle downward, and the action will not be quite as accurate when the parts move in relation to each other (FIG. 6-6D)

DEEP-LEAF TABLE

If a drop-leaf table is to take up the minimum space when folded, the center part must be narrower and the flaps wider. If the leaves are very wide and the center very narrow, there is a loss of stability on four legs only, so the flap supports incorporate extra legs, as in the Gateleg Table, which follows. Many early tables, however, had the width of the top divided approximately into three, and the four legs were heavy, with stout lower rails—all of which helped to keep the table stable. The legs also were slightly splayed, but this could not be very much if they were not to interfere with the hang of the leaves (FIG. 6-7A).

This table has the top overhanging enough at the ends to accommodate a sitter's knees, and the raised flaps are wide enough to give knee clearance at the sides, so the top rails are fairly deep for rigidity. You can fit one or two drawers at the ends. They can be deep, yet still allow for the strength of deep lower drawer rails. Drawer construction and fitting is similar to that described for previous tables, but with splayed legs it is better to leave the ends of the drawers at right angles than to conform to the slight slope of the legs. You can have tapered fillers on the sides of the legs, and you will need to arrange the runners with beveled edges to fit against the long rails. If the legs are splayed, it is advisable to make a full-size end view to check angles and the location of rails and the joints they need.

Legs can be square. You can relieve the plainness by *wagon beveling* (the edge beveling named after the way English farm wagons had their parts cut away). Where the rails come, leave the edges square, but bevel between these places (FIG. 6-7B). Alternatively, you can turn the legs between the parts left square for jointing (FIG. 6-7C).

The lower stretcher rails have simple mortise-and-tenon joints (FIG. 6-7D). If you wagon-bevel the legs, you can treat the upper angles of the stretchers in the

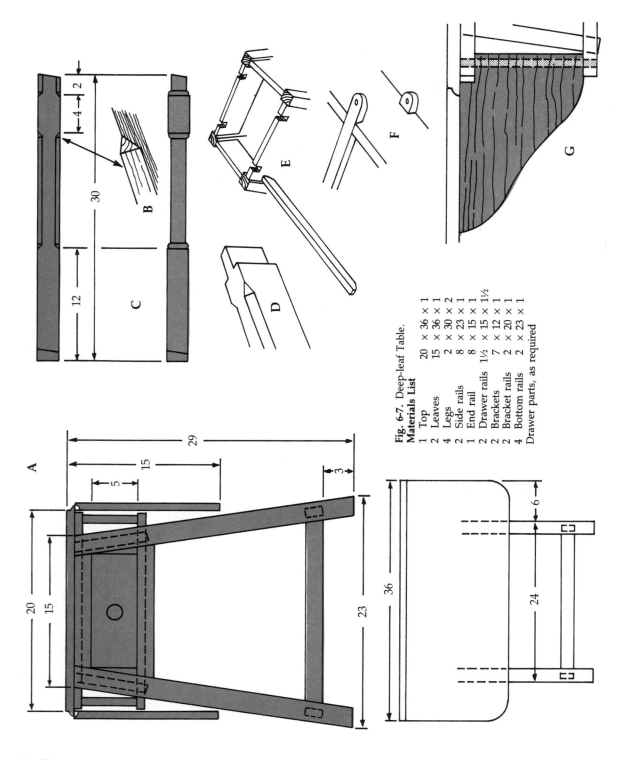

Fig. 6-7. Deep-leaf Table.

Materials List

1	Top	20	× 36	× 1
2	Leaves	15	× 36	× 1
4	Legs	2	× 30	× 2
2	Side rails	8	× 23	× 1
1	End rail	8	× 15	× 1
2	Drawer rails	1½	× 15	× 1½
2	Brackets	7	× 12	× 1
2	Bracket rails	2	× 20	× 1
4	Bottom rails	2	× 23	× 1

Drawer parts, as required

same way. With turned legs, take off the angles of the stretchers by rounding.

You can provide support for the leaves in one of two ways. You can notch the side rails to take loose cross rails, arranged about one-quarter of the length from each end. These rails are kept separate and pushed in place when needed (FIG. 6-7E). They were sometimes hung by straps under the table, hidden by the lowered flaps.

Another way is to use brackets, which could be on hinges as in the previous table, but a variation is to use central brackets pivoting on crossbars. Notch the crossbars into the top and bottom edges of the front and rear top rails (FIG. 6-7F). They should be made of close-grained hardwood because they must take a load on the short grain at their ends. The tabletop and the crossbars must extend far enough to allow the brackets to pivot on dowel pins (FIG. 6-7G). Round the back of a bracket and notch the top to clear the end of the crossbar. Round the edges of the shaped part and place a similar wedge arrangement under each leaf to allow for leveling in the raised position.

You can leave square the meeting edges between the leaves and the center of the top square or work them as a rule joint, as for the Drop-Leaf Table. Round the outer corners of the leaves—slightly, if the general effect is to be square, or with large sweeps if you prefer a rounded effect. You can leave the outer edge square, give it a slightly curved section, or mold it. It is important, however, that whatever pattern you use follows around the three parts smoothly, so finishing work on the edge of the top is best done after assembly and with the leaves raised.

Although it might seem obvious for the leaves to swing down, where gravity helps to keep them in the folded position, there have been tables of this type made where one flap swings upward. Such a table can be moved against a wall, with the upturned flap up the wall and the other down. The table then can be used as a sideboard or serving table, or as a storage place for many kitchen or dining room articles, with the upturned flap acting as a background to show off the display and prevent items from falling off the back of the table.

GATELEG TABLE

For a table to reduce to the most compact width when not needed, the center part must be narrower than the flaps. If it stands on four legs, they must be close together in the width. Stability when the flaps are up is unsatisfactory unless additional support from the floor is provided. Furniture designers in many places seem to have gotten over this problem in similar ways but independently, using swinging assemblies to take an extra leg out to each side to come under the edges of the leaves. The common name for this type is a *gateleg table*.

Gateleg tables did not come until the period of more settled conditions, so they were the products of specialist craftsmen, who had the skill and time to devote to better work than was usually possible amongst the first settlers. As a result, most originals are of a quality that would stand comparison with much modern furniture.

The first development of what became accepted as the standard form of gateleg table in America was in New England. The specimen in FIG. 6-8A is based on old gateleg tables still to be found there.

The general layout uses a central section that is about one-third of the full width. You can make the top rectangular or elliptical. The comparatively narrow central assembly has two gatelike parts swinging out to support the leaves, with legs to match the main ones and a similar pillaster acting as a pivot on each side.

If you use different sizes than suggested, do not make the side top rails as deep as might be used in a plain table, because they must be drilled for the dowel pin hinges. These and the lower rails should be thick enough to retain sufficient strength after notching for the swing legs.

Make the legs square and the same size at upper and lower joint positions. To avoid a heavy look, the parts in between and the feet are turned on most originals. There are a total of eight pieces to be turned with matching patterns. The best approach is to turn one leg after making a drawing of the intended shape. The outline might not conform exactly to the drawing, since you find curves that are more pleasing under the tool than those on paper.

From the first leg, make a rod marked with distances and diameters at various points. You also can draw an outline back from the edge (FIG. 6-8B). Some turners cut the edge to make a template, but having the diameters to set calipers and a drawing to work parallel probably gives better uniformity.

You can finish the feet completely, but leave some excess length at the top until after joints are cut. Notice that the rails for the gatelegs are closer together than the main rails, and the square parts are long enough to allow for this design, with all legs having squares of the same length (FIG. 6-8C).

To suit the action of the gatelegs, the side rails come flush with the outsides of the legs, so make them with barefaced tenons (FIG. 6-8D). The end rails need not be flush with the leg surfaces, but they will match the others if made this way. To obtain extra rigidity, make the top end rails deeper than the side ones. Since the ends show whether the table is open or folded, you can decorate the end rails rated with carving or by shaping the lower edges (FIG. 6-8E).

Mark out the upper and lower long rails together so the pivot holes and the half lap notches match. Because the distance between the pivots and half-lap cuts must match the gatelegs, delay cutting the joints until you can assemble each gateleg and try it in place.

For each gateleg, tenon lighter rails into the pillaster and leg (FIG. 6-8F). As with the rest of the table framing, be careful to assemble the parts flat and at right angles, checking with a try square and measuring diagonals. Although it is possible to use doweled joints instead of mortises and tenons throughout the table, traditional methods are stronger and more authentic. Mortises can have small dowels across for additional strength, but a glued joint that fits closely should have ample strength without dowels. If you need to remove clamps for use elsewhere before glue has set, you can drive nails across the mortises from the least obvious side, then punch them below the surface and cover them with stopping.

Holes for the hinge dowel pins need to be truly at right angles to the rails. Drilling by machine should ensure this, but if you must drill by hand, mark the hole positions around the wood and drill the holes halfway from each side. In this way, slight inaccuracies can be expected to cancel out in the center of the wood.

Place a gateleg in position and mark it through the rail holes. The pillaster lengths should make a close fit between the upper and lower main rails. Check in the assembly that the feet of the gatelegs are level with the feet of the main legs. Because it is the top of the gateleg that supports the raised leaf, see that the overall length of each gateleg is the same as the length of the main legs and that the top comes level with the top rail when folded.

The center part of the top must overlap in its width enough to allow the leaves to hang freely outside the folded gatelegs. Fitting can be with socket screws or

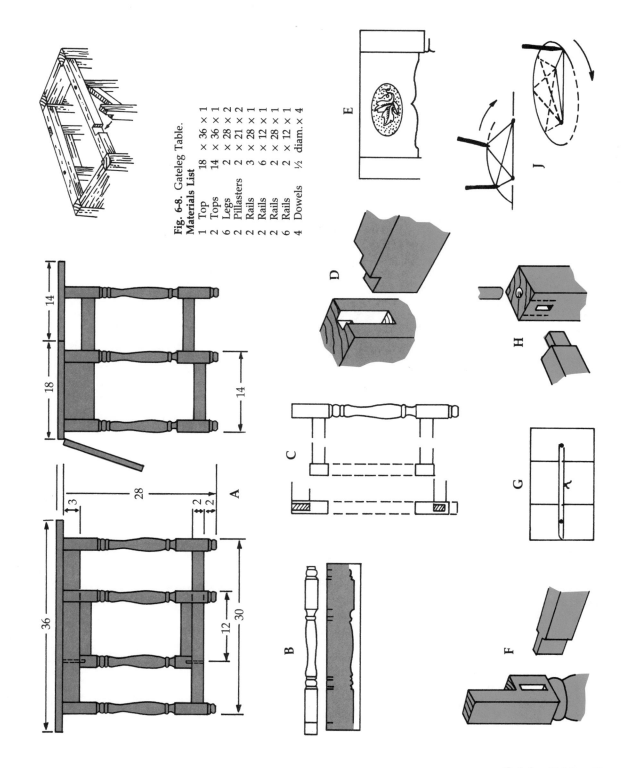

Fig. 6-8. Gateleg Table.
Materials List

1	Top	18	×	36	×	1		
2	Tops	14	×	36	×	1		
6	Legs	2	×	28	×	2		
2	Pillasters	2	×	21	×	2		
3	Rails	3	×	28	×	1		
6	Rails	6	×	12	×	1		
2	Rails	2	×	28	×	1		
6	Rails	2	×	12	×	1		
4	Dowels	½	diam.	×	4			

buttons from below, in the way described for earlier tables. The leaves can have simple hinging with square edges, but the better gateleg tables had rule joints for the better appearance with the rest of the high-quality construction.

For the greatest useful area on top, make the leaves rectangular and take the sharpness off the corners by rounding with a radius of a few inches. Many of these tables had elliptical tops, usually with the greater length across the leaves. This design gives an attractive appearance and a pleasant arrangement for setting several meal places.

The ellipse needs to be regular if it is to look right. A good way of marking it out uses two nails, a pencil, and a length of string. Put the boards for the tabletop together and upside down. Draw a centerline across them. To determine a suitable size of ellipse, experiment with the nail positions on the line. Put the nails on the line at equal distances from the end. Their position will depend on the proportions of the ellipse, but try 1 foot from each end at first. Make a loop of string around the nails to extend to one end (FIG. 6-8G). Put the pencil point in the end of the loop and work it around to the side, keeping the string loop taut (FIG. 6-8H). You will be very lucky if it reaches the side the first time. If it goes too far, start again with the nails farther apart; if it does not reach the side, move the nails closer together. Each time adjust the loop so it reaches the end of the line. When you have it right, go all the way around with the pencil, keeping the string taut from the nails (FIG. 6-8J).

After cutting the tabletop profile, you can round or mold its edges. Molding a curved edge by hand is difficult to do accurately. You can use a spindle molder or a router, but if these are unavailable it would be better to rely on a simple rounding. Check that any edge shaping follows through smoothly at the top joints. Finishing at these positions might be better left until after the final assembly.

A gateleg support has a longer reach than a swinging bracket, so the possibility of a leaf sagging is less, but you might want to include a slim wedge under a leaf to allow for wear. You can also attach small wood blocks to act as stops when the extended legs come under the center of the leaf.

SWIVEL-TOP TABLE

One way of arranging a tabletop with drop leaves—without brackets, gatelegs, or other supports for the leaves—is to have the top swiveling on the framework, which is narrow and long. The leaves hang down when the top assembly is crosswise, but if the leaves are lifted level and the top turned through a right angle, they will be held up by resting on the ends of the framework. The top parts are best joined with backflap hinges, but if ordinary hinges are used, the top can be raised on packings so the hinges clear the framework as it is turned. Metal pivots were made and modern versions can be bought, but a bolt type and a wooden pivot are described here.

Although this type of table could stand on upright legs, a more stable form has the legs splayed in both directions. The example shown is a small side table, but the method could be used for a table of any size. This example gets its stiffness from wide top rails only. With straight-grained wood for the legs and good mortise-and-tenon joints, preferably doweled through, the result is a graceful rigid table (FIG. 6-9A).

The compound angles resulting from splaying the legs both ways need not cause difficult work if you tackle them systematically. The angles in both directions need not be the same; there could be more splay in the width than the length.

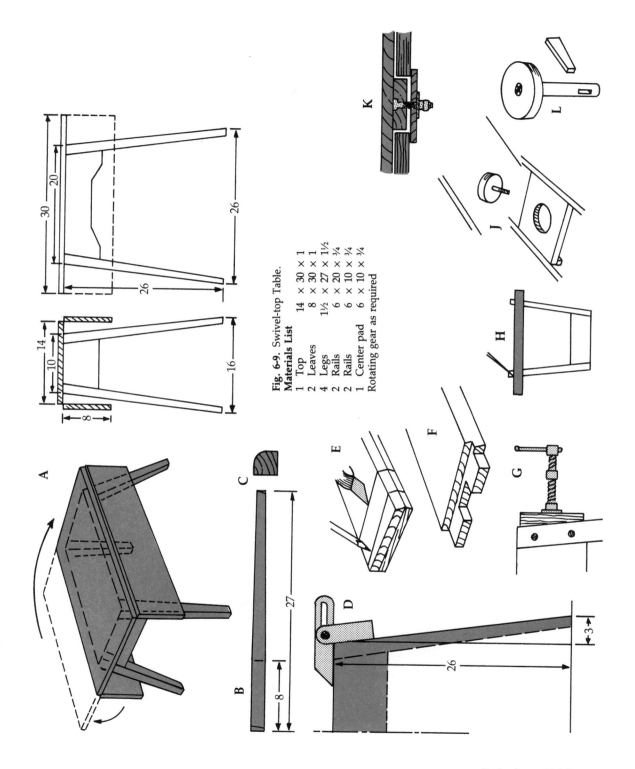

Fig. 6-9. Swivel-top Table.
Materials List

1	Top	14 × 30 × 1
2	Leaves	8 × 30 × 1
4	Legs	1½ × 27 × 1½
2	Rails	6 × 20 × ¾
2	Rails	6 × 10 × ¾
1	Center pad	6 × 10 × ¾
	Rotating gear as required	

Setting out is simpler, though, if the angle is the same both ways. Make a full-size drawing of a leg and one corner. It is helpful if the top line is at least as long as half the length of the side rail.

When a framework is splayed in two directions, the view of a leg from above remains a right angle, but the actual section becomes a diamond. With a wide splay this becomes increasingly important if joints are to fit properly, and you must use geometry to find the angles to which the legs must be planed. With a double splay of only a few degrees, as in this example, the difference between a theoretically correct section and a square section is very slight. By using bare-faced tenons in the rail joints, you avoid the slight difference between the fit of front and back shoulders of each joint, so you can make the legs to square sections.

Each leg is square and parallel to a point below where the rails will come, then there is a slight taper on each side to the bottom (FIG. 6-9B). The legs look even more graceful if you round the outer corner, starting with only a slight curve at the top of the taper and continuing to a quarter circle at the foot (FIG. 6-9C). Allow a little excess length at top and bottom of each leg.

Set an adjustable bevel to the angle shown in FIG. 6-9D. Lock it at that. It is the only angle other than a right angle you will need to test, but it should be the same throughout.

Mark the wood for the two side rails. Plane the top edges to the angle of your adjustable bevel. The bottom edges can remain at right angles. Put the two pieces together and mark across their edges the length between shoulders and a further 1 inch at each end for the tenons. Mark the shoulders on the outer surfaces with a knife and the ends of the tenons with a pencil, using the adjustable bevel (FIG. 6-9E). Cut the pieces to length, mark the widths of the tenons, and cut away the waste. Shape the tenons (FIG. 6-9F).

Mark the mortises to match the tenons and cut them. Do the same with the short rails. Do not try any of the joints at this stage. The rails must be fairly deep to provide stiffness. You can leave them full width or reduce their central areas, either by cutting back with plain curves or with a decorative outline. It might be preferable to leave the end rails full depth and only reduce the side rails. In any case, leave a good width of full-depth ends so as not to weaken the joints with short grain.

The best way to tackle assembly is to first make up the two sides, ignoring the splay in the other direction, then add the short rails to join the sides. You must pull the joints tight and make two packing blocks for the bar clamp to squeeze on. While the clamp is still on, drill through for a dowel into each extending tenon (FIG. 6-9G). Check the two side assemblies on each other. Turn one over on the other. This will show if the splay is the same at each corner. Let the glue set before proceeding.

Make all four joints the other way at the same time since the meeting surfaces will not be quite at right angles due to the double splay. Make a dry trial assembly with the tenons only entered a short distance. This will show that they are not entering quite squarely and it might be necessary to pare the side of each tenon slightly with a chisel to get a neat fit. Apply glue and clamp the joints, preferably pulling each end tighter a little at a time to keep the shape uniform. Dowel through in the same way as at the sides, and check that the corners at the top are at right angles by using a try square and checking diagonals.

The beveled top edges of the rails will show how much to cut off the tops of the legs. Measure down each leg the same amount and make a mark on the outer corner for the foot. Use a long, straight board as a guide to mark where the legs are to be cut (FIG. 6-9H). Round the edges of these cuts.

You can make up the top from three boards, preferably with rule joints and backflap hinges, but you can cut the meeting edges square and use plain hinges for a simpler construction. If you use sizes different from those given here, make the center part long enough to have a slight overhang on the framework, but wide enough to allow the leaves to hang without touching the splayed legs. The proportions are best if the ends of the framework come more than halfway under the raised leaves when the top is turned to give the full area.

The top shown has square corners and plain edges, but you could treat it in any of the ways described for the tops of earlier tables. Many of these tables had round tops; others were elliptical. Hanging curved leaves have a pleasing appearance. You can round or square edges. Much shaping goes better with turned legs, and a plainer treatment is all that is needed with the legs shown.

Glue and screw a disk to the underside of the center of the top. The disk fits in a hole in a board fitted between the framework sides. Bevel its ends to fit and support it by strips screwed to the sides (FIG. 6-9J). You can turn the disk, but perfection in its outline is not essential to its functioning, so a handcut circle will do. This also applies to the hole it fits. Providing the disk will turn in the hole, a small amount of slackness is unimportant and preferable to parts that bind against each other at some points.

Another, larger disk goes below the disk in the hole and overlaps the hole. In modern construction, this would best be made of plywood. Because it does not show, there seems little objection to using plywood, but if complete authenticity is required, it could be any thin wood unlikely to crack or split.

The best way to arrange the pivot is to use a bolt with its head let into the top disk. Attach the bolt through both disks to two nuts with a washer (FIG. 6-9K). Glue and screw the disk to the underside of the top after you insert the bolt. Adjust the nuts to allow the top to turn without undue slackness, then lock them by tightening them against each other. An original blacksmith-made bolt would have had a square head and square nuts, but you might need to use modern machine-made screws and nuts.

Some of these tables were made with wooden pivots. Drill a hole in both disks. Make a stout round wood rod and slot it at the bottom to take a long wedge (FIG. 6-9L). Glue and wedge the rod in the hole in the top disk. This must be a secure fit, and you can drive two glued wedges into the top across each other to resist the downward pull that will come later. Fit the rod through the lower disk and drive a wedge in the slot, so it will stay in place to get the best tension on the assembly.

LIGHT SIDE TABLE

In Colonial times, settled conditions, better facilities, and the skills of specialized craftsmen gradually brought more delicate treatment and tables that were more graceful, particularly those that did not have to stand up to general use. Wood for early furniture was converted from logs by equipment that would not cope with light sections, and this wood often was used before it was properly seasoned, so heavy sections also helped to resist warping and splitting. Later on, wood had time to season, and more advanced milling equipment was available to bring it to lighter sections. Experience with local woods allowed cabinetmakers to select attractive hardwoods for the better quality furniture, although much softwood was used, probably because of its easier workability with hand tools.

Lathes were usual in cabinet shops, and much decoration was provided by turned parts. This table (FIG. 6-10A) is typical and might have been made of walnut or other available hardwood, or of pine. It uses five identical spindles. The shaped parts would have been worked with a bow saw and spokeshave, but if you have a band saw, you will find it much easier to get accurate outlines than the earlier woodworker did with his hand tools only.

The four legs must be identical. The spindle forming the bottom rail does not need to be the same length, and you can lengthen or shorten the turned pattern by modifying the flowing curves. A more complex turning with many shorter patterns would not be as easy to adapt to different lengths.

Turn the spindles with dowel ends (FIG. 6-10B). It is advisable to make a full-size drawing of at least half the profile (FIG. 6-10C). You can cut a template from thin plywood (FIG. 6-10D) and use it to check the shapes as they are produced, but test frequently with calipers so diameters at various places are the same on all the parts. For the dowel ends, drill a hole of the correct size in a piece of scrap wood and use it to check the turned ends. Taper the extreme ends so they will enter easily. Be careful that overall lengths between the shoulders are exactly the same on the four legs and that the central bead really is central.

The top and bottom blocks have the same overall sizes, so mark them out together, with the hole positions and the ends matching (FIG. 6-10E). The holes for the dowels are best drilled by machine, but you can drill them by hand with an assistant sighting to check that the drill is upright. Take the holes slightly deeper than the lengths of the dowels.

Mark and cut the shapes of the feet blocks (FIG. 6-10F). You can use a half template to ensure uniformity. Drill for the bottom spindle. Be careful that the point of the drill does not break through. The dowels on this spindle could be shorter than those on the legs.

You need to notch the top blocks to take the top rails, which fit with a version of a halving joint (FIG. 6-10G). The ends of these rails and the extremities of the top blocks should have similar curves so their appearance under the top is uniform. Check the distance between the joints in the top rails with the distance between the shoulders in the bottom spindle. If they do not agree, the table will not stand upright.

In some original tables of this type, the top was screwed down into the supports, but this necessitated counterboring and plugging the holes. Plugs evenly spaced might be regarded as a decorative feature. If you prefer an unmarked top, however, you can do pocket screwing from below, although it would be simpler at the ends to have strips inside the top blocks for screws to be driven upward (FIG. 6-10H).

You can make the top from two or more boards glued together. Round corners and give the edges a curved section (FIG. 6-10J).

Do all work on the parts before assembly, including the preparation for pocket screws. Glue the spindles to top and bottom blocks to make up one end. See that it is flat and measure diagonals to check squareness. Make up the opposite end and check it by putting it in the correct relative position over the first end. Put a board and weight over the two assemblies and leave them for the glue to set. Fit the bottom spindle and the top rails. Check for squareness, both from the side and from above, by measuring diagonals, as well as by standing back and viewing the work.

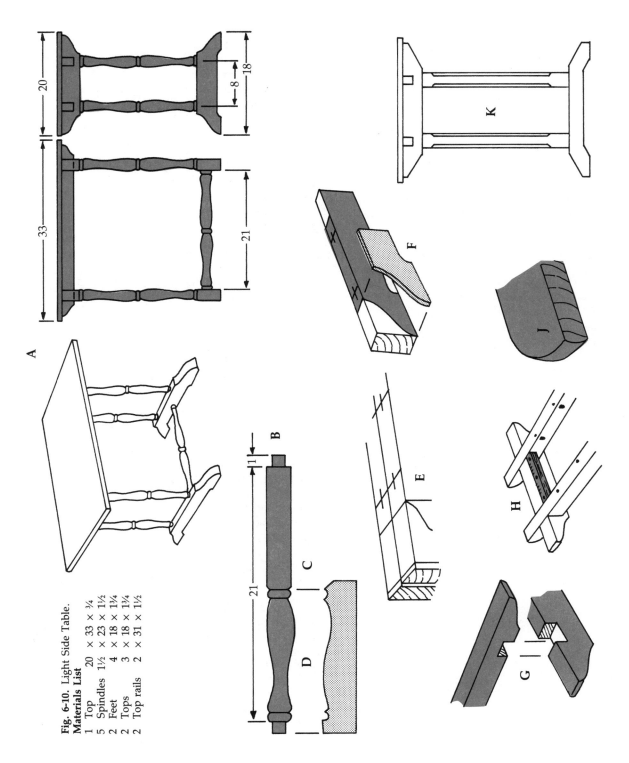

Fig. 6-10. Light Side Table.
Materials List

1	Top	20	× 33	× ¾
5	Spindles	1½	× 23	× 1½
2	Feet	4	× 18	× 1¾
2	Tops	3	× 18	× 1¾
2	Top rails	2	× 31	× 1½

It will probably be best to leave all this work until the glue is hard, then invert the assembly on the tabletop so you can see the correct position and drive the screws downward.

Similar tables were made without the use of a lathe. You can use square-sectioned pieces instead of the turned spindles for the legs and central bottom stretcher. To relieve plainness, chamfer the edges, either the full length or by using wagon beveling stopped short of the joints (FIG. 6-10K). This type of construction looks better with a more angular treatment of the blocks.

TRESTLE COFFEE TABLE

The basic type of trestle table goes back a long way before the settlement of America. There are tables of this type in many ancient castles and houses in Europe. Most are quite large and would be unsuitable for modern homes. Even one of dining table size, but otherwise in the usual proportions, might tend to look rather heavy in a small room. Trestle tables of this type were made by early American craftsmen, with larger versions in meeting houses and similar places, and more modest overall sizes, but still stoutly built, in private homes.

Although a full-size trestle table of this type could be built today and might have uses in some circumstances, the example shown to illustrate the basic method of construction is of a suitable size to serve as a coffee table (FIG. 6-11A). You can adapt the proportions to suit available wood or the intended purpose. If you make modifications, you should arrange the feet to spread almost as wide as the top, and the central post at each end should be wide enough to have its end joints strong enough to take the considerable leverage that might come on them if the edge of the tabletop is pressed hard.

Work from a full-size half drawing of an end (FIG. 6-11B). This gives the location of the parts in relation to each other, and you should draw it using the actual pieces of wood for sizes. Prepare the wood for the two trestle assemblies first. It is easiest to cut the joints before you do any shaping of these parts.

Mark the lengths and mortise positions on the two feet pieces. The profile and cutaway between the feet can be marked for cutting later (FIG. 6-11C). The crossbars under the top need not be quite as long as the bottom pieces, but you should mark similar mortise positions and draw the profile. In both cases, it is advisable to use a card or plywood template to mark the curves. Even if shapes will be cut with a band saw, it is advisable to mark the outlines on both sides to serve as guides when cleaning off the curves with spokeshave, Surform tool, or sandpaper.

Mark the two posts together. Distances between shoulders are the important sizes, and you should cut them with a knife all around the wood. Mark where the stretcher will come (FIG. 6-11D).

Strength comes from having the tenons as thick as reasonably possible. Because the cross members are wider than the thickness of the post, the rule about having a tenon one-third the thickness of the wood does not apply. Instead, cut the tenons with narrow shoulders. They should be as long as can be conveniently cut. They need not go right through the cross members, although that would allow wedging for maximum strength. Otherwise they can go about three-quarters of the way through and have foxtail wedging for security. Do not cut back the tenons from the post edges—the wider the spread of the tenons, the greater will be the resistance to bending loads on the table edge (FIG. 6-11E).

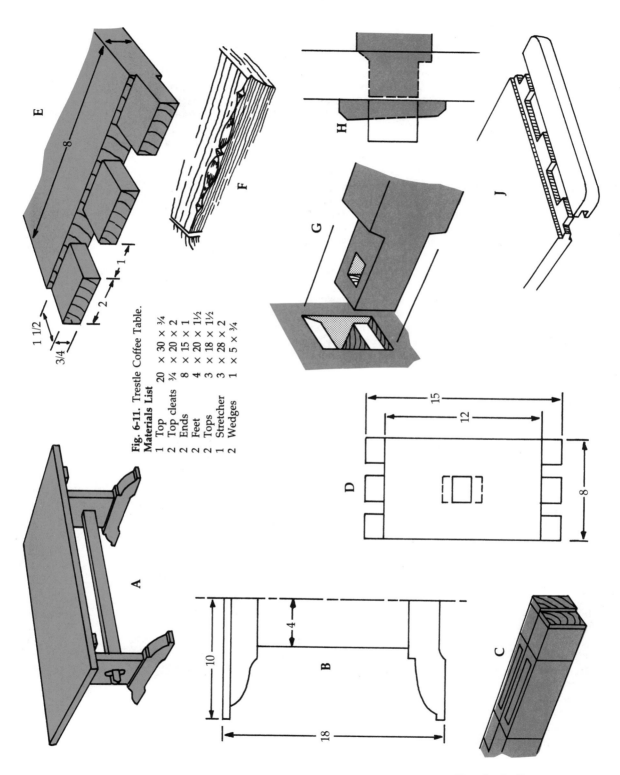

Fig. 6-11. Trestle Coffee Table.

Materials List

1	Top	20	×	30	×	¾
2	Top cleats	¾	×	20	×	2
2	Ends	8	×	15	×	1
2	Feet	4	×	20	×	1½
2	Tops	3	×	18	×	1½
1	Stretcher	3	×	28	×	2
2	Wedges	1	×	5	×	¾

After you have cut the tenons and mortises, you can shape the parts. Some tables have very ornate outlines cut in the posts, but it is inadvisable to cut away the edges very much. The decoration shown in FIG. 6-11F is a form of wagon beveling worked with a chisel. A similar pattern could be worked on the feet, but with a curved profile it is better to merely sand the sharpness off the edges.

There need be no lengthwise top rails, although some tables had them let into the top crossbars of the trestles. Instead, lengthwise rigidity comes partly from the stiffness of the top and mainly from the central stretcher. This is of fairly stout section, so its depth resists lengthwise loads. It was traditionally fixed with a *wedged tusk tenon*, which probably originated with the need for takedown furniture when families moved on. In medieval England, it was usual for the nobility on tour to take much of their furniture with them. In pioneer America, it was convenient to dismantle furniture when moving west. In this table, the wedged tenon does not serve that purpose since the tabletop does not come off (unless it is merely screwed on), but wedging gets maximum tightness and rigidity in the joint.

A wedged tusk tenon (FIG. 6-11G) is made with the stretcher on edge. In addition to the tenon proper, which goes right through, there is a step cut in the shoulder below the tenon, a wedge from the shoulder below the tenon, and a wedge from the shoulder line to the same point above the tenon. These cuts must be matched in the mortise. Such a construction is not really essential, unless the reproduction is to closely match the customary original joints. The alternative is to make the joint with the shoulders of the tenoned piece cut straight to abut the post.

The tenon goes through far enough for a slot to take a wedge, then enough wood outside that for the end grain to resist the pressure from driving the wedge. So the wedge will pull the stretcher tight when it is driven, cut its slot so the inner edge is below the surface of the post (FIG. 6-11H). In most tables and other furniture using wedged tenons, the wedge was usually plain, although there are examples with shaped top profiles and some with carved ends. The stretcher can have wagon beveling or a rounded edge. A full-size table that had been much used would have its stretcher edges rounded from contact with many boots.

Put together the end assemblies in stages. Make sure each post stands upright in the foot section. You can draw a line at right angles to the edge of a piece of plywood and use it as a guide. Measure diagonals from the extremities of the cross piece to the center or matching points on the post. Add the top crossbar and clamp the parts tight. If the tenons go right through, drive wedges into saw cuts in their ends. You can use small foxtail wedges inside for stub tenons. The alternative to wedging is doweling through, but wedges are preferable.

The wedged tusk tenons were traditionally left without glue. It was then possible to draw them tighter if age or shrinkage caused loosening. This is unlikely in the coffee-table version, so you can glue the joint and wedge.

The top of a full-size trestle table might have been made from a full-width board, if the builder was lucky. More likely, it was made up from several boards. In the coffee table, it might be made from two or three boards with interesting grain markings joined to make up the width. In the simplest version, leave the top in that form, with corners and edges slightly rounded, but to obtain a neater finish for modern use cleat the ends. Use similar wood to the top for the cleats and groove them about one-third their thickness. Reduce the ends of the top to this thickness, and carry them farther as tenons at intervals (FIG. 6-11J). Leave the cleats a little thick and reduce them to their final thickness after you have glued the joint.

Although it would be possible to fix the top by deeply counterboring screws driven upward through the supports, in this case it would be nearer to the original method to drill downward, so plugs over the screws are leveled on the top surface and show as part of the constructions and decoration.

Draw the stretcher tight to the posts with the wedges. Have the tabletop upside down and invert the assembly on it. Experiment with its position. See that the two end assemblies are parallel by measuring between their tops and bottoms, and check that they are upright on the top before marking where they come on the top and drilling through for the screws.

TAKEDOWN TRESTLE TABLE

The original idea of making tables and other furniture to take apart for storage or transport can be used today. A table made in this way will pack flat when not needed, yet make a more substantial piece of furniture than many modern tables made to fold or disassemble for camping and similar purposes. Even where the table is kept in constant use for long periods, it is convenient to be able to reduce its size when not needed temporarily, as when rearranging the furnishings of the home or when moving.

This table is of fairly light construction, although it is of sufficient size for dining. It also would make a useful table in a children's room. It could be made of hardwood, but if taking down and moving will be frequent, it is better to use a softwood, such as yellow pine, for lightness. Much depends on the intended use. Softwood will have a good life with careful use, but hardwoods will take a better finish and might be needed to match existing furniture. They will also stand up to rougher use. This type of table can be used outdoors on a patio, but a durable wood must be used if it is to stay out in all weathers.

The general construction is very similar to the Trestle Coffee Table, although the proportions and profiles are different (FIG. 6-12A). The rail or stretcher provides lengthwise stiffness. Do not connect the top crossbars of the trestles directly to the top. Instead, use braces across the underside of the top against these rails and hold them to the rails with pegs, which can be withdrawn for disassembly. The braces also stiffen the top and prevent it from warping.

The feet and top rails could have many different outlines. Those shown are easy to cut. Instead of the feet tapering toward the floor directly, they are given an upward curve, then pads are added to bear on the floor. This appearance of solidity around the feet prevents the table from looking excessively light (FIG. 6-12B).

Match the uprights with the parts they tenon into. Prepare and cut the joints before doing any shaping (FIG. 6-12C). As with the Trestle Coffee Table, keep the tenons thick and let them come to the extreme width of the wood to get the benefit of maximum resistance to bending. The tenons may go through the top rail, or only part way, as in the feet, but a tenon length of about 1 1/2 inches is needed for adequate strength, particularly in softwood. Original tables of this type usually had pegs through the tenons. These pegs often were rounded only roughly from square section, then driven into round holes. Their uneven outline can be seen on the surface of some old furniture. You can still make and use pegs in this way, but it will be simpler to use pieces of dowel (FIG. 6-12D).

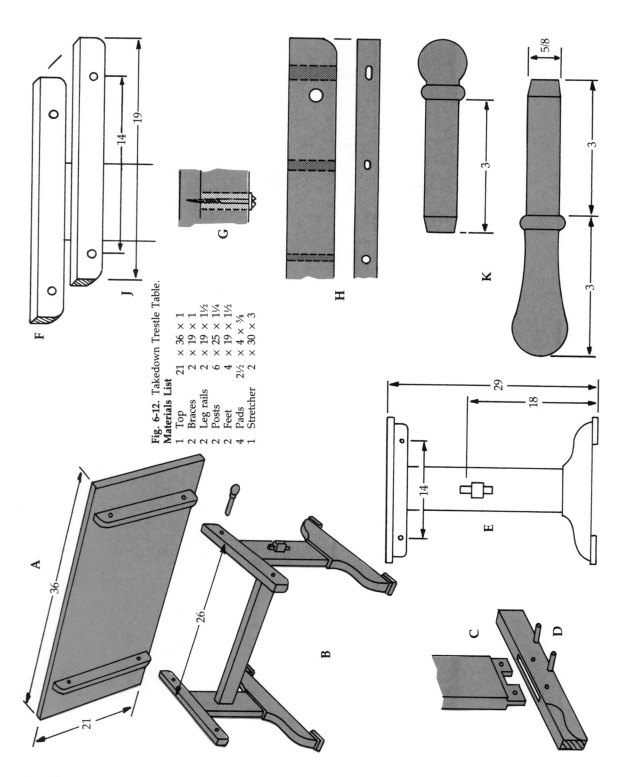

Fig. 6-12. Takedown Trestle Table.

Materials List

1	Top	21	×	36	×	1	
2	Braces	2	×	19	×	1	
2	Leg rails	2	×	19	×	1½	
2	Posts	6	×	25	×	1¼	
2	Feet	4	×	19	×	1½	
4	Pads	2½	×	4	×	⅝	
1	Stretcher	2	×	30	×	3	

Fit the stretcher above half the height (FIG. 6-12E). Shape its ends as wedged tusk tenons, in the same way as described for the Trestle Coffee Table. Fit the joints carefully so the assembly stands with the trestle legs upright when the wedges are tightened. Put the assembly on a flat floor and sight across the top rails to check for twist.

The top is a plain rectangle, which can be made up of several boards if necessary. The braces need not be as thick as the top rails of the trestles, but they should have similar outlines (FIG. 6-12F).

A pine top is likely to expand and contract in its width more than most hardwoods might. You should allow for this process in fitting the braces by using slot screwing. Expansion and contraction is most noticeable near the full width and is less obvious near the center of the board. This means that movement which must be allowed for its slightest close to the middle. With slot screwing, there are slot holes made in the brace, usually by drilling two holes and cutting away the waste between them. Screws go through the slots into the top and have washers under their heads, so any movement of the top causes the screw to slide along its slot (FIG. 6-12G).

In this table, there is one screw through a round hole at the center, two others with slots about 1/2 inch long, and two farther out about 3/4 inch long (FIG. 6-12H). Locate the braces on the underside of the top so they fit easily over the tops of the trestles. Check the whole table for squareness, particularly that the trestles are upright in relation to the top, before fixing the braces.

Hold the top to the trestles by pegs, or *trunnel pins*, through holes. It might be possible to have only one central peg at each end, but wear might cause the top to wobble. It is better to have two pegs in each place, spaced fairly widely (FIG. 6-12J). The pegs could be pieces of dowel given a slight taper at one end for ease in driving. If a lathe is available, however, you can turn pegs with knobs (FIG. 6-12K)—either round ends for gripping to pull or longer handles that might be better for twisting to remove. In either case, it probably will be necessary to use a hammer or mallet to drive out the pegs when they have been in place for a long time.

Only in exceptionally accurate work or by a great deal of luck will the top reverse on the framework and the peg holes line up properly again. It is better to mark the way the peg holes were drilled, so the table is always assembled the same way. An X-cut with two crossing chisel cuts on the adjoining brace and trestle will be better than a mark with a pencil or pen.

TRESTLE DINING TABLE AND BENCH

Large trestle tables were often of massive construction, and a full-size reproduction might be considered rather clumsy for use in a room with normal modern furniture. The design shown in FIG. 6-13A has its sections lightened, but is otherwise made in the same way as many early trestle tables that had to serve for most purposes, as well as dining, in the early homes. Although the wedged stretcher, essential to retain the characteristic appearance, has been retained, much of the stiffness of the table is a result of the deep central lengthwise rail directly under the top.

Later tables of this type were given decorative outlines on the legs. Some possible designs are shown in FIG. 6-13B. If you choose another outline, it is important to keep the wood to its greatest width at the ends so you can make tenons of the full width. Although it is possible to cut away quite a lot around

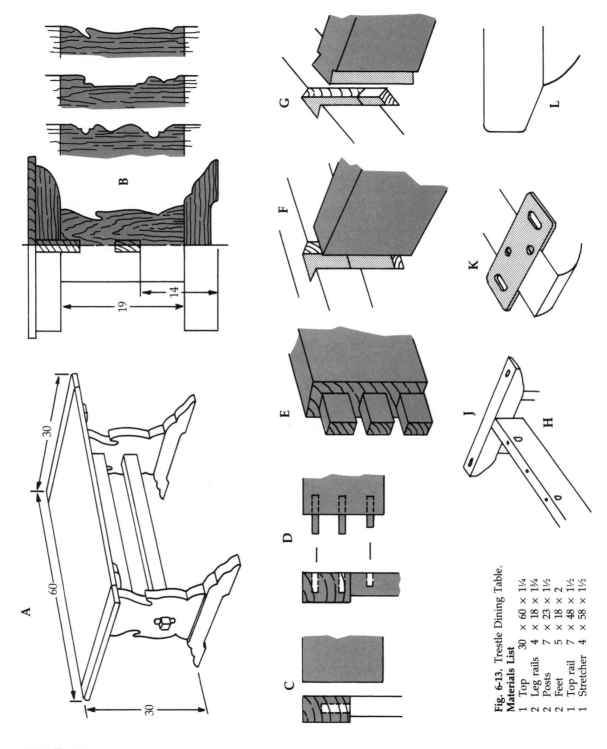

Fig. 6-13. Trestle Dining Table.
Materials List

1	Top	30	× 60	× 1¼
2	Leg rails	4	× 18	× 1¾
2	Posts	7	× 23	× 1½
2	Feet	5	× 18	× 2
1	Top rail	7	× 48	× 1½
1	Stretcher	4	× 58	× 1½

the centers of the edges, always leave sufficient width to ensure rigidity. It is also possible to cut decorative holes in the legs, but shaping the edges was more usual.

Decoration of the uprights can be reflected in similar edge decoration on the stretcher. Do not take this decoration into the wood too deeply, or its stiffening effect will be impaired.

Lay out the two trestles, cut the joints, and assemble the parts in the same way as for the previous two tables. The mortise for the stretcher should be just above half the height for the best appearance. (If it is exactly halfway, an optical illusion will make it appear below halfway.) On each trestle, the inner surface of the top rail should be level with the leg for ease in fitting the lengthwide rail (FIG. 6-13C).

The way to fix the lengthwise rail to the trestles depends on your skill and preference. Whatever method you used, the details of the joint will not be apparent in the finished table. The simplest method is to cut the ends of the rail squarely and join it with dowels (FIG. 6-13D). Another way is to have short tenons (FIG. 6-13E). They cannot be very long unless they are to go right through and their ends be left showing. There could be a groove to take the end of the rail (FIG. 6-13F), but it would not have much useful glue area and you would need to provide strength by giving the groove a dovetail form, so the rail entered from the top (FIG. 6-13G).

A broad hardwood tabletop could have cleated ends. The tendency then for the wood to expand and contract might not be much, and the construction would be satisfactory, but if you use softwood, make allowance for changes in the width. There should be firm fastenings along the central rail. You can drive counterbored screws from above and plugged or pocket screws from alternate sides (FIG. 6-13H).

These screws will keep the top securely in place, but further screws are needed at the extremities of the tops of the trestles to further hold the top and prevent warping. They should be in slots to allow for changes in the top width. You can arrange the design of the ends to allow for slots and inconspicious countersunk screws (FIG. 6-13J). Another method that was used and is still a good one is to have metal plates with slots. Notch the wood to take the plates, screw on the plates, then use roundhead screws through the slots secure the tabletop (FIG. 6-13K).

A solid top of good width must be fairly thick for stiffness, but you can make it look lighter by beveling around the underside (FIG. 6-13L). Molding the edges of the tabletop is inappropriate for this traditional table. A small curve at each corner and rounded edges are all that should be done.

Trestle tables date from the days when chairs for everyone were unusual. The head of the house might have had a chair, but most others sat on stools or benches.

It was usual to sit at the table on benches that matched the style of the table. Sizes varied, but a convenient sitting height was between 15 inches and 18 inches for eating off a tabletop 28 inches to 30 inches high. The higher seat would be preferable now, but only a few generations ago, our ancestors had shorter legs than we have, and seats were generally lower. Their full height was also much less, as you will find when ducking your head to go through a doorway in a very old house.

Benches were made to the same length as the table (FIG. 6-14A). This one has the stretcher and its wedged tusk tenons to give rigidity, but sitters might put considerable strain on a bench, so there are rails under the top, with strips between to give further support to the top (FIG. 6-14B).

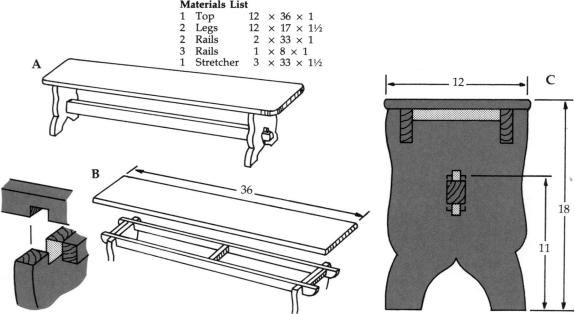

Fig. 6-14. Trestle Bench to match the Trestle Dining Table.
Materials List

1	Top	12	× 36	× 1
2	Legs	12	× 17	× 1½
2	Rails	2	× 33	× 1
3	Rails	1	× 8	× 1
1	Stretcher	3	× 33	× 1½

Having strips across allows you to make the legs without tenoning on. There is no need to make feet, but you should cut back the bottoms of the legs so only the outer edges rest on the floor (FIG. 6-14C). Any outline shaping of the legs should match the decoration used on the table.

You can use a single board for the bench top or make it up from two or more boards and there may be cleated ends similar to the tabletop. A bench is often lifted by its top, so the joint between top and framing should be secure. You can use glue, but you should also attach screws upward into the top, arranged to go as deeply as possible without breaking out the grain on the top surface.

DROP-LEAF TRESTLE TABLE

Trestle tables were not made with flaps to drop at the sides and certainly were not made in a form comparable to a gateleg table. It is possible to arrange a means of supporting side leaves, but trestle tables that could be enlarged were more usual with leaves at one or both ends. Two leaves could be arranged so they almost doubled the length of the top when raised. Usual supports were central swinging brackets, and their size was limited by the need to keep with the width of the tabletop when swung back for folding, so a raised leaf should not extend too far past the bracket if there is to be sufficient strength.

The table shown in FIG. 6-15A is a suitable size to use as a side table, for sewing sewing with enough area for laying out patterns, or for occasional dining use. It looks best in hardwood, but is equally suitable for pine.

The general construction is very similar to the Takedown Trestle Table. Shape the feet and cut them away to bear at their ends on the floor. Keep the top rail of each trestle parallel so it can more easily be used for slot screws. Make a central

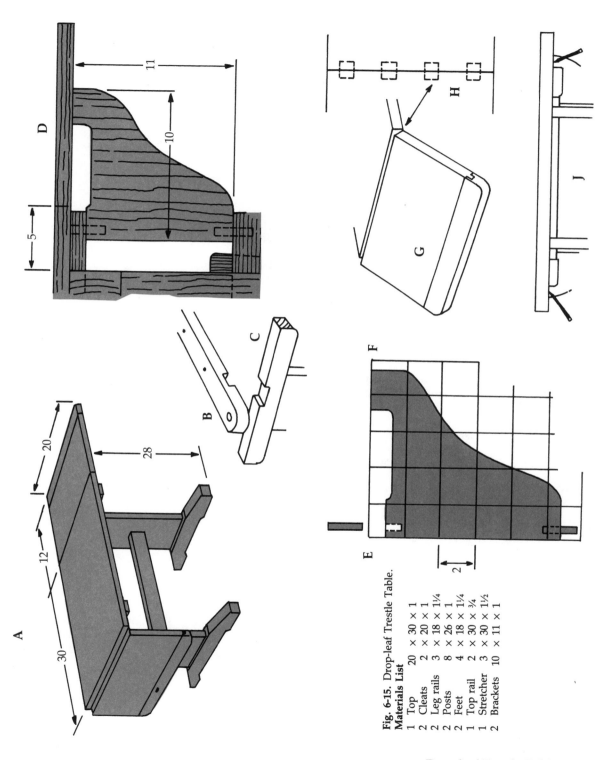

Fig. 6-15. Drop-leaf Trestle Table.
Materials List

1	Top	20 × 30 × 1
2	Cleats	2 × 20 × 1
2	Leg rails	3 × 18 × 1¼
2	Posts	8 × 26 × 1
2	Feet	4 × 18 × 1¼
1	Top rail	2 × 30 × ¾
1	Stretcher	3 × 30 × 1½
2	Brackets	10 × 11 × 1

shallow lengthwise rail and notch it through the trestles to provide a pivot for the bracket at each end. This rail also adds to stiffness and can be screwed through into the top (FIG. 6-15B). Cut only a little out of the rail to give a positive location in the trestle without weakening the wood (FIG. 6-15C).

The stretcher is above halfway. It supports the bracket and you might need to arrange its exact position to suit the wood available for the bracket. The overhang of the tabletop at the ends must be enough to allow a leaf to hang down clear of the bracket and the end of the stretcher. It is advisable to draw this detail full size to get the dimensions of the parts right (FIG. 6-15D). There must be enough of the stretcher past the wedge to take a hole for a pivot. It is the extension necessary for this that decides on the amount of projection for other parts. Allow the ends of the lengthwise rail to extend as far as possible to obtain the maximum strength in the end grain outside and pivot hole.

The bracket has its grain upright. Drill holes for pieces of dowel rod on which it pivots (FIG. 6-15E). Even if the main parts of the table are softwood, the dowels should be hardwood. A close-grained hardwood is better for the lengthwise rail than a softwood because there is considerable load on the short grain outside the pivot dowel at each end. At the ends of the stretcher, the loads on the pivot are inward, so bursting forces are not as great there.

Only the outer part of the bracket is at the supporting height (FIG. 6-15F). Cut back the rest of the top so it does not bind under the table end. There is no need to round the inner edge of the bracket much, except where it might touch another part. Leaving it as near square as possible makes for strength.

The main top and its leaves should be of similar wood and the grain pattern should continue across all three if you choose a wood with prominent grain. The three parts are best cut from one piece, if possible. In any case, the grain on the leaves should run in the length of the table, so the leaves are smaller in the direction of the grain than they are across it. These are circumstances in which warping is more likely, if nothing is done to prevent it. Cleat the outer edges (FIG. 6-15G). Support the inner edges by using a greater number of backflap hinges than would be usual if the meeting edges were along the grain. In this size table you could use four, let in flush so they do not interfere with the action of the bracket (FIG. 6-15H).

With the meeting edges end grain, it would be difficult to plane a rule joint, so this type of table was allowed to have square meeting edges.

Although it is as important as always for the table to be properly squared up by testing diagonals, and the trestles to stand upright, the most important consideration, for utility and appearance is for the full length of the top to be level when the leaves are up. To ensure this, make the brackets with their ends high at first. Assemble the main part of the table framework completely. You can fix the lower dowel of each bracket, but slip the upper dowel in loose through the top pivot point in the lengthwise rail. Swing the brackets into their support position and place a piece of wood with a straightedge along to represent the tabletop and leaves. Use a pencil along this wood to mark the supporting position on the brackets (FIG. 6-15J). Remove and trim the brackets to size. If they are correct when tried again, glue the upper pivot dowels into the brackets. You can put candle grease or graphite in the pivot holes for easy working.

Assemble the leaves to the top and make a trial assembly on the framework. If the leaves and brackets function properly, fix the top with screws from below. This type of table looks best with the corners and edges left square, except for sharpness being sanded off. There could be some rounding, but molding would be inappropriate.

SAWBUCK TABLE

Sawbuck table is an American term, resulting from the similarity of the leg arrangement to the common support used for supporting logs being sawn by hand. The design is European, where a sawbuck is more often called a *sawing trestle* and this name was not applied to tables. It was more likely to be referred to as an *X-leg* or *X-frame* table. These tables are found in many old houses and castles in Europe, but they are sometimes called *Swedish* tables in America because many were made by Swedish immigrants who settled in the Pennsylvania area.

The parts used in the construction of the leg assemblies must be of fairly substantial section because they are weakened by being cut away to make cross-lap joints and are further cut away for the mortise at the end of the stretcher. Although some sawbuck tables were made with crossed pieces of straight section, the majority had the legs with shaped outlines. This breaks up the heavy appearance and gives some grace to what would otherwise be a rather clumsy assembly—appropriate to a sawyer's clearing in the woods but unwelcome in a home.

The design shown in FIG. 6-16A could be made full size as a dining table. A smaller version could be regarded as a model and used as a coffee table. Benches for use with the table often were made in the same way, so it would be appropriate to use a similar construction for a seat.

Draw an end view full size (FIG. 6-16B) without first considering any shaping. Crossing two straight pieces shows where parts come in relation to each other. Draw on the end view of the stretcher and note where to cut the mortise, balancing its size between the need for a strong tenon and the need for sufficient wood to be left around it in each of the crossing pieces. The strongest joint comes when the width of the table is about the same as its height (FIG. 6-16C). A table that is much higher than it is wide gets very acute angles in the crosslap joint (FIG. 6-16D). Normally, it is also best to have the crossing near the middle of the legs. If it is higher or lower, it affects the spread. If the crossing is below the center, the feet do not spread as much as the top, and if too low, the table becomes unstable (FIG. 6-16E). If the crossing is to be off-center, it is better to have it slightly higher than the middle, then the feet spread wider than the tops of the legs. This difference can be compensated for by using a wider tabletop (FIG. 6-16F).

The full-size drawing gives the shapes and angles of the parts, which should be identical, except that the cutout of the cross lap should be on opposite sides of each pair (FIG. 6-16G). Carefully remove the waste wood so a cross-lap joint goes together with the two surfaces level. Make up both ends in this way. Check across the ends with a straightedge and mark around all sides (FIG. 6-16H), then cut off the ends. Separate the part and do the shaping to the edges. Glue and clamp the center joints.

Make the stretcher in the same way as for trestle tables, cutting the ends as wedged tusk tenons. Mark and cut the mortises in the legs after the glue has set in the half-lap joints. Make a trial assembly, check diagonals, and see that the legs stand on all four corners and are upright when viewed from the side.

In the simplest construction, braces attached to the tabletop go across beside the tops of the legs and are screwed or doweled to them (FIG. 6-17A). This is a satisfactory arrangement and is found in some early examples of these tables.

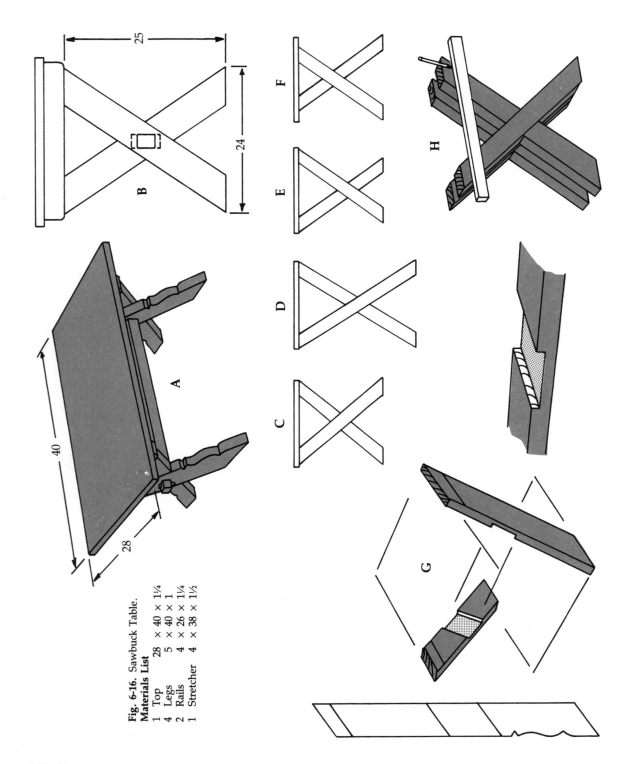

Fig. 6-16. Sawbuck Table.

Materials List

1 Top   28 × 40 × 1¼
4 Legs   5 × 40 × 1
2 Rails   4 × 26 × 1¼
1 Stretcher   4 × 38 × 1½

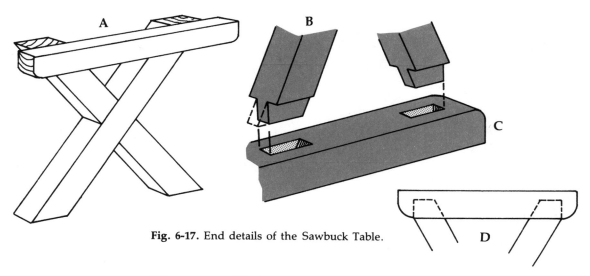

Fig. 6-17. End details of the Sawbuck Table.

When a more skilled woodworker made a sawbuck table, however, he tenoned the tops of the legs into the brace. If you use this method, it is advisable to complete the half-lap joints and treat each end assembly as a single unit, rather than deal with loose pieces of wood.

The crossed pieces of wood need to enter mortises at right angles to the edge of the brace so the inner edge of each leg retains its angle, but the outer edge has its tenon cut at right angles to the edge that will enter the brace (FIG. 6-17B). It is advisable to cut the tenons completely before marking the mortises from them (FIG. 6-17C). The inner ends of the mortises match the slope of the legs, but otherwise cut the joints in the usual way (FIG. 6-17D).

The tabletop is the same as in earlier tables and can have its ends cleated. In this table, it is stout enough to support itself, but in some tables you might need to use lengthwise rails.

SAWBUCK SIDE TABLE

Traditional sawbuck tables mostly require wood of quite large section, but the method of construction was used for small tables that were for occasional use, or for serving, sewing, or writing use. A light square sawbuck table was suitable for playing cards. This table has the crossing slightly above center height, so the extremities of the feet come under the edges of the overhanging tabletop (FIG. 6-18A) for proper stability, when there is little weight to assist in keeping the table steady. Draw an end view full size (FIG. 6-18B). From this, mark and cut the cross-lap joints and the ends of the legs.

Fix the top rails or braces to the legs with dowels or tenons. In addition to the stretcher fixed in the usual way through the cross-lap joint, there are two more cross-lapped rails under the top (FIG. 6-18C). They assist the stretcher to provide lengthwise rigidity. Locate them just inside of where the legs join the braces.

Lay out the joints in these rails and the stretcher together so distances between the joints match. Notice that in the stretcher joint there is not enough

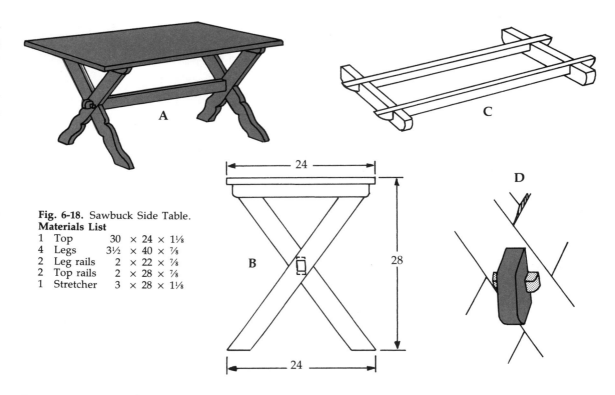

Fig. 6-18. Sawbuck Side Table.
Materials List

1	Top	30	× 24	× 1⅛
4	Legs	3½	× 40	× ⅞
2	Leg rails	2	× 22	× ⅞
2	Top rails	2	× 28	× ⅞
1	Stretcher	3	× 28	× 1⅛

thickness for a wedge slot to be cut vertically and the wedges are driven across (FIG. 6-18D). This direction of wedging is found in some larger and heavier tables, but vertical wedging when there was sufficient thickness of wood was more usual.

Some light sawbuck tables were made with the legs straight, but the one shown has shaped outlines below the joint. You can use any method of decorating edges, but when the wood is of light section do not cut it away too much or it might be weakened.

HEAVY SAWBUCK TABLE

Much ecclesiastical tables and chairs in Europe incorporated crossed legs. Many old monasteries and cathedrals have examples of crossed-leg furniture many hundreds of years old, although their users would not recognize the term *sawbuck*. Many settlers in America would have known these tables and chairs, which were usually large and of quite heavy construction, so when they were faced with the need to make furniture for public buildings and churches, they reproduced these designs. A modern reproduction of this type might be regarded as a reproduction of a reproduction.

Much of the beauty of these tables was in the legs. Exact reproductions of many of them would be too large to use in a modern home, as well as require sizes of wood that might be almost impossible to obtain, but lighter versions can be attractive. The full-size version was usually a *refectory table*, the communal table around which the monks sat to eat a meal. A smaller version makes a good dining room table with plenty of character (FIG. 6-19A).

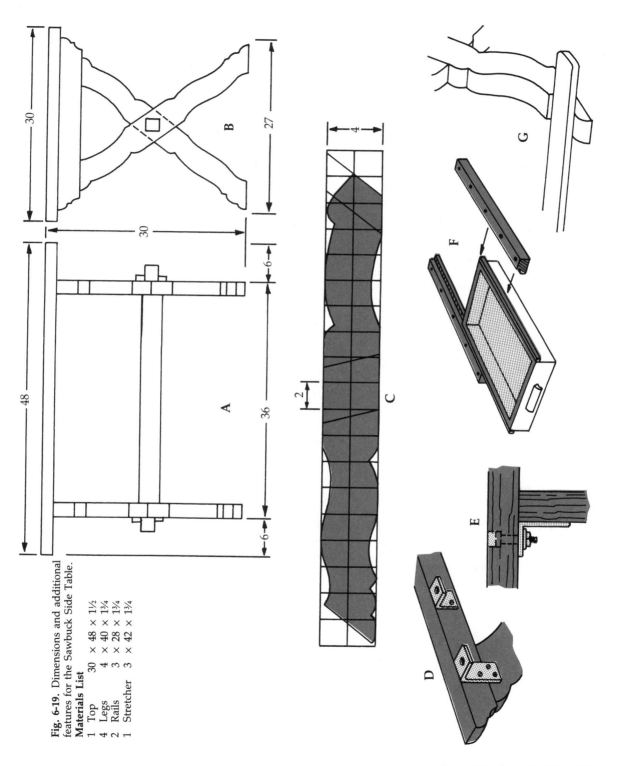

Fig. 6-19. Dimensions and additional features for the Sawbuck Side Table.

Materials List

1	Top	30 × 48 × 1½
4	Legs	4 × 40 × 1¾
2	Rails	3 × 28 × 1¾
1	Stretcher	3 × 42 × 1¾

The method of construction is the same as for the Sawbuck Table, but because of the steadiness from the weight there is no need to spread the feet as wide as the top. Tenoning of the legs into the top rails was usual and is advisable today, since maximum strength is needed for a heavy table that could put excessive strain on joints if mishandled or dropped when moving. The type of decoration shown in FIG. 6-19B comes from an ecclesiastical table, but it is appropriate to a dining room.

A full-size drawing gives the angles of joints and cuts, but it is probably advisable to make a template for marking the shaping so all four legs are identical (FIG. 6-19C). They are most simply cut with a band saw, but you can remember the hard labor and skill of the original craftsmen by using hand tools. Make sure all signs of machine sawing are removed from the decorated edges. In addition to sanding, scrape with a metal scraper or the edge of a broken piece of glass to remove saw marks from the more awkward parts of the design.

The tabletop must be fairly thick, and you will need to build it up from several boards glued edge to edge. So far as possible select wood where the end grain of one board is the opposite way to the next, to minimize any overall tendency to warp. With modern glues and even clamping, a simple edge-to-edge joint will suffice, but for further security you can use dowels between boards or work the edges with tongue-and-groove joints. Even if the boards have all been machine planed, you will need to hand-plane the top surface. Something might be done with a power sander, but there should be no signs of its action in the finished surface. You will need to spend some time getting the top smooth, but this and the shaping of the legs are the outstanding features of the design.

Because of the weight of even this lightened version, it is unwise to depend only on wood screws to hold the top to the leg rails. Instead, it is advisable to follow what was customary in the heavier originals. Iron angle brackets go inside the top rails (FIG. 6-19D). Those above the legs should overlap onto them so two or three stout wood screws can be driven. The original brackets would have been made by a blacksmith, but you should be able to adapt iron shelf brackets that will look sufficiently authentic. The originals would have been black from forging, so bright modern brackets would not look right. The number of brackets depends on their size, but four should be enough.

To hold the top, bolt through these brackets, but before drilling any holes invert the assembled legs and stretcher over the reversed top. Get its position correct and check that the framework is square and the legs are upright. When you are certain everything is as accurate as you can get it, mark through the bolt holes in the brackets. Drill through with an undersize drill from the underside. This will give the location on the top without the risk of grain breaking out, which might happen with a larger drill.

Use carriage bolts to fix the top. Counterbore enough to sink the head far enough below the surface to allow for plugging, then follow through the small pilot hole with a drill to suit the bolt (FIG. 6-19E). Insert all the bolts, then tighten progressively all around until the top is tight. Make the plugs from the same wood as the top. Their grain should be across to match the top.

Some refectory tables were fit with shallow drawers for cutlery. Because there was no framing between the legs immediately under the top, they were easy to fit. One type of drawer could be opened from either side, and this would be useful in a modern dining table version. Make the drawer in the usual way, but with what amounts to two fronts. Dovetail the two fronts and fit them with handles.

Hang it from slides fixed under the tabletop. Attach square strips along the top edges of the drawer sides. Screw rabbeted pieces below the tabletop as runners (FIG. 6-19F). On a long table, you could have more than one drawer, but keep them shallow so as not to impede the knees of sitters.

Other additions to some refectory tables were footboards (FIG. 6-19G). These were intended to provide somewhere to put the feet a few inches above the ground. There is no real need for footboards on a reproduction, but you could provide them if desired.

TILT-TOP AND CANDLE TABLES

Many tables were made so the top could be tilted completely to an upright position. In addition to being an alternative to a drop-leaf table for reducing the size when out of use, this method allowed the top to form a screen. A large top might protect occupants of the room from drafts. Some tables had a small, flat area exposed when the top was tilted, and this would be a place to put a candle, then the tilted top acted as a draft screen and a reflector. Because a candle did not spread its light very far, it had to be located where needed, and there were many small tables made to take a candle, and placed alongside a chair, bed, or elsewhere.

These tables serve as attractive occasional or bedside tables and for use in places too small for a larger table. Even if not needed for supporting a lamp or books, such a table makes a good stand for a plant pot or a vase of flowers.

Large tilt-top tables were often made on a single central pedestal in a similar way to the smaller candle tables. Others were arranged on legs, and there was a storage box exposed when the top was lifted. Some of these tables could be used as seats, with the tabletop forming the back of a chair arranged with a seat at a suitable height between the legs. The seat top might then lift to expose a storage chest.

There is less need for tilting tops today, but many of the designs make satisfactory tables with fixed tops. Not all of the originals tilted, in any case, and there are examples of tables of similar appearance, some of which had rigid tops, while others tilted.

Many pedestal tables had turned parts, with the central post in patterns that varied from rather basic conical sections to elaborate designs with many beads, quirks, and curves. Some of these tables are adaptable to construction without the use of a lathe, but many of the candle tables, in particular, are attractive turning exercises, well within the capacity of a light lathe. The large tables with turned pedestals might require a larger lathe, although most lathes that will accept up to 30 inches between centers can be used.

Pedestal tables usually were made with three legs. Less common were four legs. A three-leg assembly could stand firm on any surface, while four legs might wobble (even a slight wobble could be a nuisance or a danger with a candle or oil lamp).

Whatever the method of construction, the arrangement of three equally spaced legs involves the same preparatory geometry. The three legs need to be at 120 degrees to each other around the pedestal (FIG. 6-20A). If a lathe has a dividing head or there are other means of spacing mechanically, you can divide with precision. If a radius is stepped off around a circumference, it goes six times, so on a circle of the size of the pedestal, the leg positions are at alternate marks (FIG. 6-20B). Another way is to wrap a strip of paper around the wood and push a spike through the overlapping parts (FIG. 6-20C). Open the paper and divide the distance between the holes made by the spike into three (FIG. 6-20D). Put the paper back around the wood and transfer these positions.

Draw lines along the cylinder to give the positions of the legs. You can do this step in the lathe. Bring the tool rest close to and parallel to the wood. Get a mark in position and draw a line along the tool rest with a pencil (FIG. 6-20E). If joints must be marked away from the lathe, join two narrow parallel pieces of wood to an angle—it will probably be a right angle, but it does not matter if it is not. What is important is that the edges are parallel with the joint and with each other. Bevel the edges (FIG. 6-20F). If this tool is put on a cylinder with an edge on a mark, a pencil line along the edge will be parallel with the axis of the cylinder.

The alternative to a cylindrical pedestal with three legs is a hexagonal pillar. The problem then is to get all six faces the same width and all angles of the section the same. Stepping off the radius around the circumference gives the six points of a regular hexagon (FIG. 6-20G). This is one way to get the shape. If you start with a square piece of wood, the size circle to work on is the distance across the flats of the square. The distance across the points of a hexagon is obviously more than the distance across the flats, so you cannot include the existing flat of a square piece, but if you start with wood wider than it is thick, you can use two faces as part of the hexagon. In that case, draw a circle to touch the edges (FIG. 6-20H) Shaping can be done by planing, in the way that would have been used by the original craftsmen, but the tilting fence of a table saw or jointer will enable you to true the six faces with less effort and more precision.

The part of the pedestal where the leg joints come does not need to be parallel, but laying out the joints is easier if it is. There could be a regular slight taper, but decorative beads and other turned shapes are better kept away from the area of the joints.

Original construction used mostly mortise-and-tenon joints. Making a full-size drawing of a section of the pedestal will show how deep the tenons can go. They should not meet, as that might weaken the pedestal, but they should go as deep as reasonably possible. This sort of joint cannot be strengthened by dowels across the tenons, and it is important to give as large a side-grain glue area as possible (FIG. 6-21A).

You can undercut the shoulders of the tenoned legs where they come against the pedestal to make a close fit (FIG. 6-21B). This was sometimes done, but a more usual way was to flatten the pedestal for the width of each leg, so shoulders were cut squarely (FIG. 6-21C). In most cases two narrow tenons are better than one long one on a leg (FIG. 6-21D).

You can arrange dowels in a similar way to tenons, with the pedestal cut flat to give a good bearing for the leg. Plane the leg to fit closely (FIG. 6-21E).

In most constructions, the legs meet the pedestal a short distance above its bottom. This method should be stronger than having them level with the end. Some originals have the legs level with the end of the pedestal. You could dowel or tenon them, but it is possible to use open slots, with the reduced ends of the legs sliding in (FIG. 6-21F). The strength then will be comparable with tenons, but you can strengthen the joints more by giving them dovetail sections (FIG. 6-21G).

A problem with this type of tripod construction comes in pulling the joints tight and holding them while the glue sets. It might be sufficient to press the joints in by hand. Some legs were designed with patterns that gave a bearing for the pad of a clamp opposite the joint, but most legs had flowing curves with

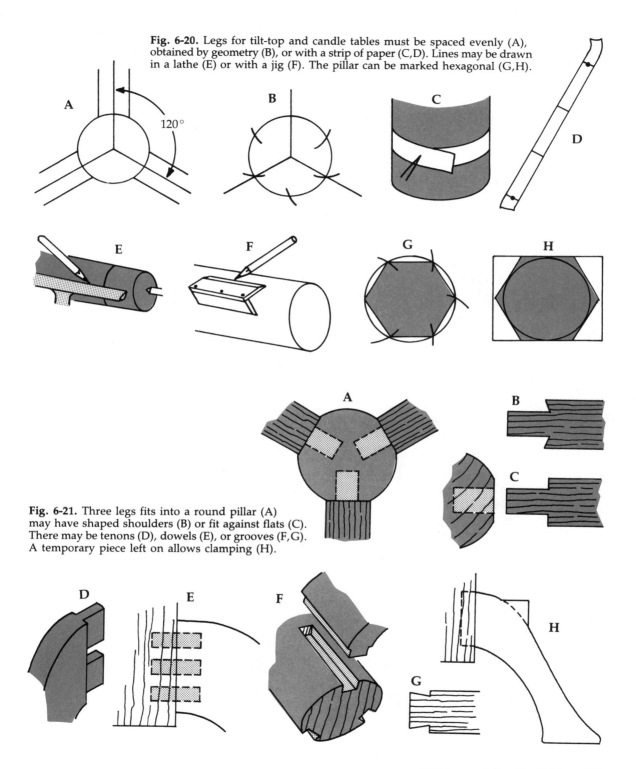

Fig. 6-20. Legs for tilt-top and candle tables must be spaced evenly (A), obtained by geometry (B), or with a strip of paper (C,D). Lines may be drawn in a lathe (E) or with a jig (F). The pillar can be marked hexagonal (G,H).

Fig. 6-21. Three legs fits into a round pillar (A) may have shaped shoulders (B) or fit against flats (C). There may be tenons (D), dowels (E), or grooves (F,G). A temporary piece left on allows clamping (H).

Tilt-top and Candle Tables 115

nowhere for a clamp to give effective pressure. Sometimes a temporary block of wood was glued on to take a clamp, but a better way is to leave a small area of the actual leg (FIG. 6-21H). The clamp squeezes against that and it is not difficult to cut it off afterward and fashion the surface to the final shape when the joint is secure.

HEXAGONAL CANDLE STAND

This design is based on an early original when the cabinetmakers probably did not have access to a lathe (FIG. 6-22A). The top was arranged to tilt, but a fixed alternative is also shown.

The central hexagonal piece is parallel in the length, but a little decoration is provided above and below the leg joints in the shallow V-shaped cuts. Make them with a backsaw, using two guidelines (FIG. 6-22B). You can bevel the projecting bottom, but cut the top carefully so it is at right angles to the sides.

The legs sweep upward, and the outer curves are sufficiently near parallel over the joints for clamps to be used over scrap wood. Use a template or make one leg and use it as a pattern for the others (FIG. 6-22C) if you cannot cut all of them at one time on a band saw. Arrange the wood so the grain is diagonal. If there is any curve in the lines of grain, arrange it to follow the shapes of the legs. Be careful that the edge which meets the pedestal is at right angles to the foot of each leg.

Because the grain in the legs would come across any tenons, thus reducing their strength, it is better to use dowels in these leg joints (FIG. 6-22D). Prepare the joints, but wait to put the parts together until work at the top of the pedestal has been finished.

For a tilt top, fix a square block to the top of the pedestal. In some originals it was nailed on, but screwing would be better. You can also glue in four small dowels (FIG. 6-22E). The square block supports the top when the top is raised or lowered. Even if the rest of the table is a softwood, it would be better if this and the pieces that frame it are made of close-grained hardwood. Glue the pedestal assembly and test that it stands upright. If the legs are identical and carefully fitted, there should be no difficulty, but check with the feet on a level surface and use a large try or set square in three directions. You can make corrections by planing the bottom of a leg.

The top can be round, elliptical, or hexagonal. Curves were more popular than angular shapes, possibly because there was slightly less risk of anyone passing and knocking the table over. A circle is shown in FIG. 6-22A. You can make up the top from several boards, then arrange the underframing across its grain to provide some resistance to warping.

Fix two braces to the top, parallel and on each side of the supporting block on the pedestal. They should be across the grain of the top and in the same direction as the grain of the pedestal block. Taper the ends almost to nothing so they are not obvious when the top is down. Tenon into these braces another piece between them (FIG. 6-22F). When the top is central on the pedestal, this piece comes loosely over the block. Fix the parts to the top with glue and counterbored and plugged screws.

Mark for pivot screws and drill small pilot holes through the braces into the block. The points marked on the block are the centers the curve of the top edge of the block. Use a compass to draw the curves, then round the top edge

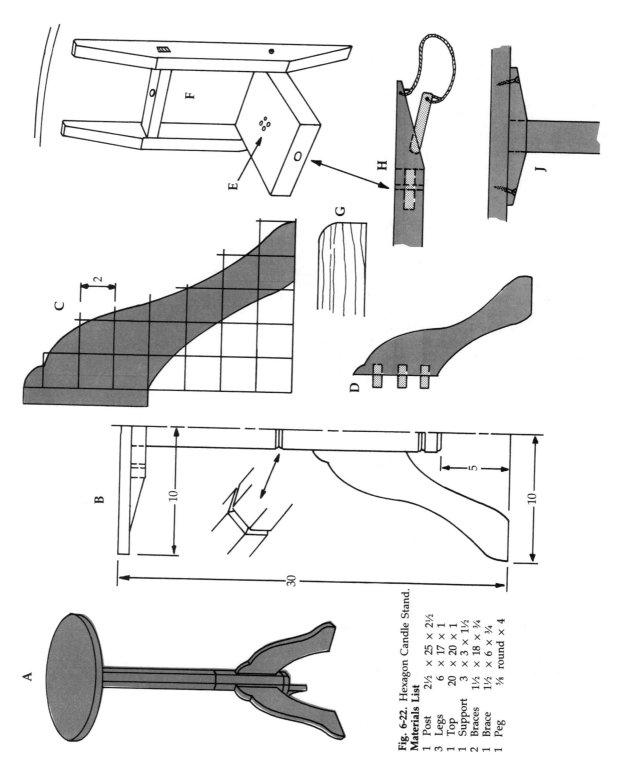

Fig. 6-22. Hexagon Candle Stand.

Materials List

1	Post	2½ × 25 × 2½
3	Legs	6 × 17 × 1
1	Top	20 × 20 × 1
1	Support	3 × 3 × 1½
2	Braces	1½ × 18 × ¾
1	Brace	1½ × 6 × ¾
1	Peg	⅝ round × 4

(FIG. 6-22G) to allow the top to tilt. Enlarge the holes to suit large roundhead screws. For a larger table, the pivots could be dowels or iron rods.

There are metal catches available to hold the tabletop in the down position, and fittings of this type were available quite early, so using one is not necessarily a departure from authenticity. A simpler and older method of locking the top in position was a peg (FIG. 6-22H) pushed into a hole. This could be turned or hand whittled. It might have a hole in the end for a cord to another hole in a brace so it does not become lost.

For a fixed tabletop, the support does not need to be square, so you can make a round or hexagonal piece of wood to fit on the top of the pedestal. Tapering toward its edges will improve its appearance and allow for screws upward into the top (FIG. 6-22J).

SIMPLE ROUND CANDLE TABLE

Many candle tables and their larger counterparts had turned pedestals. Some also had turned tops, but this is only possible if the lathe has a sufficient swing. Turned tops usually have raised edges or are molded around the rims. Leg shapes were related to the turned spindles. The plain turned spindles of a Shaker table had legs in simple curves, while a spindle with a bulbous outline and much turned decorations had legs with more flourishing outlines.

The plainly turned Shaker candle table gets its beauty from its proportions and fitness for purpose. Because most of the lines are plain, accurate workmanship is important. Flaws will show up more in a plain design than in an intricate design. You might need to modify sizes to suit materials or the size of lathe, but the drawing is of normal proportions (FIG. 6-23A).

The bottom of the spindle is parallel. Keep it as thick as the wood allows for strength in the joints. After curving in, the taper toward the top is straight, then an enlarged part takes the top bolster on a dowel end (FIG. 6-23B). Make a hole of the size to be used in the bolster as a gauge for the size of the dowel.

The top bolster is also turned. You can mount the wood on a faceplate, with the side that will be against the tabletop toward a plywood pad (FIG. 6-23C), or you can drill the hole first and push the wood onto a temporary mandrel (FIG. 6-23D).

The feet follow simple curves (FIG. 6-23E), with the grain following the long way as far as possible. The best joint is a dovetail, sliding in from below (FIG. 6-23F).

The top is a plain disk. Either turn it or carefully cut it by hand. Assemble the legs to the spindle and fix the bolster centrally under the tabletop. Arrange its grain to come across the grain of the top, so the two mutually prevent warping. Glue might be sufficient, but you could use a circle of screws upward through the bolster into the top.

With the tabletop inverted, fit the dowel of the pedestal in place and use a try square to check all around that the spindle is at right angles to the top. Leave the assembly for the glue to set, then stand the table on its legs to see if it is upright and with the top parallel with the floor. Adjust by planing the bottoms of feet, if necessary.

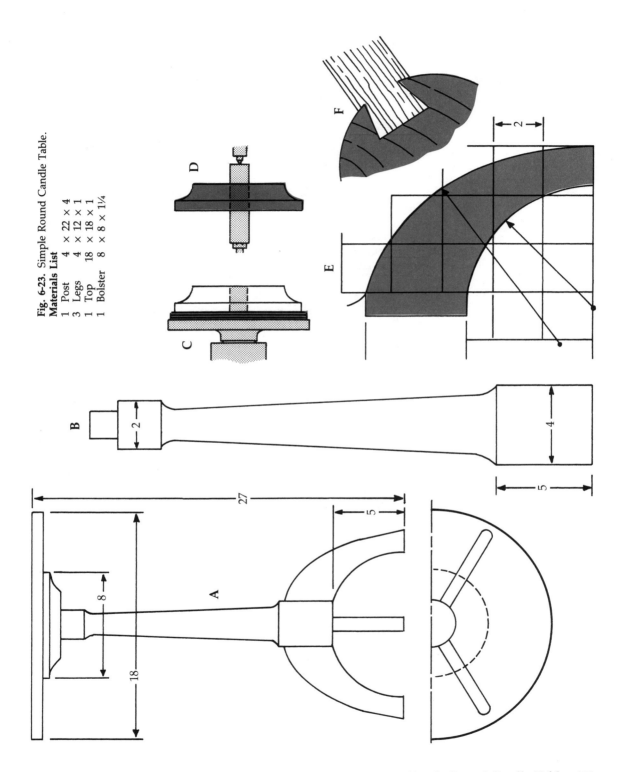

Fig. 6-23. Simple Round Candle Table.

Materials List

1 Post	4 × 22 × 4
3 Legs	4 × 12 × 1
1 Top	18 × 18 × 1
1 Bolster	8 × 8 × 1¼

Simple Round Candle Table   119

ROUND TILT-TOP CANDLE TABLE

Most wood turners produced more elaborate spindles than those used by the Shakers. The example in FIG. 6-24A is typical and there were a great many variations, but general designs were similar. In this table, the method of fitting and tilting the top is the same as for the Hexagonal Candle Stand. Differences are in the lower parts, although tops were often turned with raised rims when a large-swing lathe was available.

The spindle is at its maximum diameter at three points (FIG. 6-24B): at the bulbous part, just above the part where the legs come, and at the top. The lower part is a parallel cylinder, but the main length follows classical lines. The sweep of the curve toward the top is broken by a single bead. At the top, the end is turned to a large dowel to fit into the top block on which the tabletop pivots.

The legs (FIG. 6-24C) are of the type where a pad should be left for clamping. Tenons are the correct joints to use. Cut the wood to the outlines, then mark and cut the tenons. Chisel flats on the cylinder so the shoulders will come level when you pull the joints tight. Do all the work on the joints, but do not assemble them yet.

The legs look best if they are given a rounded section. Only the last parts close to the pedestal remain angular. To get an even curve, do the rounding in stages. First bevel the same amount all around. Use a notched piece of wood with a pencil to mark the bevel (FIG. 6-24D). Work the bevel with a chisel, spokeshave, or Surform tool.

When the bevel is the same all around (FIG. 6-24E), remove its sharpness and round the edges further by sanding (FIG. 6-24F). A suitable cutter in a spindle molder or router would also do the bulk of the shaping, but the final finish should be by hand. Under curves are not as important, but a good smooth flowing curve should be on the outside of each leg and the foot against the floor should show an almost elliptical outline. Get all three to the same shape for a neat finish.

Of course, the clamping pads will delay complete shaping of each leg. Glue the mortise-and-tenon joints. To avoid damage to the cylinder, make a curved block to go under the clamp (FIG. 6-24G). Although it is possible to glue all three legs in place at the same time, positioning the clamps becomes difficult and it would be better to glue and clamp the legs one at a time. Cut away the clamping blocks and complete the shaping of the legs.

When the pedestal has been assembled, completion of the table is the same as for the Hexagonal Candle Stand.

OTHER CANDLE TABLES

Although three shaped legs around a central spindle or post made up the usual arrangement for a small candle or lamp table, there were other constructions. Two feet could be cross lapped and the post tenoned or doweled at their center (FIG. 6-25A). With a basically deep section, there was strength and weight at the center, then the extremities were tapered. The underside could be shaped, but it was simpler to put pads under the ends.

With this arrangement of feet, it was logical to attach the post in the same way under a fixed top. For a tilt top, a solid block was used. With four feet the spindle could be just a square post (FIG. 6-25B); it could have wagon beveling, be made octagonal, or be turned.

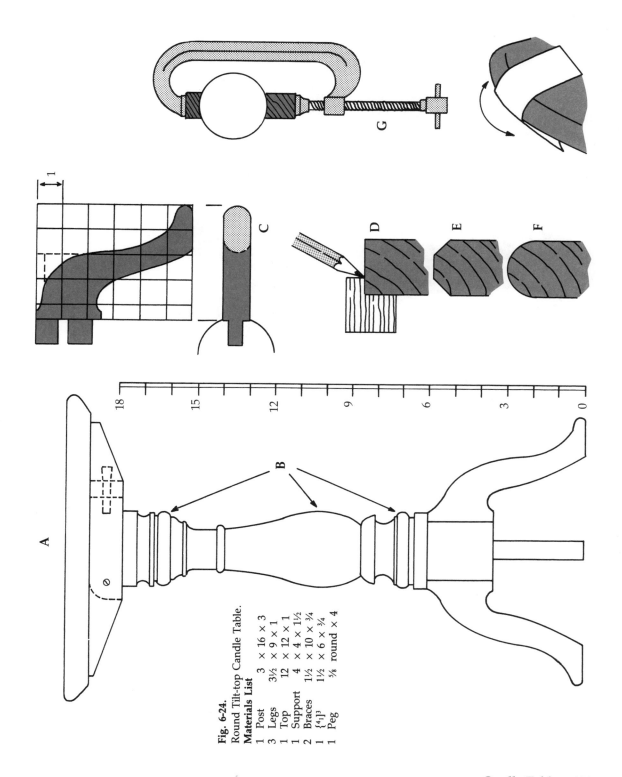

Fig. 6-24.
Round Tilt-top Candle Table.
Materials List

1	Post	3	× 16	× 3	
3	Legs	3½	× 9	× 1	
1	Top	12	× 12	× 1	
1	Support	4	× 4	× 1½	
2	Braces	1½	× 10	× ¾	
1	{⁴₁]³	1½	× 6	× ¾	
1	Peg	⅝	round	× 4	

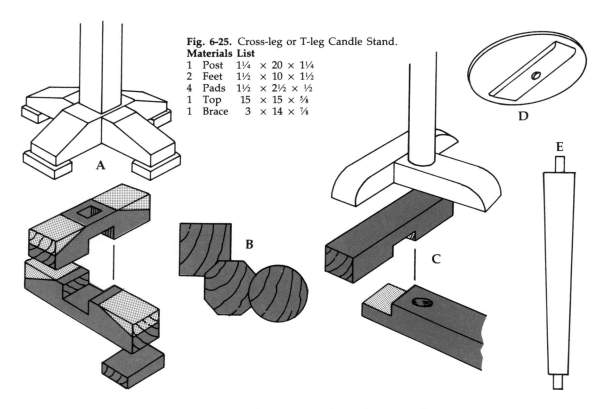

Fig. 6-25. Cross-leg or T-leg Candle Stand.
Materials List

1	Post	1¼	×	20	×	1¼
2	Feet	1½	×	10	×	1½
4	Pads	1½	×	2½	×	½
1	Top	15	×	15	×	⅝
1	Brace	3	×	14	×	⅞

Four feet are acceptable on modern flat floors, but on the early uneven floors, three feet were almost obligatory. An interesting Shaker variation of the cross-lapped feet had only three bearing surfaces. It had the two pieces joined in a T-shape, with the spindle or post on the leg of the T (FIG. 6-25C).

The top of a fixed table has a single bar across the underside, in a direction to control any tendency to warp (FIG. 6-25D). In a Shaker table, the turned spindle had no concessions to decoration, except a slight taper, which could be larger at the top or the bottom (FIG. 6-25E). Dowels made the joints at the ends.

REVOLVING TILTING TABLE

Tilting tables of many sizes were common in Europe and America, but a type of table that would revolve as well as tilt was more particularly American. This was arranged with a *bird's cage* or *crow's nest* at the top of the pedestal. This piece consisted of two square pieces with corner posts and was arranged to revolve on the shaft projecting from the pedestal, while the tabletop pivoted on the top square piece. Most of the tops were round, and the construction was used for tables of dining size, as well as for smaller tables for lamps or candles. The specimen shown in FIG. 6-26A is for a candle table, but a dining table could be made with a thicker and longer spindle under a larger top.

The feet and the lower part of the pedestal are similar to those in tables already described. The three feet are fitted into dovetail slots or mortises in the post. The

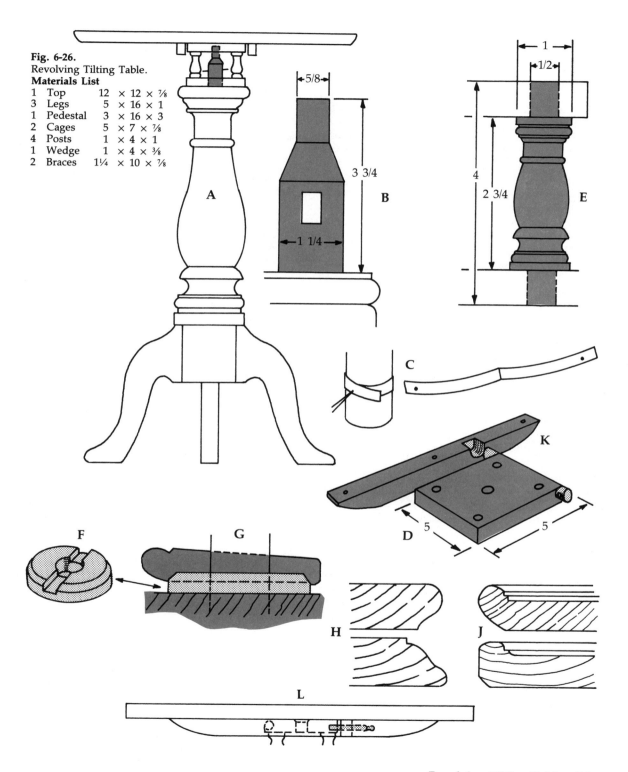

Fig. 6-26.
Revolving Tilting Table.
Materials List

1	Top	$12 \times 12 \times \frac{7}{8}$
3	Legs	$5 \times 16 \times 1$
1	Pedestal	$3 \times 16 \times 3$
2	Cages	$5 \times 7 \times \frac{7}{8}$
4	Posts	$1 \times 4 \times 1$
1	Wedge	$1 \times 4 \times \frac{3}{8}$
2	Braces	$1\frac{1}{4} \times 10 \times \frac{7}{8}$

A

B

5/8

3 3/4

1 1/4

E

1

1/2

4

2 3/4

C

K

D

5   5

F

G

H

J

L

turned design is generally similar to a previous table, but the top is turned with a shaft extension in two diameters and a slot is cut through to take a wedge (FIG. 6-26B).

To get the slot marked accurately on opposite sides of the shaft, wrap a piece of paper around the shaft and push a spike through the overlap. Remove the paper and fold it midway between the spike holes (FIG. 6-26C). This represents half the circumference. Put the paper back around the shaft and mark the spike hole and fold positions. Use them to locate the setting out of the slot.

The bird's cage is made of two boards. One is a plain square, but the other is the same size with two dowels cut to project from it (FIG. 6-26D). Traditionally the dowels were cut in the solid wood. If you make the projections square, then draw circles on their ends, you can carefully pare them and sand them round. Round the top edge of the board to allow the tabletop to tilt. Drill a hole in the center of the lower board to fit over the lower part of the shaft. Drill a hole in the upper board to fit the narrower upper part of the shaft.

The upper and lower square boards are held the correct distance apart by four spindles with dowel ends. Drill a hole near the corners of both boards (FIG. 6-26D) to take the spindles. Turn the spindles to patterns that match those of the main pedestal (FIG. 6-26E). The heights of the spindles at the corners of the square boards should hold them at a distance apart so when the assembly rests on the central shaft the top of the shaft does not quite pass through the top board. It probably will be best to make the central shaft too long at first and trim it to length after assembly.

To prevent the bird's cage, and the tabletop attached to it, from lifting off, there is a wedge through the slot in the shaft. A load on the rim of the tabletop can put considerable bending strain on the bird's cage at the pivot. To spread this load, you need a wooden washer under the wedge. This washer could be a square of wood under the wedge, but it is better if it is turned (FIG. 6-26F). The wedge, or *key*, is long enough to pass over the washer and project slightly (FIG. 6-26G). The wedge must thrust against the top of the slot in the shaft. If necessary, trim the lower edge of the slot to give clearance and to prevent the wedge binding there instead of pressing on the washer. Make the groove across the washer an easy fit on the wedge. Check the fit and action of the bird's cage on the shaft before making and fitting the tabletop.

The top is a circle, preferably turned on a lathe. If you must cut it by hand, you can make it a plain circle with rounded edges. If you are turning the top, you can give it a molded edge (FIG. 6-26H) or a lip and a sunken center (FIG. 6-26J).

Arrange two braces across the underside of the top, at right angles to the direction of its grain and at a suitable distance apart to fit each side of the bird's cage. The projecting dowels from the top square are level with the surface, so recesses for them must touch the top edges of the braces. You can cut these recesses most easily by drilling, then trimming with a chisel (FIG. 6-26K). You use a commercially made catch to hold the table down, you can fix the braces with glue and screws independently to the top, but if you use a peg, add a cross brace (FIG. 6-26L).

Check the action in all positions. If necessary, lubricate with graphite or candle grease. Do not use oil or mineral grease. Disassemble as much as possible for finishing with stain and polish.

TIER TABLE

Early table makers who had developed their skills with simple treadle lathes expanded their turned work to produce tables with tops at two levels—usually with a smaller top above the main top so the assembly could act as a side table for foods to be served on the main dining table, or for fruit or candies. You can make a tier table without turned parts, but it has a more graceful appearance if the main parts are made on a lathe.

Several variations are possible. The main support could be a central pedestal with three legs, then a turned pillar continues to support the upper tier. The lower part could be a table made in another way, possibly with three legs, then the central pillar taken up to the upper tier. Some tables had a further turned piece extending a short way above the top tier, to act as a handle for lifting a light table, to serve food to guests.

You can make the central-pedestal version similar to one of the tables described earlier, then dowel a spindle to the upper tier into its center (FIG. 6-27A). Make a bolster like the one below the main tabletop, and attach the spindle into it. Make the wood above the bolster to match the larger piece (FIG. 6-27B).

On a three-legged version (FIG. 6-28A), the main feature is the central pillar assembly, but it is logical to also turn the legs. However, some of these tables had the legs made with square or octagonal sections and a moderate taper.

If you turn the legs, make them with simple outlines, so as not to detract from the central turnings. Give them dowel ends and fit them into angled blocks at the top (FIG. 6-28B). These angled blocks under the tabletop allow for accurate setting of the slopes of the legs and make stronger joints than having the doweled ends going directly into holes in the tabletop. The method also avoids the need to cut the shoulders of the turnings at an angle where they meet the flat wood.

FIGURE 6-28 shows an extension of the central turned pillar above the top tier for use as a handle, but you can omit this piece to give a clear surface if the stand is intended to be used for a large dish or a plant pot. Although the underside of the table is not normally visible, it is good craftsmanship to arrange another turned piece below its center (FIG. 6-28C). This is not essential, but it gives a good finish to the piece of furniture (FIG. 6-28D).

The method of construction depends on facilities available to make the two large-diameter disks. If they are too large to be turned on the lathe, you can give them plain outlines, carefully saw them, then round or bevel the edges, depending on available tools. A spindle molder can work a pattern, but follow by enough handwork to disguise the method used. The alternative for making without a lathe is to cut the wood six- or twelve-sided (FIG. 6-28E).

Make central holes through the disks to suit dowels turned on the spindle parts. Increase the bearing surfaces of the turned parts with thin turned disk; otherwise there is a danger of rather narrow jointed areas weakening and becoming loose after some use. These pads or washers need not be round, but they continue the entire theme of the design if they are (FIG. 6-28F). The two are similar to each other, but the upper one can be slightly smaller and thinner.

Give the main pillar a classical taper (FIG. 6-28G). If there will not be a turned part below the lower tier, make a dowel end long enough to go through the tier and pad below. If you will use a turned part below, it is easier to turn the parts so the main pillar has holes for dowels at both ends. Getting the parts to assemble accurately depends on the fit of the joints, and it is wiser to turn the ends of the main spindle so they are slightly undercut and so the bearing against the disks or pads is at the rim and not at a high spot near the dowel.

Use a long dowel for the lower turning. Drill its pad for screws to be driven downward into it and for three or more screws to pass upward into the tabletop and supplement glue in the joint (FIG. 6-28H). Deal with the top turning in a similar way. It is shown with a knob for ease in lifting (FIG. 6-28J), but if the unit is not to be lifted, you can give it a taper or omit it. In the final assembly, screw the pad to the main pillar, which is inverted under the top tier for screwing to it. Then assemble the other parts.

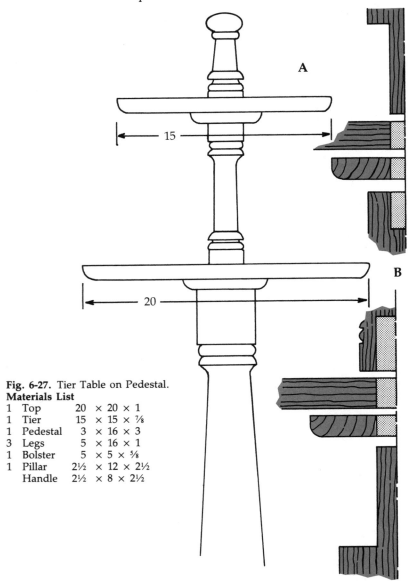

Fig. 6-27. Tier Table on Pedestal.
Materials List

1	Top	20	× 20	× 1
1	Tier	15	× 15	× ⅞
1	Pedestal	3	× 16	× 3
3	Legs	5	× 16	× 1
1	Bolster	5	× 5	× ⅝
1	Pillar	2½	× 12	× 2½
	Handle	2½	× 8	× 2½

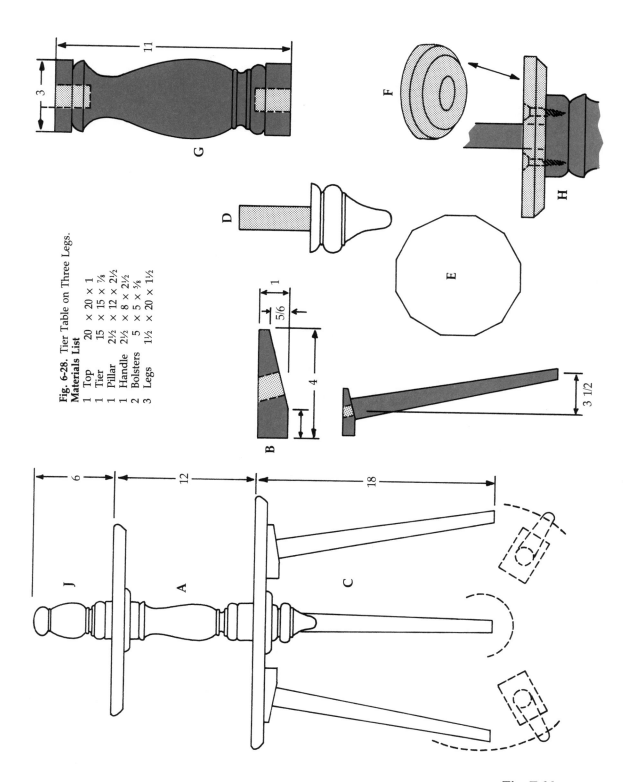

Fig. 6-28. Tier Table on Three Legs.
Materials List
1	Top	20	× 20	× 1
1	Tier	15	× 15	× ⅞
1	Pillar	2½	× 12	× 2½
1	Handle	2½	× 8	× 2½
2	Bolsters	5	× 5	× ⅝
3	Legs	1½	× 20	× 1½

It is advisable to fit legs into their blocks and let their glue set before attaching to the tabletop. You can probably push the central assembly tight by hand if the joints are a good fit. Clamping is difficult, because of the large disks. The original makers probably squeezed the two doweled joints in a cider or cheese press. You can support the assembly on a bench and use weights instead of clamps.

TILT-TOP BOX TABLE

A table that combined its normal purpose with storage had obvious uses. A drawer under allowed cutlery and other things of comparatively shallow depth to be stored and be accessible. For larger items, it was possible to arrange a box under a tilt top. The weight of things inside might contribute to stability, but the contents could not be reached while the table was in use. Box construction also contributed to the rigidity of the assembly, which was an advantage when the material and facilities of the early makers were not of a very high standard.

Tables of many sizes were made so the tilted top exposed a storage box below. Methods of construction varied. The example chosen here (FIG. 6-29A) is a side table of simple trestle form, with the box between the ends.

You can vary sizes to suit available material; they are not critical. Make the legs first (FIG. 6-29B). Make the feet wider and shape them so end pads rest on the floor. If you want to avoid sawing the underside to shape, you can build up the thickness. The original joint at the feet would have been tenons, taken right through (FIG. 6-29C). In a reproduction table, you could use a doweled joint (FIG. 6-29D), if that is more convenient to work.

The sides of the box overlap notches in the legs. Many early tables were simply nailed or screwed (FIG. 6-29E). A better construction uses a rabbet so nails can be driven both ways (FIG. 6-29F). Check for squareness after you have attached the box parts to the legs.

In a modern construction, you could let a plywood bottom into plowed grooves during assembly (FIG. 6-29G). Since the edges of the plywood would not be visible, this might be an acceptable alternative. In the most primitive construction, the bottom was made of boards nailed from below, but for a neater appearance the bottom was made of thin boards with their grain across the box, supported in strips around the sides and ends (FIG. 6-29H).

The top pivots on two pegs or dowels. You can use plain pieces of dowel, but they are more authentic if turned (FIG. 6-29J). Lay out the pivot corner full size. Keep the holes fairly close to the box sides and at the center or lower on the top braces; otherwise the top will not swing clear and finish in an upright position. If you are using softwood, you can use reinforcing strips across inside the tops of the legs. Draw a curve to indicate the swing of the top over the edge (FIG. 6-29K). This curve shows the amount the back of the box must be rounded to provide clearance.

The top could be a rectangle with rounded corners, or it could be round or elliptical (FIG. 6-29L). It is best to glue the braces and hold them with counterbored screws from below. Their distance apart should allow free movement over the box. If you are using a tilt-top metal catch, arrange it centrally to engage with a slot in the box side. Another method of securing is to drill the opposite side of the leg tops for pegs. To avoid confusion, these could be slightly smaller and turned with knobs for ease of withdrawal (FIG. 6-29M).

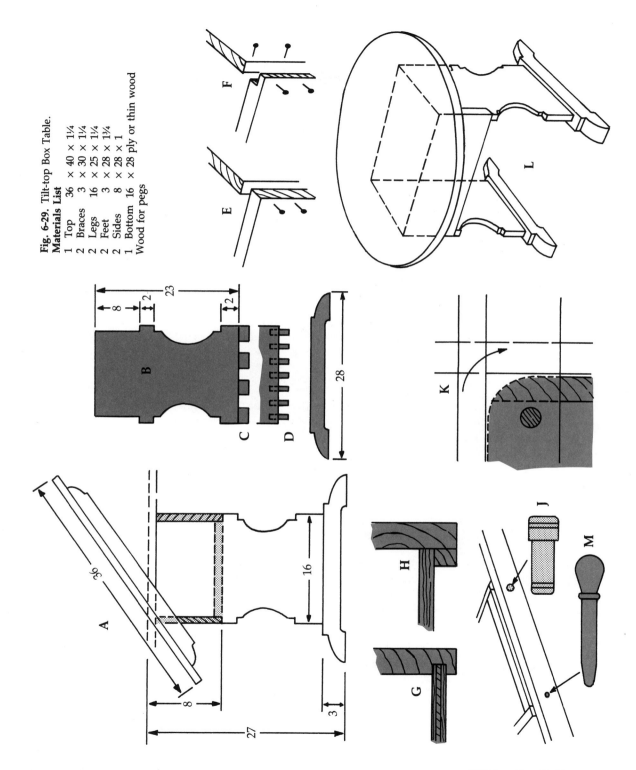

Fig. 6-29. Tilt-top Box Table.
Materials List

1	Top	36	× 40	× 1¼
2	Braces	3	× 30	× 1¼
2	Legs	16	× 25	× 1¼
2	Feet	3	× 28	× 1¾
2	Sides	8	× 28	× 1
1	Bottom	16	× 28 ply or thin wood
Wood for pegs				

SEAT TABLE

When a tilt-top table had the top swung to a vertical position to take up less space against a wall, there was obviously an advantage in arranging for it to then have a second use. Several tables were designed so they became seats. There had to be supports for the top when in the horizontal position, so the ends could not follow a more normal armchair shape. However, the piece of furniture offered reasonable comfort as an additional chair in a home where seating might otherwise be inadequate. The space under the seat was made into a box or chest with a lifting top to give a further use.

Some of these combination pieces of furniture were made like chests, with the ends extended upward to support the tilting top. A lighter version is shown, with the box shallower on legs (FIG. 6-30A).

Sizes for a dining table are shown, but other sizes are possible. For normal use, the seat level should be not less than 14 inches from the floor, whatever the size of the table, unless it is for a child's use. The top should be 28 inches to 30 inches from the floor; a side table could be lower. The load of a person leaning back on the vertical top must be taken on the pegs and the leverage from the amount the top extends down the back posts, so allow enough of an overhang on the top to allow for this.

Make the two end assemblies first. You can cut the shaped lower parts of the legs from solid wood, but it is more economical and easier to glue on pieces to make up the width (FIG. 6-30B). You can use solid wood for the ends of the box, and tenon them into the legs (FIG. 6-30C). Another method uses framed ends, with panels fitting into grooves (FIG. 6-30D). The original panels were solid wood, thinned at the edges to go in the grooves (FIG. 6-30E). The top rail should be wide enough to overlap the seat.

You could make the front and back of the box overlap the legs, with nailed or dado joints, as in the Tilt-top Box Table. Alternatively, you can fit the front and back between the legs and attach them to strips of wood inside (FIG. 6-30F).

At the seat level, place narrow end pieces (FIG. 6-30G) on each side of the top, which is a single board. Attach braces below the top and hinge it over the box back. The front edge should extend over the box front and be rounded. Cut the top back toward the ends (FIG. 6-30H). This design makes for comfort and gives a grip for lifting.

Cut the tops of all four legs the same and drill holes for pegs near their tops (FIG. 6-30A). So the tabletop will swing without binding, the curves of the tops have their centers at the holes.

You will need to make up the tabletop from several boards. The braces can have slotted screws through to allow for expansion and contraction. The pivot pegs and locking pegs are similar to those for the Tilt-top Box Table. Check the action with a trial assembly before sanding and applying a finish.

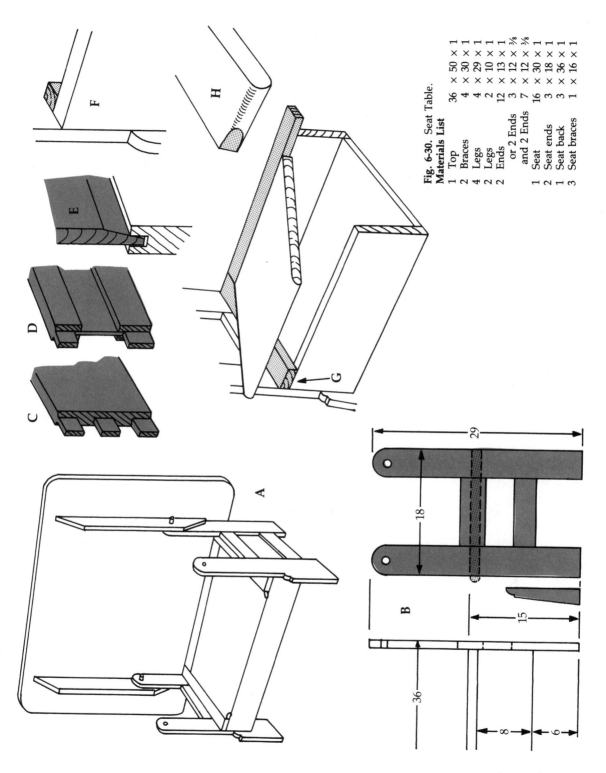

Fig. 6-30. Seat Table.

Materials List

1	Top	36 × 50 × 1
2	Braces	4 × 30 × 1
4	Legs	4 × 29 × 1
2	Legs	2 × 10 × 1
2	Ends	12 × 13 × 1
	or 2 Ends	3 × 12 × 3⁄8
	and 2 Ends	7 × 12 × 3⁄8
1	Seat	16 × 30 × 1
2	Seat ends	3 × 18 × 1
1	Seat back	3 × 36 × 1
3	Seat braces	1 × 16 × 1

JACKSTAND

Many early woodworkers became intrigued with the adjustable action of a carriage jack, many of which used a ratchet and pawl movement. Small tables were made to adjust in height with this action. Candle holders were made with several sockets around the top. Others were made quite tall and arranged to support a hanging lamp. With light sources of only small output, there was a need to be able to adjust them to the best advantage.

The jack adjustment provides an interesting design. The most generally useful form today would be in the form of a small table or candle stand (FIG. 6-31A). The idea obviously predates the modern electric floor lamp, so the jack adjustment could be included in an electric stand, but could hardly be described as a reproduction.

The two posts (FIG. 6-31B) and the center shaft (FIG. 6-31C) are similar sections. Make the base of two fairly heavy-sectioned pieces to provide stability. They should extend a little farther than the diameter of the top. Half-lap them together. You can cut them back below to form feet, or add pieces for the feet, if that is easier (FIG. 6-31D).

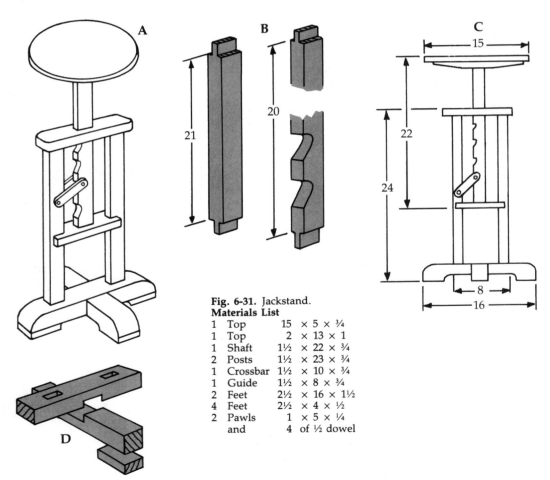

Fig. 6-31. Jackstand.
Materials List

1	Top	15	× 5	× ¾
1	Top	2	× 13	× 1
1	Shaft	1½	× 22	× ¾
2	Posts	1½	× 23	× ¾
1	Crossbar	1½	× 10	× ¾
1	Guide	1½	× 8	× ¾
2	Feet	2½	× 16	× 1½
4	Feet	2½	× 4	× ½
2	Pawls	1	× 5	× ¼
	and		4 of	½ dowel

Tenon the posts into the top crossbar, and mark the crossbar with the mortises into the base, to get the spacing the same. For design, you can use tenons showing through the crossbar, or shorter stub tenons. Do not assemble these parts yet.

At the bottom of the shaft, there is a guide joined on with a mortise-and-tenon joint (FIG. 6-32A). Notch its ends to slide easily on the post. There is a mortise slot in the crossbar that lets the shaft slide through. Rigidity of the table depends on the notched ends of the guide and the fit of the shaft mortise. Mark these parts carefully on both sides of the wood (FIG. 6-32B) and cut away the waste carefully from both sides. You can use a round or octagonal tabletop. Stiffen it with a batten across the grain (FIG. 6-32C) that is mortised to take a tenon on the top of the shaft.

Some jackstands had the pawl made as a single piece let into a slot in one of the posts, but for a stronger and more rigid assembly, make the pawl with two cheeks and two dowels (FIG. 6-32D). One dowel goes through the post, while the other engages with the notches.

Draw the center part of the assembly full size to the actual sizes of your wood and the mortise spacings. Allow for the pawl being mounted just below half the height of a post. The lowest position is when the guide rests on the base. The next move can be 3 inches above this position so the first notch comes opposite the pawl there. The highest position is when the guide almost reaches the pawl, so allow for another notch there. You can space other notches between these points at 2- to 3-inch intervals (FIG. 6-32E).

Because of the difficulty of getting at all parts satisfactorily for finishing after complete assembly, it is best to make up subassemblies and paint, varnish, or oil them before final assembly. Waxing on rubbed-down varnish is better than using a high gloss finish. Make sure the shaft will still slide freely after finishing. For lubrication, use candle grease or one of the antifriction sprays. Suitable subassemblies are: the top attached to the shaft, but the guide left loose; the base, crossbar, and posts made up; and the pawl left with one side off.

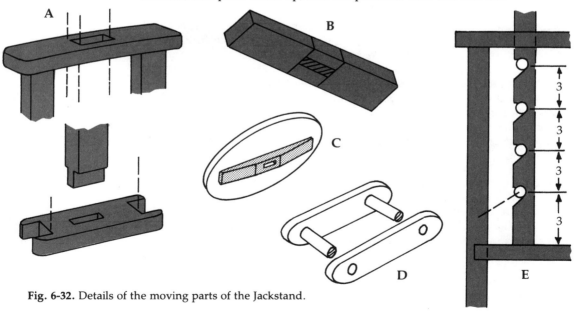

Fig. 6-32. Details of the moving parts of the Jackstand.

7

Chairs and Seats

STOOLS AND SIMPLE BENCHES that are no more than extended stools might have served for seats while there were things of more importance to occupy early settler craftsmen, but these things do not offer much comfort and there would soon have been a demand for chairs, settles, and other forms of seating that most immigrants would have known in Europe.

Unfortunately, a chair that is to provide a high degree of comfort is not an easy thing to make, and many early craftsmen with high degrees of skill in many aspects of their occupation would have found that making chairs which were fully functional did not come as readily as they might have expected. Chair making has always been a specialized branch of furniture making, and many craftsmen are still occupied almost solely in this branch of cabinetmaking. It would have been so in the days when people from all walks of life decided to make a new home in America.

Consequently, there are some examples of early chairs and seats that reflect the inability of their makers to produce something fully up to the standards of what they could remember in their home lands. Whether some of these are worth reproducing or not depends on other aspects of the particular items, which might have artistic merit or features of particular interest, even if they are not as fully functional as their makers had hoped.

Upholstery, as we know it, was uncommon at first. Any softening of seats and backs would have been by draping blankets over them or by having loose cushions. In the later, more settled, period when many people expected to live in greater comfort and with more amenities, there were craftsmen making American equivalents of Chippendale chairs and working to the designs of other famous European cabinetmakers.

Gradually the designs were adopted and a local influence became apparent, so chairs and other pieces of furniture could be identified as American and not imports from England. The American chairmaker was also influenced by designs from countries other than England, so features he liked might have been incorporated in something that was basically of English design, to produce the start of a new series of designs.

Chairs that reproduce the better type of style and design of the later period are difficult to make, and it would be inadvisable for the average amateur to attempt them. There are plainer chairs that provide reasonable comfort and are much easier to make. These might be all wood with softening by loose cushions; some of them include upholstery of a type that is easy to apply. If you are new to chair making, you are advised to start with a simple design, before going on to try a reproduction of an advanced type that is contoured to give support at just the right parts of the human anatomy and still be a thing of beauty.

Another consideration might be the number of chairs. Chairs are normally in sets of four or more, possibly with one or more matching armchairs. When a single chair is made, there can be variations from errors or the need to adapt construction to suit the size of a piece of wood, but more skill is needed if several chairs must be made identical.

Some chairs and benches are little more than stools with backs built in. These obviously are a little more comfortable, but better chairs have shaped wooden seats, or the part that takes the sitter's weight is either made slightly flexible or is padded. Further steps are contouring of the back and the addition of arms. Early chairs were made in all these ways and can serve as prototypes for reproduction work.

PEASANT CHAIR

Many European countries—notably Germany, Austria, and Switzerland—favor a stool type of seat with a solid back having its decoration provided by shaping around the edge. The Pennsylvania Dutch remembered their German origin and produced chairs of this type in the early days of settlement when most available wood was in thicker sections. The example chosen here (FIG. 7-1A) should be kept to thick wood to retain authenticity and to provide sufficient strength in the joint between the seat and the back. If thinner wood is used, there would not be sufficient rigidity without additional brackets or other strengthening.

The seat is a plain slab with its grain running front to back. You can make the sides parallel or slightly wider at the front, with the corners taken off (FIG. 7-1B). You can leave the edges square or round them, preferably with more rounding on the top edge than the bottom (FIG. 7-1C). Some chairs were molded (FIG. 7-1D). At this stage, leave the rear edge too wide and untreated.

There can be considerable load on the angle between the seat and the chair back when the sitter leans back, so the joint must be secure. The best is a multiple mortise-and-tenon joint, with tenons on the back passing through a series of mortises in the seat. Because both parts are meeting with their grains in line, arrange the tenons so their greater lengths are in the direction of the grain (FIG. 7-1E). This design is stronger than having the tenons wider. Mark out and partly cut the joint before you fit the legs and cut the outline of the back.

The back should slope at about 10 degrees. Set an adjustable bevel to this slant and use it instead of a try square when marking across the edges of both pieces of wood to transfer the joint details to the other sides (FIG. 7-1F). Cut the tenons carefully, watching the lines on both sides and tilting the saw. Similarly, drill out waste with the bit at a slight angle and trim the mortises from both sides toward the center of the thickness of the wood. Let the tenons be slightly too long so they can be trimmed level with the underside of the seat after the final assembly.

With the joints cut, but not finally fitted, you can undertake the rest of the work on making legs and shaping the back. Fixing the back to the seat should be done as the last assembly process. When you reach this point, do any final trimming with a chisel and drive and glue the tenons into the mortises. Make saw cuts in the tenons so you can drive wedges from below. Leave the glue to set before trimming off the ends of the tenons and finally truing the back of the seat, which should be allowed to project enough for the end grain to resist the load on the joint. If the chair is made of softwood, the seat should project about 2 inches behind the joint, but this can be reduced to nearer 1 inch for a hardwood such as birch, beech, or maple.

The legs do not have rails. Make them fairly stout. You can turn them on a lathe with a simple outline and a dowel top (FIG. 7-1G). Early examples made this way were either fit into the seat with foxtail wedging in blind holes (FIG. 7-1H), or taken right through and wedged on top (FIG. 7-1J), before being planed off level. It is important that all four legs splay the same amount. You might be able to set up a tapered support to make the holes uniformly on a drill press, but if you drill by hand, use an adjustable bevel or a piece of wood cut to the angle as a guide (FIG. 7-1K).

Make the legs with a tapered square section, having the sharpness taken off the corners to produce an irregular octagon section. Although it would be possible to use dowels into the seat, a stronger joint is made with a tenon. Cut the tenon with its shoulders at an angle. Marking and cutting the tenon is most easily done before the legs are tapered or beveled (FIG. 7-1L).

You will need to cut mortises in the seat. As with the holes for dowels, you can have them go only part way and tighten the tenons with foxtail wedges, or you can have them go right through and wedge them on top. Saw cuts for the wedges should be at right angles to the grain of the seat and not at right angles to the tenons. This puts the spread of the tenon against the seat in the direction best able to resist it (FIG. 7-1M).

The back is shown with a typical outline (FIG. 7-1N). The hollows suit the cords of cushions tied on. It might be advisable to make a template of half the back so you can cut both sides uniformly. The band saw will be the best tool to cut the outline, but the first makers did the work by hand, and a bow saw or jigsaw will get around the outline, even if your muscles have to be exercised to the full. Clean the edges with a Surform tool and plenty of sanding. Cut the hole at the center with a jigsaw or saber saw.

Many of these chairs have the outline left square across in section with the sharpness taken off the edges. Others have the front edge well rounded. Some have the outline thoroughly rounded to a semicircular section.

When assembly is completed, stand the chair on a level surface and trim the legs so it stands without wobbling and with the seat parallel with the floor. Round the bottoms of the legs so they will not mark carpets or other floor covering.

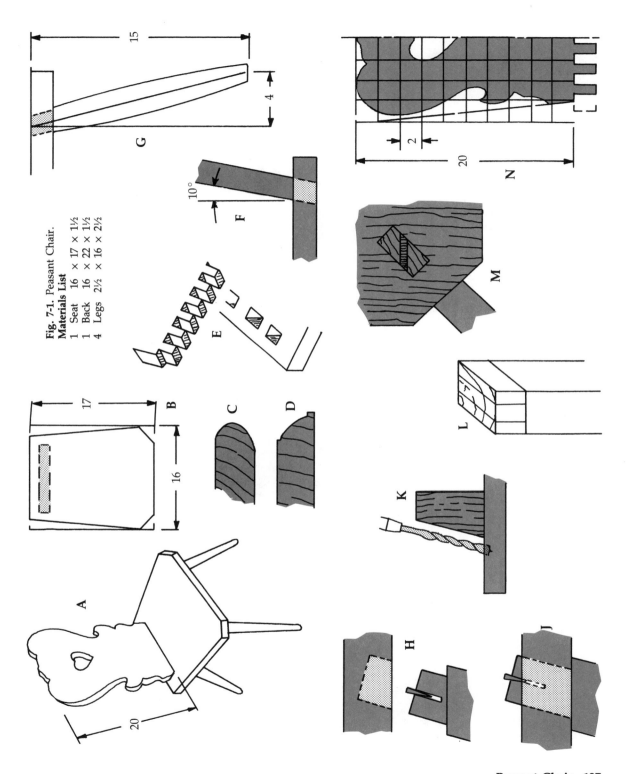

Fig. 7-1. Peasant Chair.
Materials List
1 Seat 16 × 17 × 1½
1 Back 16 × 22 × 1½
4 Legs 2½ × 16 × 2½

LADDERBACK CHAIR

Chairs with slats across the back have been popular for a long time, and modern versions are still being made. The term *ladderback* obviously comes from the ladderlike appearance of the back.

Many early ladderback chairs had the rear posts arranged at right angles to the floor, so the support for the sitter's back was upright. This form was probably easiest to make and assemble, but it gives an unnatural and uncomfortable posture. The design is improved by letting the rear posts slope back at a slight angle. This method does not affect stability. Some old chairs and many new ones, have the rear posts curved, so the part forming the leg below the seat is upright, but the curve above produces a slope. Some posts were steamed and bent around jigs. This would be the only way of producing a bent turned leg, but for a square section it is possible to cut the shape from a flat board with a band saw.

Many old ladderback chairs had high backs, and all parts except the slats had been turned on a lathe. Some of the old treadle lathes had a long capacity, but many modern lathes will only handle a length of about 30 inches and a high-back chair needs more than this—spindles near 4 feet for the rear posts are usual. The first example shown here (FIG. 7-2A) has a lower back within the capacity of most lathes. The back slopes. Draw a full-size side view to obtain the sizes of the parts (FIG. 7-2B).

Turn the rear posts and the front legs from 2-inch-square wood, so the greatest diameters will finish about 1 3/4 inches. The front legs are simple cylinders with the bottoms slightly rounded and the top finished in a shallow knob. While the wood is revolving in the lathe, it is helpful for further work to use a pencil on the tool rest to lightly mark at each position that will need to be drilled for rails. The side rails are at a slightly different level to the front rails. Staggering the holes allows the dowel ends of the rails to penetrate farther and produce stronger joints. The four top rails around the seat must be at the same level for working the seat (FIG. 7-2C).

Turn the posts parallel up to slightly above seat level, then give them a slight taper toward the top. Use one of the front legs as a guide to pencil the rail positions while the post is in the lathe. Also pencil the positions of the tops and bottoms of the mortises for the back slats (FIG. 7-2D). The posts are plain turnings, but you can add some decoration at their tops.

The rails can be plain parallel cylinders reduced at the ends to form dowels (FIG. 7-2E). It is unusual in these chairs for the rails to be turned with beads or other decorations. One small amount of shaping that was sometimes used was to have the centers of the rails slightly thicker than the ends (FIG. 7-2F).

Some chairs were made with flat slats and these are shown in FIG. 7-2G, but shaped slats are more comfortable, and you could use them for this chair. (They are described for the Ladderback Armchair.) Cut flat slats to the outline. You can use a template, or make one slat and use it to mark the others. Mark the lengths between shoulders of the tenons to match the lengths of the turned rails for the back (FIG. 7-2H).

To make holes, use a drill press, an electric drill, or a bit brace. Draw a line along a post or leg to get all holes in line. Deal with the mortises and the holes across the back and front of the chair first. These are all at right angles. If drilling is by hand, have a try square alongside, and get an assistant to sight the drill, so drilling is as accurate as possible. Drill some of the waste from the slat mortises and trim them to shape with chisels.

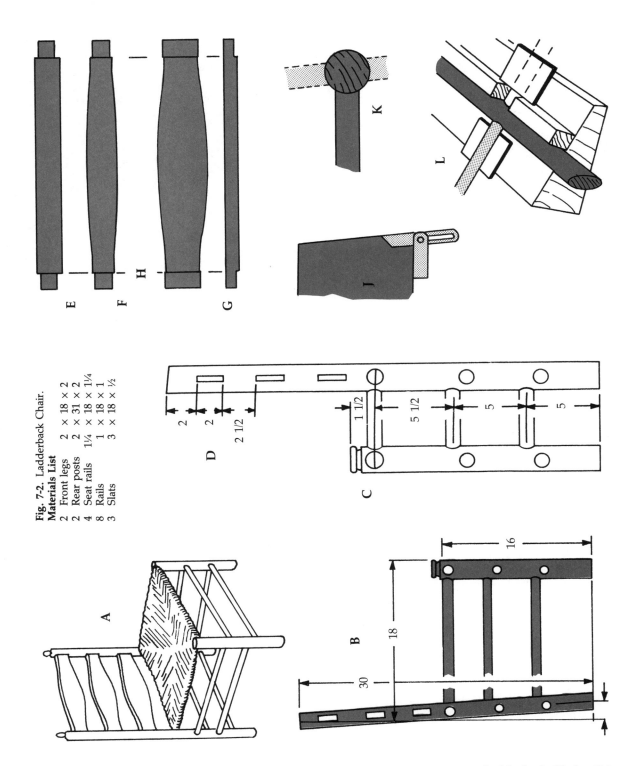

Fig. 7-2. Ladderback Chair.
Materials List
2 Front legs 2 × 18 × 2
2 Rear posts 2 × 31 × 2
4 Seat rails 1¼ × 18 × 1¼
8 Rails 1 × 18 × 1
3 Slats 3 × 18 × ½

Because the chair seat is wider at the front than the back, you must drill the other holes at something other than a right angle to the first holes. Draw half a plan view of the seat sufficient to get the angle between front and side rails. Set an adjustable bevel to this angle (FIG. 7-2J). Place a rail in one of the holes. The bevel will give the angle the other holes are to be. Use the obtuse angle for the back posts and the acute angle for the front legs (FIG. 7-2K). If you use a drill press, it would be helpful to make up a jig to hold the post or leg with a rail in position as a guide to the angle and an extension each way to allow the jig to be used for obtuse and acute angles (FIG. 7-2L). The amount the rail holes differ from a right angle at the sides into the rear posts is not enough to matter.

Assemble the chair in stages. Join the legs with their rails. To check squareness, use a try square and measure diagonals. To check that there is no twist across the assembly, put it on a flat surface and see that it does not wobble. Assemble the two rear posts and their slats and rails. Use the front leg assembly to check the rear assembly by putting it over the matching part. Also check the rear assembly for squareness and lack of twist in the same way. Do not do any more assembly until the glue for these parts has set.

Fit all the side rails into the front assembly. Put glue on all the joints into the rear assembly, then bring all the parts together. Use bar clamps where necessary to get joints tight. Sight across the chair to see that rails are parallel, then stand the chair on a flat surface and check diagonals across the seat. You cannot use a try square there, but the diagonals should measure the same. You can use a try square on the sides—it is important that the front legs stand upright. Put a board across the seat with a weight on it to hold the parts in shape until the glue has set.

The traditional seats were made of *rushes* (cattail leaves) gathered from the waterside and dried, but moistened just before use. Rushes were twisted into ropes as the seat was formed. You can still use this method, but there are prepared ropes available that produce a very similar effect. They also are much more convenient to use because they are in long lengths and used dry. There are art fibers and plastic ropes, as well as sea grass, which is a rushlike imported rope for the purpose. The method of working is the same whatever material is used, except you must add rushes constantly and twist them as you go.

Although the traditional form of seat hides its method of construction when it is complete, the work is actually quite simple and the pattern of strands mitered from the corners builds up automatically. If you use any of the continuous ropes, it is helpful to make a few rough wooden spools (FIG. 7-3A) to wind the material on. The only other tool needed is a pointed stick for the last few turns. This could be a square or round rod about 3/4 inch across sharpened to a point.

Tie a knot in one end of a strand and tack it inside a rail. Take the shuttle over the next rail, underneath, and back over the rail you tacked to (FIG. 7-3B). This is the complete action you need to know—further steps merely repeat it. Keep the tension on that first corner and go across to the next one—over the opposite rail, into the center and over the one you have just crossed alongside (FIG. 7-3C). Continue around the stool, doing this at each corner and keeping a good tension on the next strand, particularly when it goes from one corner to the next.

After a few times around you will see the pattern building up. It will be the same above and below the seat, and the strands going from one corner to the next eventually will be hidden inside the seat.

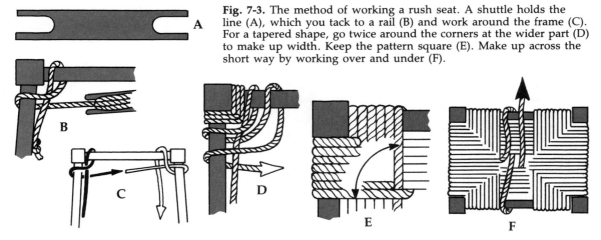

Fig. 7-3. The method of working a rush seat. A shuttle holds the line (A), which you tack to a rail (B) and work around the frame (C). For a tapered shape, go twice around the corners at the wider part (D) to make up width. Keep the pattern square (E). Make up across the short way by working over and under (F).

If you continued all the way in this manner, the narrow rail at the back would fill with strands first, leaving a gap at the wider front one. To cure this, go around each of the front corners twice (FIG. 7-3D) about every third time you come to them, until the gap left along the front rail is the same as the one at the back. Use the edge of a piece of wood to push the strands tightly toward the corners and aim to keep the angles between strands at each corner reasonably close to a right angle (FIG. 7-3E).

If you must add new line, tie it to the old line anywhere between corners. The knot will then be hidden.

It will be satisfactory to continue in this way until the pattern fills the seat and many chairs are finished in this way, but to get a firmer seat, you can stuff the seat with oddments of rush or the material used. When the seat is about half completed, you will see pockets between the top and bottom patterns. You can push pieces of the covering material into these pockets with a stick and add more as the work progresses.

As the pattern continues toward the middle, you will reach a point where the shuttle cannot be passed through. From here on, you will need to use the line in a long length and push its end through the hole. Use the pointed stick to force a sufficient gap.

Nearly always, the pattern fills up on one pair of opposite rails before the other opposite pair. To fill the second pair, continue to thread through in a figure-eight pattern (FIG. 7-3F) until the rails are covered. Tack the last turn under its rail and push a few inches of the end inside the seat.

LADDERBACK ARMCHAIR

Using wood of square section instead of round section for the legs and posts of a chair is slightly stronger because the bearing surfaces in the joints are increased a little. Working on a flat surface when marking and cutting joints also makes for accuracy with less trouble. In the case of a high-back chair, the avoidance of round sections for the posts means there is no need for a lathe of increased capacity.

This chair (FIG. 7-4A) has the wood of square section throughout for legs, posts, and rails. The slats could be flat, as in the previous chair, but they are shown

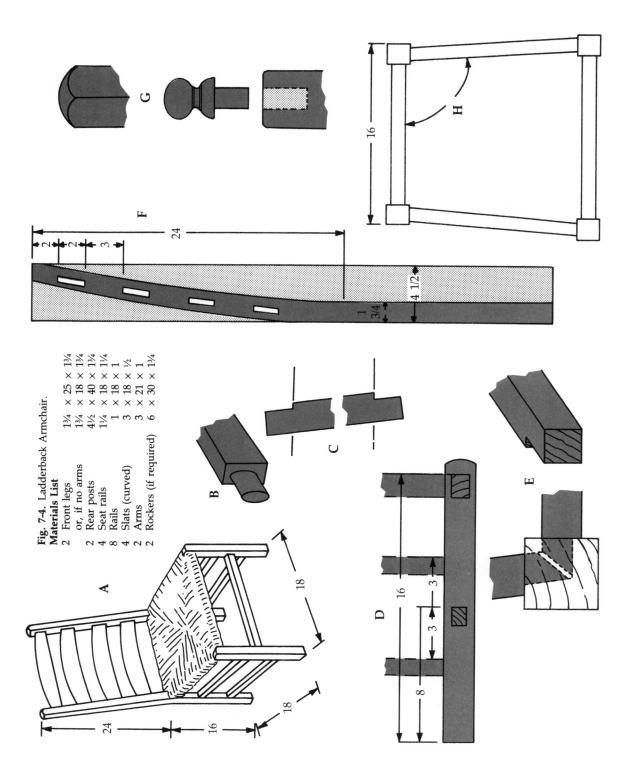

Fig. 7-4. Ladderback Armchair.

Materials List

2	Front legs	1¾	×	25	×	1¾	
	or, if no arms	1¾	×	18	×	1¾	
2	Rear posts	4½	×	40	×	1¾	
4	Seat rails	1¼	×	18	×	1¼	
8	Rails	1	×	18	×	1	
3	Slats (curved)	3	×	18	×	½	
2	Arms	3	×	21	×	1	
2	Rockers (if required)	6	×	30	×	1¾	

curved in the way most of these chairs were produced. It would be possible to make the chair in the way just described, using turned parts. The overall sizes and the method of construction could be the same.

Joints may be doweled. A doweling tool for use in a bit brace can cut dowels directly on the ends of rails, or you can glue pieces of dowel rod into holes in the ends of the rails (FIG. 7-4B). Dowel diameters should be about two-thirds of the thickness of the rails.

Better joints are mortises and tenons. The rails could be shouldered both sides of the tenon, but they are easier to cut if barefaced and the obtuse and acute angles are easier to fit closely (7-4C). The tenons should be only slightly less than the thickness of the rail: one-third of the thickness of the legs and post would be about right.

Start with the front legs (FIG. 7-4D). Leave some surplus length at the top until after you have cut the mortises. Mark the positions of the mortises or dowels for the rails. Note that the side and front rail positions are staggered, so the mortises do not meet. For the seat rails, you can cut the mortises to meet, then miter the ends of the tenons or dowels. Allow a slight gap (FIG. 7-4E), however; otherwise it might be difficult to bring the shoulders of the rails tight against the legs.

Cut the rear posts from a wide board, either one post from one board, or (less wasteful) both from a wider board if that is available. The lower part is upright and matches the front legs, then the upper part sweeps back (FIG. 7-4F). The upper part may taper both ways slightly. You can finish each top in a simple rounding or plug in a turned finial (FIG. 7-4G).

The rails on each panel are all the same length. Mark all the side rails together and mark the back and front ones in sets. It is the distance between shoulders that is important. All of the ends of doweling and the shoulders for tenoning may be cut square, but for the best fit and appearance the side rail angles should match the shape of the seat. To find the angles, use a full-size drawing (FIG. 7-4H). Round the edges of the seat rails around which the rushes will be wrapped.

The slats go squarely into the posts, but curve them in their length, and cut them to a profile in their depth (FIG. 7-5A). They can all be the same, but top slat in the better type of older chair has more curve than the lower ones, with the amount of curve tapering (FIG. 7-5B). This gives more curve toward the top of a sitting person's back and less below his waist. If the rear posts are parallel, all slats are the same length between shoulders, but if the posts taper, you must make the slat lengths to suit. One way of keeping all slats the same length with tapered posts is to keep the inner surfaces of the posts parallel and only taper the outer surfaces.

If possible, cut all slats from one solid block of wood. Mark around it to indicate the overall length and the distance between shoulders. Draw the curves to be cut with a little waste between for sawing (FIG. 7-5C). If you are cutting the slats from more than one piece of wood, mark the shoulder length on all pieces at the same time. Cut the curves with a band saw, if possible. A belt sander is a convenient tool for smoothing the curved surfaces. Slats in some early chairs were made slightly thinner at the top than the bottom.

Profiles for slats followed many simple patterns. This type of chair was not made with elaborate twists and curls to the outlines. Whatever the outline, bring the ends straight just before the projecting tenon (FIG. 7-5D). Some chairs had the slats taken their full thickness into the posts, but it is neater to thin the tenon

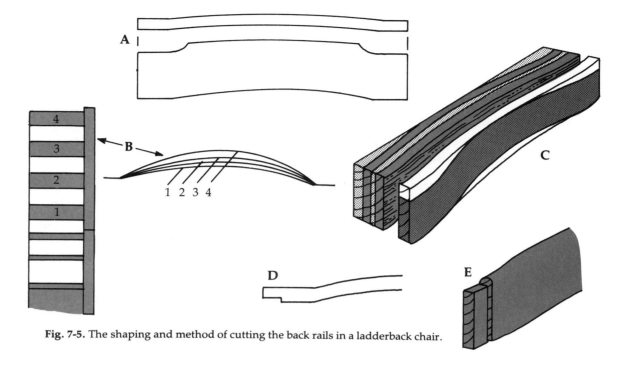

Fig. 7-5. The shaping and method of cutting the back rails in a ladderback chair.

slightly. Since the wood is already quite thin, particularly if the thickness tapers, it is best to cut a barefaced shoulder on the front only (FIG. 7-5E). Round the tops of the slats thoroughly and either do the same with the bottom edges or take the sharpness off the square edges.

Assemble the chair in stages, as described for the previous chair, and work a seat in the same way. If you are making an armchair, the front legs must continue upward. It is also possible to make one of these chairs into a rocker.

For an armchair, the front legs continue upward (FIG. 7-6A), but are otherwise the same as for a plain chair. They could be square and tenoned into the arms (FIG. 7-6B), or you can turn the upper part and finish each of them with a dowel into the arm (FIG. 7-6C).

The arm is flat and parallel in thickness, but has a tapered curved outline when viewed from above (FIG. 7-6D). Cut the pair to the same outline, but make sure you cut the joints before completing the shapes. Under the front there is a mortise or hole bored to take the top of the leg. At the back there can be a tenon into the rear post (FIG. 7-6E). Some arms, particularly when they join round posts, have the arm section tapering to round, so the arm itself becomes a dowel. This goes into a hole and the joint may be reinforced with a screw from the back (FIG. 7-6F).

Round the upper edges of the arm well and take the sharpness off the angles below (FIG. 7-6G). The arms are a prominent feature of the chair, so use care in their shaping, particularly the finish at the front of the chair.

Converting the chair to a rocker involves fixing pieces to the bottom. These need not extend far forward of the legs, but they must go far enough back to

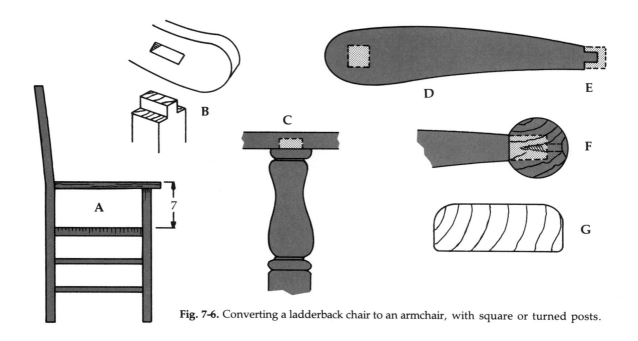

Fig. 7-6. Converting a ladderback chair to an armchair, with square or turned posts.

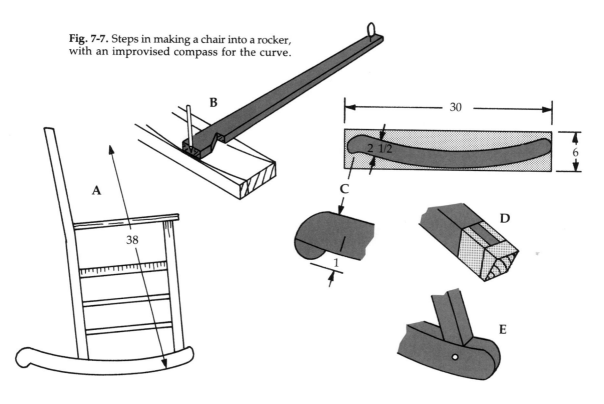

Fig. 7-7. Steps in making a chair into a rocker, with an improvised compass for the curve.

prevent the chair from tipping in that direction. The amount of curve is slight—too much curve would cause the chair to go too far with only slight movement and there would be more risk of falling over backward. The curve shown in FIG. 7-7A suits the chairs just described. If you are making rocking feet for chairs of other sizes, choose a center for the curve about 2 feet above the seat and toward the back (FIG. 7-7A).

You can draw a curve of this size on a piece of wood turning on an awl with a pencil against the end (FIG 7-7B) if compass or trammels of sufficient reach are unavailable. Give these feet a small projection at the back to serve as a stop and warn the sitter that he has gone far enough back (FIG. 7-7C).

Cut both feet and see that they match. Use the actual feet to mark the bottoms of the legs. The chair will come to rest when out of use with the back tilted slightly more than it does when standing on the legs alone.

Transfer the sloping lines of the shoulders of the leg tenons around the wood (FIG. 7-7D) and cut the tenons. This can be done on a completed chair, but if you are building it as a rocker, you can assemble the pair of sides and add the feet before the chair is finally assembled with the other crossing rails and slats.

Locate and mark the mortises on the feet. The tenons go fairly deeply into the feet and a modern glue might be all that you need to hold them securely, but dowels or pegs through the joints were usual (FIG. 7-7E) and may be added. Round the edges of the feet between joints and see that the bottom is smooth, with no sharp edges to mark the floor covering.

SPINDLE CHAIR

Many Colonial chairs were made almost entirely by turning the parts on a lathe. It seems that having bought or made lathes, the furniture makers looked for projects that would make the fullest use of them. Probably a point in favor of turning was the comparative ease with which a competent craftsman could produce a good surface on round work, yet getting as good a surface with the planes and sanding equipment of the day was much more difficult. This applied particularly to wood that had not been fully dried during seasoning. Turned work in "green" lumber can be brought to a reasonable finish, yet the same wood worked under a plane would be liable to tear up and leave a poor surface, no matter what direction it was planed. Since sufficient time could not be allowed between felling trees and converting their wood into furniture, these qualities associated with the lathe must have had considerable appeal.

The ladderback chairs have turned parts, but their outlines are plain and utilitarian. Other chairs were given decorative turnings along the lengths of spindles. If made in attractive hardwood and polished, these chairs were attractive pieces in a dining room and could still be used for that purpose. Most followed the early tendency to make the backs upright. Seats were often rush, worked in the manner described for the Ladderback Chair, but some were given lift-out panels that either supported a cushion or were upholstered. The example shown in FIG. 7-8A has this type of seat, but giving it a rush seat instead would only involve the substitution of suitable seat rails.

The main motif in all the turned parts is a series of large beads, with very few small quirks of angular sections. The lower parts of the rear posts were left plain, except for the feet, but they could be turned like the front legs if the back of the chair was likely to be visible in normal use.

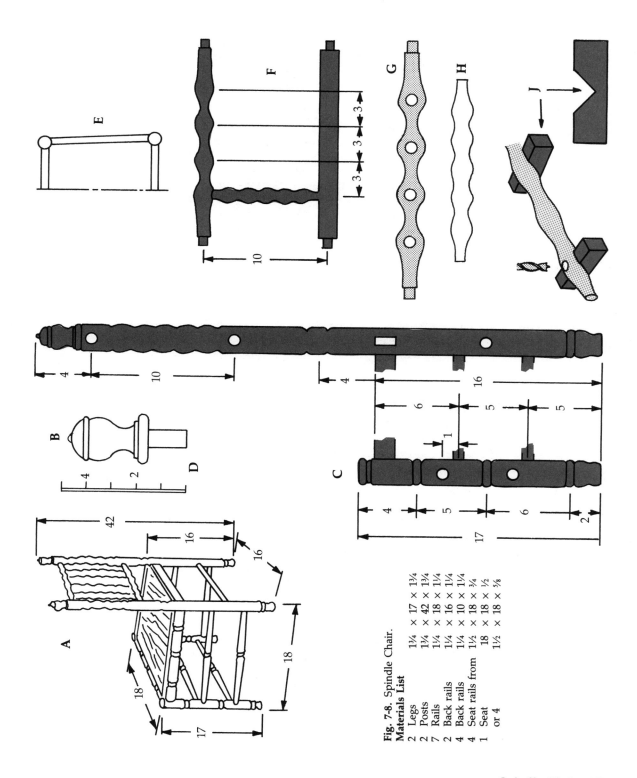

Fig. 7-8. Spindle Chair.

Materials List

2	Legs	1¾ × 17 × 1¾
2	Posts	1¾ × 42 × 1¾
7	Rails	1¼ × 18 × 1¼
2	Back rails	1¼ × 16 × 1¼
4	Back rails	1¼ × 10 × 1¼
4	Seat rails from	1½ × 18 × ¾
1	Seat	18 × 18 × ½
	or 4	1½ × 18 × ⅝

Make the front legs. Note that the parts that will be drilled for rails are parallel (FIG. 7-8B). Mark the rail positions with lightly penciled rings while the wood is rotating in the lathe. Make the rear posts (FIG. 7-8C) using the front legs as a guide to the centers for drilling rails. As with the legs, keep the parts that will be drilled parallel. Some of these chairs had quite tall spindles projecting at the tops of the posts, but the more squat finial shown in FIG. 7-8D was typical of a more compact decoration. You should turn this finial as part of the post, but if the post length is near the capacity of the lathe, you could drill its end and make the finial separately with a dowel for plugging in.

The front legs and rear posts stand upright, so the side joints are at right angles. When viewed from above, the front of the chair is wider than the back. This means that you must use care when drilling to always have the drill at right angles to the length of the spindle being drilled, although it might need to be a few degrees away from a right angle in relation to other holes because of the taper of the seat. As with the ladderback chairs, draw the seat shape full size to get the corner angles (FIG. 7-8E).

Instead of slats, the back is made up of two horizontal spindles and four upright ones (FIG. 7-8F). Make the horizontal spindles with the same distance between shoulders as the lower rails, and space the beads to suit the upright spindles (FIG. 7-8G). Pencil around where the holes are to come, although some chairs have a line cut around with the long point of a turning chisel.

Turn the upright spindles without shoulders at their ends (FIG. 7-8H). In this way, you can make some adjustment in the joints to allow for slight errors in the diameters of the horizontal spindles or the spacing between the holes for them in the posts.

If you drill the horizontal spindles by hand, hold the wood in a vise and stand a try square beside each hole in turn so the drill is always as near upright as possible. If you drill the spindles in a drill press, it is helpful to use V-blocks. They may be a metal engineering type or made of wood. Accuracy in the V is not important, so long as both blocks are identical, as they should be if cut together on a band saw (FIG. 7-8J).

Drill the holes in the legs and posts at the correct angles in relation to each other, either with an adjustable bevel alongside for hand drilling or on a drill press using a similar jig to that suggested for the ladderback chairs (FIG. 7-2L).

The chair rails could be a rabbeted square section (FIG. 7-9A) to take the seat panel. An alternative is to fasten one piece inside another (FIG. 7-9B). If you want a turned effect alongside the seat, you can use a split turning.

Make two opposite parts at the same time. Prepare two strips that will make up a square when put together (FIG. 7-9C). Glue them with paper between (FIG. 7-9D) and let the glue set. Turn this spindle to the pattern for the seat rails. Avoid very great differences in diameter between parts of the spindle (FIG. 7-9E). Let the ends of the design be straight and leave a little excess length for trimming to make joints. Remove the wood from the lathe and split the pieces apart along the paper line with a knife or chisel. Scrape and sand away any remaining paper.

Glue on a strip to form the ledge inside the turned part (FIG. 7-9F). Join whatever type of seat rails you use to the legs and posts with mortise-and-tenon joints. Assemble the chair in a similar way to the ladderback chairs. Make up the assembly of spindles in the back and join them to the posts with the lower rails before the glue in any joint has set, then the upright back spindles can adjust to the other parts. Check diagonals and flatness, then allow to set—under weights if necessary.

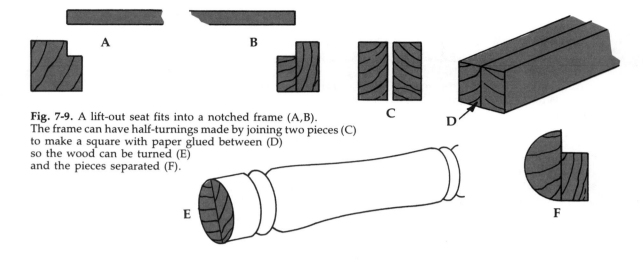

Fig. 7-9. A lift-out seat fits into a notched frame (A,B). The frame can have half-turnings made by joining two pieces (C) to make a square with paper glued between (D) so the wood can be turned (E) and the pieces separated (F).

Do the same with the chair front, then join with the side rails, checking that the chair stands upright and does not wobble.

In its simplest form, the seat is a plain board, making a loose fit on the rails (FIG. 7-10A). In modern furniture it would be plywood, but if you use a board as in an original chair, you can place battens across the grain below and cut them back to fit inside the rail frame.

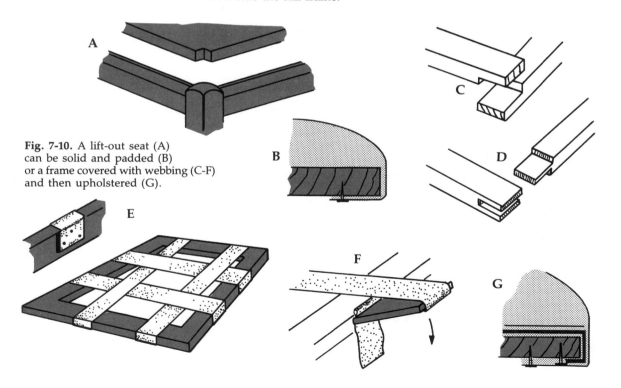

Fig. 7-10. A lift-out seat (A) can be solid and padded (B) or a frame covered with webbing (C-F) and then upholstered (G).

The plain wooden seat can support a loose cushion, or you can give it its own padding. This would have been sheep wool or pieces of cloth, but a modern version would be better with plastic or rubber foam. Stretch cloth over and tack it underneath (FIG. 7-10B), neatly folding the corners of the cloth around the corners of the board.

Such padding only gives limited comfort. A further step was to use an open frame with the padding supported on strips of canvas, webbing, or leather. Make the frame a loose fit in the recess, and cross-lap the corners (FIG. 7-10C) or join them with open mortise-and-tenon joints, sometimes called *bridle joints* (FIG. 7-10D). Interlace the straps tightly and tack them below (FIG. 7-10E). You can put tension on with one of the modern upholstery webbing stretchers, but the simplest way is the original one: levering with a piece of wood (FIG. 7-10F). Tack a piece of cloth, such as burlap, above the webbing, then put the padding on, pull the cloth cover over, and tack it in the same way as for a plain board bottom (FIG. 7-10G).

SHAPED CHAIR

If a wooden chair is to provide maximum comfort without the use of cushions or upholstery, it must be contoured to the human form in many ways. There are modern molded seats that blend into the figure, but when strips of wood must be made into a chair, there cannot be much shaping and the parts must be disposed and arranged so they give support where they touch the body. Other parts of the construction are arranged to contribute to this support. Some curving of parts might be possible, but to avoid complications, most of the parts are straight.

To a certain extent, the making of chairs is an art, rather than a craft, insofar as the skilled chairmaker works by eye and knows from the look of the assembly and by previous experience that it will be right. Working from a drawing is difficult, mainly because there are some compound curves involved, which are difficult to portray and interpret on a flat piece of paper.

One type of solid wood chair that was common and reasonably comfortable had a beauty in its form, but it was more for the kitchen than the important rooms of the home (FIG. 7-11A). The front legs splay slightly. The back posts curve in their length when viewed from the side and curve outward slightly toward the top when viewed from the front. The piece at the top of the back is flat with its front edge curved to the body, and the slats below it curve to fit into the small of the back. This means that there are few straight lines to work from, but if the construction is approached systematically it is not difficult. A band saw lessens the labor of cutting curves in thick wood and hand tools provide the shaping.

The seat (FIG. 7-11B) is a solid piece of wood with its grain running front to back. The front corners are curved and the sides may have a slight curve. The top could be flat, but these seats were hollowed to a shape something like the human posterior (FIG. 7-11C) with an adze or a curved drawknife. You can also use a broad gouge. The depth does not need to be great, but you must use care to keep the two halves matching. Work toward the deepest parts from a penciled outline. A curved scraper will remove tool marks. Follow with a coarse then a finishing grade of abrasive paper.

The two front legs are simple turnings. Keep the diameters near parallel for the parts that will be drilled to take the rails (FIG. 7-11D). The dowel tops usually go through the seat and are wedged on top. The exact amount of splay is not as important as getting both legs splayed the same amount. An adjustable bevel alongside the drill will guide it correctly.

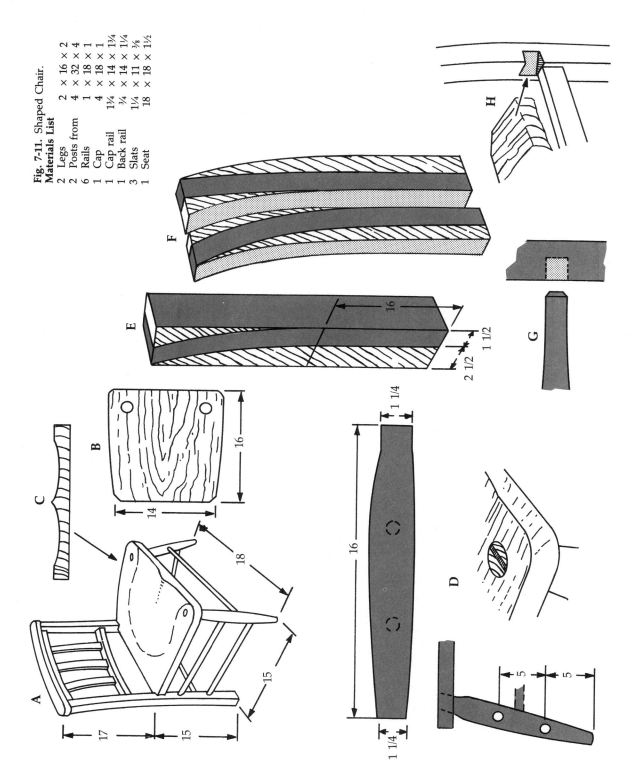

Fig. 7-11. Shaped Chair.
Materials List

2	Legs	2	×	16	×	2			
2	Posts from	4	×	32	×	4			
6	Rails	1	×	18	×	1			
1	Cap	4	×	18	×	1			
1	Cap rail	1¾	×	14	×	1¾			
1	Back rail	¾	×	14	×	1¼			
3	Slats	1¼	×	11	×	⅜			
1	Seat	18	×	18	×	1½			

Shaped Chair   151

Cut the rear posts from a wide board (FIG. 7-11E), then plane them to match in side view. Next, modify their thickness so they form parallel legs up to the seat level, then flare outward slightly toward their tops (FIG. 7-11F).

Remove all signs of saw marks and clean up the posts. See that they finish with their surfaces at right angles to each other in cross section. The upper parts should retain the same width all the way to the top. This type of chair does not have tapered posts.

You can either make the rails plain cylindrical ones or turn them with a thicker part at the center. It was usual to not shoulder the ends, but to turn them parallel with a slight chamfer to push into the holes (FIG. 7-11G) to allow adjustment. It would be difficult to get every shouldered rail correct when dealing with flared and curved legs and posts; holes are drilled slightly too deep to allow for this. Although some guidance might come from the use of an adjustable bevel, you must use a certain amount of judgment to determine the correct angle to hold the drill for some holes.

If there are slight errors, you can modify holes with a gouge or pare the end of a rail with a chisel. Joints should make tight fits, however. Glues are not sufficiently gap-filling to retain their strength if required to fill spaces. You can mix sawdust with glue that has to go into a space. Many old chairs that have been dismantled have shown shavings in joints, proving that not all early furniture makers got their joints right every time.

Tenon a rail between the posts to support the seat. Notch the seat into the posts, also (FIG. 7-11H). There are no rails under the seat sides or front. Tenon or dovetail a curved piece into the posts, then cap the back with a piece of wood having a hollowed front edge, by attaching the wood over the curved piece with glue. Hold it down (FIG. 7-12A) with screws into the posts. Many chairs had the plugs over the counterbored screws turned with curved tops standing above the surface (FIG. 7-12B). The best way to mark the curved piece under the capping is to make it too long, then make a temporary assembly of the lower parts, so you can hold the wood against the flared posts and mark the compound angles.

Another rail crosses between the posts lower down (FIG. 7-12C). Curve it to match the top one and tenon it into the posts, slightly nearer the front than the top one.

Between these rails are narrow curved slats, which you can make in one of two ways. You can curve them by cutting with thick wood with a band saw or alternative handsaw (FIG. 7-12D). In original chairs, they were more likely made flat and bent. Larger pieces would have to be steamed, but you can boil these small pieces to make them sufficiently pliable. One way of bending is to use one piece of wood to push a slat against two more in a vise (FIG. 7-12E). A better curve is obtained by shaping two blocks and squeezing the wood between them (FIG. 7-12F). Whatever the method, make the slats too long and trim from both ends, as the ends tend to straighten. If you boil the wood, leave it to dry completely before you build it into the chair.

Fit the slats into mortises in the two curved rails. Do not shoulder them to make tenons, but their full width fits in. A slight taper on the back allows adjustment (FIG. 7-12G).

As the first step in assembling the chair, make up the back parts. Put the curved laths into their mortises, with glue, and assemble their rails and the lower rails between the posts. Pull these parts together and check symmetry by measuring diagonals. If you tenoned the rail under the capping, fit it at the same

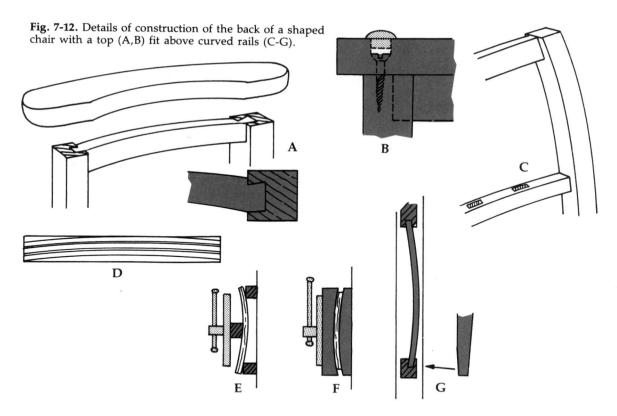

Fig. 7-12. Details of construction of the back of a shaped chair with a top (A,B) fit above curved rails (C-G).

A B C D E F G

time, but if you dovetailed it, get the other parts together. Sliding the dovetails in from the top should pull the assembly tight. Glue and screw on the capping.

Fix the rail between the front legs and join the legs into the seat. Bring this assembly up to the back and add the side rails as you fit the seat into its notches in the posts. Settle it with glue on its back rail. You might need to use a few counterbored screws through the seat into the rail.

FIREHOUSE ARMCHAIR

Armchairs shaped to fit around the body are sometimes loosely referred to as *Windsor chairs,* but the true Windsor chair has an arched back (see the next example). The Firehouse Armchair gets its name from its common use in early days in the quarters of volunteer fire departments. There are a great variety, but the specimen shown in FIG. 7-13A is chosen because it can be made without steaming wood.

Some chairs had flat seats; others were shaped as in the Spindle Chair; and others were shaped from back to front, while remaining straight across (FIG. 7-13B). The front edge is straight, the grain is across the seat and the back is a part of a circle (FIG. 7-13C).

The seat is the key member of the assembly. Make it first. Locate the leg positions on the underside. On the top, pencil a line around parallel with the edge, and position the spindle locations on this line. Note there is an even number and spacing is uniform (FIG. 7-13D).

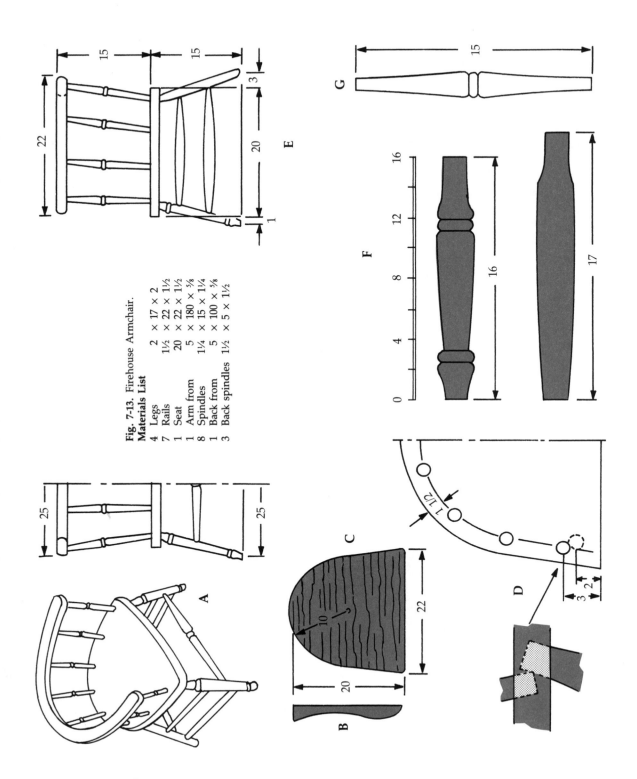

Fig. 7-13. Firehouse Armchair.
Materials List

4	Legs		2	×	17	×	2
7	Rails		1½	×	22	×	1½
1	Seat		20	×	22	×	1½
1	Arm from		5	×	180	×	⅝
8	Spindles		1¼	×	15	×	1¼
1	Back from		5	×	100	×	⅝
3	Back spindles		1½	×	5	×	1½

The front legs are upright when viewed from the side, but are splayed when viewed from the front. The rear legs have the same splay as the front legs when viewed from the front, but from the side they are seen to have considerable splay toward the rear (FIG. 7-13E). It is difficult to arrive at the exact sizes of the legs, so turn the tops with parallel parts to adjust in the seat holes, and arrange the bottoms so that final trimming to length will not affect their appearance (FIG. 7-13F). In this case, the front legs are decorated with beads, but the rear legs are plainer.

Turn the spindles with thicker centers. You can use beads to match the front legs (FIG. 7-13G). In effect, the underassembly and seat can be regarded as a stool and be put together without reference to the parts above the seat. You can assemble these parts before proceeding with the arms and spindles, if you wish.

Laminate the combined arms and back with two or three thicknesses. The shape must match the seat, and the inner edge should be just within the outline of the seat (FIG. 7-14A). Use any convenient lengths of wood. Let them abut and arrange joints to come at different places in each layer (FIG. 7-14B). Cut each piece to shape with a little to spare. Glue the part together and put them under pressure until set. After that, you can treat the laminated part as a single piece of wood. Trim its profile, but do not do any cross-sectional shaping at this stage.

Transfer the spindle locations from the seat to the arm. The spindles will flare out slightly. Let the front pair flare in the width, but be upright when viewed from the side, then space the hole positions for the others around the centerline of the arm piece (FIG. 7-14C).

The eight spindles are all the same. Allow a little excess length and keep the ends parallel and to the hole size, so they will still fit if trimmed to length.

You can complete the armchair at this stage, but many chairs were given an extension backrest. A modern method of construction would be to laminate many thin pieces of wood around a mold, but the older glues were not suitable for this method, so the backrests were built up by laminating more flat pieces in a similar

Fig. 7-14. The back and arms of the Firehouse Armchair.

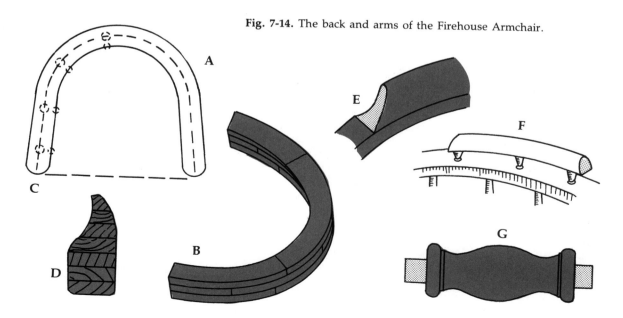

way to the arm piece (FIG. 7-14D). You can work the backrest with spokeshave and plane to a comfortable section. Mount it on top of the arm piece (FIG. 7-14E), with dowels or screws from below.

This method of mounting does not give high support to the back. Another method of mounting the backrest is to use short spindles located above and between the main spindles (FIG. 7-14F). Turn these with dowel ends (FIG. 7-14G) and stand them upright between the two parts.

The front ends of the arms should be well rounded. Most of the rest of the shape also should have a rounded section. Drill the holes for the spindles connecting to the seat at angles judged by eye, with appropriate adjustment later with gouge and chisel, if necessary.

When the arm is to be attached to the seat, have all the spindle ends glued and lightly inserted in place in the seat. Bring the arm into place and get the spindle ends located in their holes. Use a piece of scrap wood under a hammer or mallet to work around the arm a little at a time, driving the parts together. When all of the spindles have entered a short distance, check that the arm is parallel with the seat and that the assembly when viewed from the front is not flaring more one way than the other. Continue driving progressively around the arm until all the joints are fully closed and the chair looks symmetrical.

WINDSOR CHAIR

The Windsor chair originated at High Wycombe in Buckinghamshire, England, a town that is still situated amid beech woods. The main parts of the chairs were made from this wood, with the arched bow of the back made of yew. The name comes from nearby Windsor, with its royal castle, and a medieval monarch who used the chairs gave them this name. The type was well known to those who sailed to America, and many chairmakers produced local variations from very different woods. No British Windsor chairs were made of softwoods, but some American versions were.

There are a great many designs of Windsor chairs, but all have the characteristic bow back and a number of upright rods or spindles. Many British Windsor chairs had a central "splat" in the back, decorated with profiling and fretting. This was less common in American Windsor chairs. The ordinary Windsor chair does not come high enough to provide a headrest. Some chairs were made with some of the rods extending through the bow to a shaped top high enough to come behind the head. These were *comb-back* Windsor chairs.

Some of the best Windsor chairs are examples of a high degree of craftsmanship. It is unlikely that even the most skilled amateur woodworker could make one, since these chairs are the result of years of experience making nothing else. Even the more basic types are complex to the extent that much of the work has to be done without guides, and only experience will show if the action was right. Consequently, the first attempt at a full Windsor chair might not be successful.

The bow at the back of many Windsor chairs continues to complicate the attaching of armrests. This complication can be avoided if a version without arms is made (FIG. 7-15A). Up to seat level, the chair can be made with splayed legs as described for the Firehouse Chair, or with almost any arrangement of rails. The top is traditionally hollowed to suit the sitter's posterior, but some specimens were made with shaping back to front only in a "plank" seat.

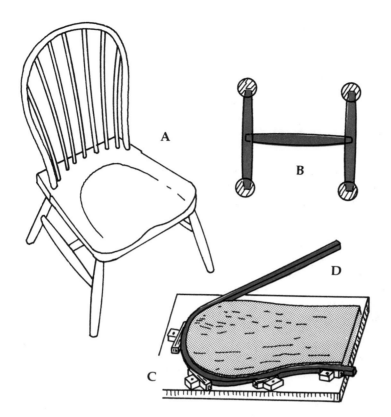

A

B

Fig. 7-15. Windsor Chair, showing how to bend the back.

Materials List

4	Legs	1¾ × 16 × 1¾
2	Rails	1½ × 18 × 1½
1	Seat	20 × 20 × 1½
1	Bow	1¼ × 80 × 1¼
	or 3	1¼ × 80 × ⅜
7	Spindles	⅝ × 30 × ⅝

D

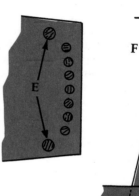

E

F

C

The example has turned legs doweled into the seat and single rails between back and front legs, then a stretcher between them (FIG. 7-15B). Thicken the rails at their centers to allow for a hole deep enough to provide strength in the joints.

You can make the bow of solid wood, such as hickory or ash, if you can steam the wood. A steam chest is made of four boards nailed together into a box, a little longer than the wood for the bow. Add some sort of water container and a source of heat, then place a tube into one end of the box. Surround the tube with cloth or other packing, with more at the other end, except for a small space for steam to escape. The wood must steam long enough to become flexible without risk of breaking. This may take an hour.

Make a mold from scrap wood to the intended outline. Have blocks of wood screwed on and wedged ready for tightening (FIG. 7-15C). With the help of an assistant, get the wood from the steam chest and pull it around the mold as quickly as possible, working from the center toward the ends (FIG. 7-15D). Leave this for at least a day.

A modern way of making the bow without steaming is to laminate from three thin pieces. Use full-length pieces, coat them with glue, and pull them around the same mold, then wedge them in the same way as for steaming. This assembly would not be authentic, but when cleaned up and rounded, the glue joints would not be obvious to the casual viewer.

You could tenon the ends of the bow into the seat, but many ends were rounded and pushed into holes like dowels.

Some spindles were slender turnings with beads around, looking something like bamboo. Others were given a slightly bulbous shape. Slender turning needs careful support. An alternative is to use parallel prepared dowel rods.

To give stiffness to the back of a Windsor chair, have the ends of the bow forward of the holes for the bottoms of the spindles (FIG. 7-15E). The spindles look best if given a slight curve. This is achieved by drilling the holes in the seat nearer upright than is estimated as the angles toward the bow, then bending the spindles as you bring them into place.

To find the actual positions of holes in the bows, you must use trial and error. Mount the bow in its holes on the seat. The center spindles are easy to locate. Put them in their seat holes and pull them back to a pleasing position on the bow (FIG. 7-15F). Pencil the location on the bow and remove the bow. Take the lines to the inner surface of the bow and drill holes. Trim the spindles to length and reassemble with them in their holes. Do the same with the next pair outward, giving them a slight fanning. Continue in this way with the other spindles. As you reach the outer pair, you will need to take the holes acutely into the bow.

Round the edges of the bow, particularly parts that come toward a sitter's back. Assemble with glue and check symmetry and the slope of the back in relation to the seat. Hitting the top of the bow, with a piece of scrap wood to spread the blow, will bring the parts together. Forcing the top of the bow backward or forward slightly will adjust the dowel rods in their holes.

If you are making a Windsor chair with a central splat, the method is similar, except the splat fits into mortises in the back of the seat and the center of the bow, and takes the place of two of the spindles.

WAGON-SEAT BENCH

Seats for two or more people economized on space and material, and were a convenience in a room where the family gathered around a fire. A bench like an extended stool had its uses, but for comfort there had to be a back of a reasonable height. Farm wagons often were equipped with bench seats across their width, and this idea was adapted in a variety of ways to broad seats for use in the home. Wagon-seat benches were popular for use on an exterior porch. Those for use indoors acquired refinements as they developed later into settees and love seats.

The majority of early seats of this type were made of wide boards nailed together with only elementary joints. Better seats had screws counterbored and plugged, and this would be the best method for a reproduction wagon bench seat. The example in FIG.7-16A is built this way.

You can alter sizes to suit available boards, but if you modify the design, take care to see that the legs extend to near the full length of the seat and go out to at least its width to minimize the risk of tipping.

Draw a full-size front view of one end (FIG. 7-16B) to get the angles for the legs and arms. Overall sizes are governed by the size of the board that makes the seat.

Make the two legs and check that they match and that angles on their edges are the same (FIG. 7-16C). Notch them for the rails, but you do not need to let in the notches for their full thickness (FIG. 7-16D). The rails look best if their lower

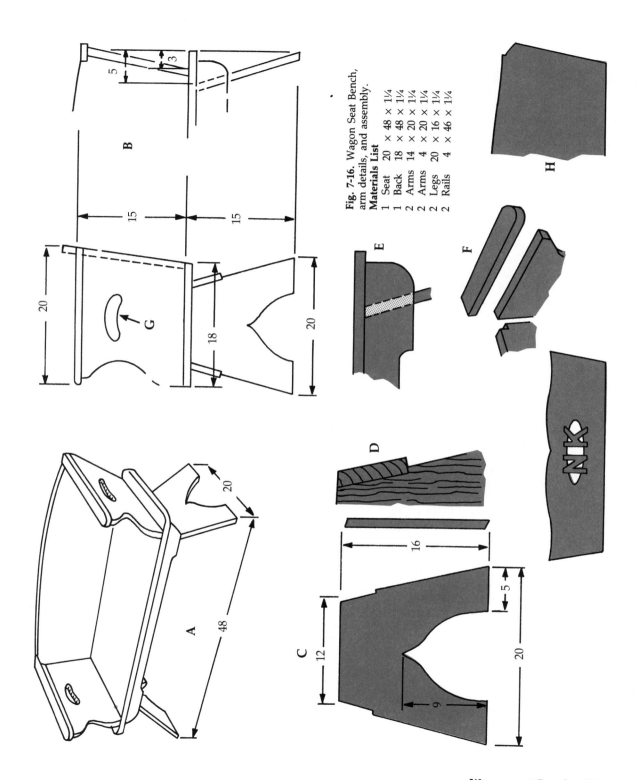

Fig. 7-16. Wagon Seat Bench, arm details, and assembly.

Materials List

1	Seat	20	× 48	× 1¼
1	Back	18	× 48	× 1¼
2	Arms	14	× 20	× 1¼
2	Arms	4	× 20	× 1¼
2	Legs	20	× 16	× 1¼
2	Rails	4	× 46	× 1¼

edges are shaped (FIG. 7-16E), although the back rail can be left parallel if the bench is to go against a wall.

Assemble the rails to the legs and check squareness and that the feet stand level. Do not fit to the seat board yet, although you can cut the seat board to size and try it in position.

Note that the back comes between the arms, so the load of anyone leaning against it is taken across the screws and not in a direction that would pull them endwise. Plane the back board at an angle to fit on the seat and give the arms a slight flare. Shape the fronts of the arms. You can round their tops or make them more comfortable by widening with top pieces (FIG. 7-16F).

The ends can be pierced for two reasons. The holes may be decorative, but they also serve as hand grips when two persons want to move the bench about (FIG. 7-16G). Many outlines of holes were used, so you can shape piercing to suit personal preference.

You can decorate the back in many ways, but because it is likely to be fitted with cushions, you might only need a plain board. If it is a bench for outdoor use, with all of the wood visible, there could be more decoration to the body of the board. Many benches had the backs straight, with rounding at the ends; others were given a slightly wavy outline (FIG. 7-16H). There could be holes pierced that continue the same theme as the holes in the ends, or you can include initials or a date (FIG. 7-16J).

LOVE SEAT

Many seats were really double-width chairs, and some of the chairs already described could be widened in this way. The broader seat and larger load meant there was some tendency to strain the construction in the width, so although the arrangement of rails from back to front might be little different from a chair, there had to be stronger bracing across the width. The example shown in FIG. 7-17A is a double-width seat on four legs, but it is of a Pennsylvania Dutch style that was finished by painting brightly. Others were made wide enough for four people, with support below coming from as many as eight legs. For that number of legs to stand firmly, the floor must be absolutely flat.

In the example, the front legs stand upright when viewed in any direction, but the rear legs are splayed both ways. In order for the side rails to be level and parallel with the seat, you must lay out the parts so front and back legs cross in front view at the rail position (FIG. 7-17B). The spindles supporting the back are also upright in front view, but the arms spread to sloping spindles at the front. Drawing two views of the end of the seat full size will show the angles you will need to cut. This is also an opportunity to get a pleasing shape to the arm and see that it blends into the other parts (FIG. 7-17C).

Hollow the plank seat back to front, but make it straight across and flat underneath (FIG. 7-17D). Leave the top surface flat at the back.

Turn the front legs (FIG. 7-17E) as you would table legs. At the positions of the broad front rail, the taper should be straight so the mortise-and-tenon joints can be most simply made. The four legs are plainer (FIG. 7-17F). Since the front legs are upright, their tops can have a definite shoulder where they are doweled into the seat, but because of the flare of the rear legs it is better for the shaping to blend into the dowel end, so there is no need for handwork cutting a sloping shoulder across the turned wood. You can mark the positions of the rails with a pencil while the front legs are revolved in the lathe. The rail positions on the

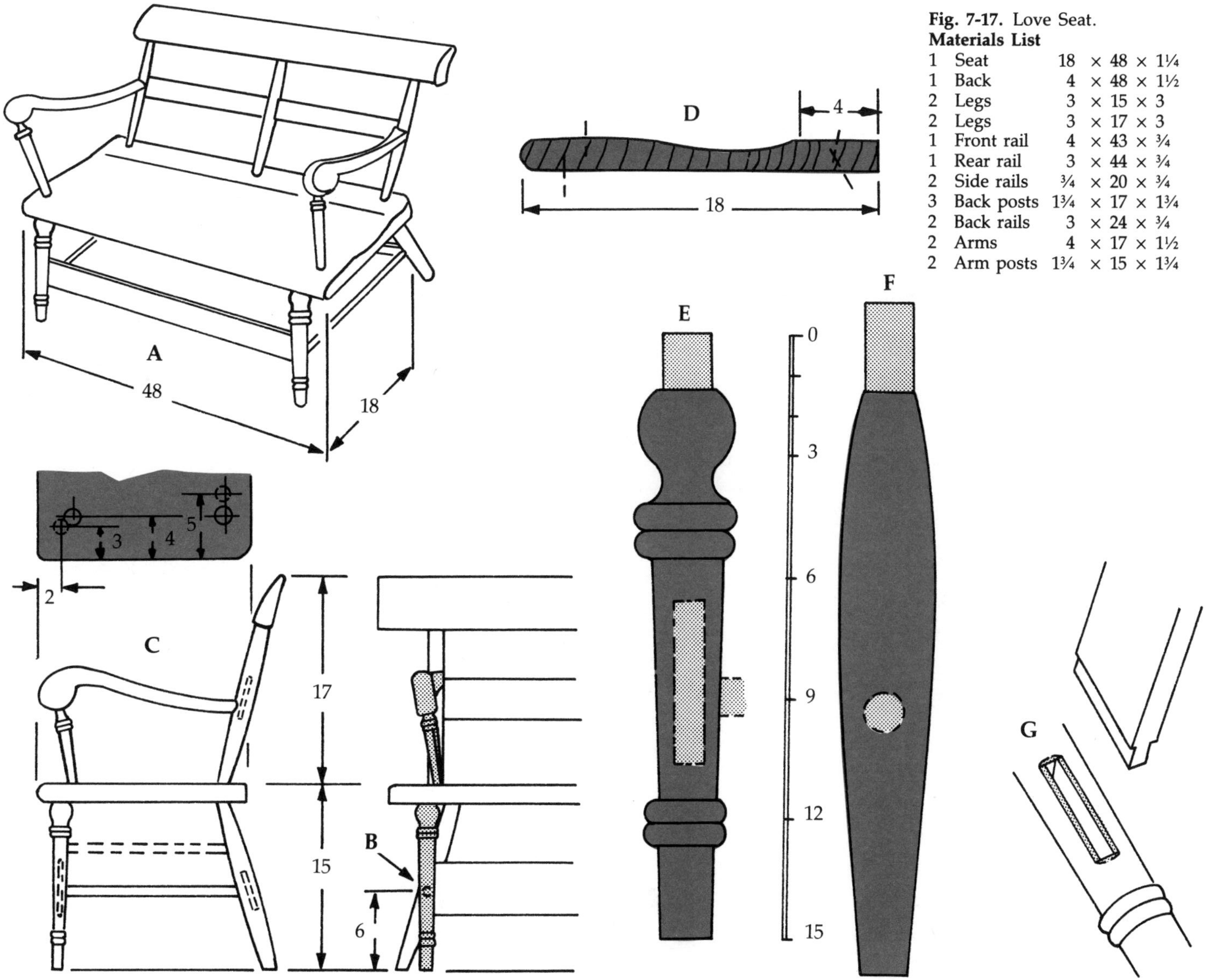

Fig. 7-17. Love Seat.

Materials List

1	Seat	18	× 48	× 1¼
1	Back	4	× 48	× 1½
2	Legs	3	× 15	× 3
2	Legs	3	× 17	× 3
1	Front rail	4	× 43	× ¾
1	Rear rail	3	× 44	× ¾
2	Side rails	¾	× 20	× ¾
3	Back posts	1¾	× 17	× 1¾
2	Back rails	3	× 24	× ¾
2	Arms	4	× 17	× 1½
2	Arm posts	1¾	× 15	× 1¾

rear legs are the best found during a trial assembly. With the rear legs temporarily plugged into the seat, hold the wood for the rails in position parallel with the seat and mark the joint positions marked on rails and legs.

Drill holes for the side rails, at right angles into the front legs, but at estimated angles into the rear legs, using the full-size drawing as a guide.

For the flat rails, the joints are mortise and tenon, but it is advisable to flatten the legs in each place for an area to match the section of the rail, then cut and fit the joints (FIG. 7-17G). Without this flattening, it would be necessary to cut the tenon shoulders to a curve to get a close fit.

Above the seat there are spindles supporting the back and the arm. Make the back straight in its length, but curve its front (FIG. 7-18A). Some originals had the rear surface hollowed, but this is difficult to do and is not essential.

Fit the spindles squarely into the back with dowel ends (FIG. 7-18B). Taper the lower ends into thicker dowels, long enough to go right through the seat, for maximum strength.

Fig. 7-18. Arm and back details for the Love Seat.

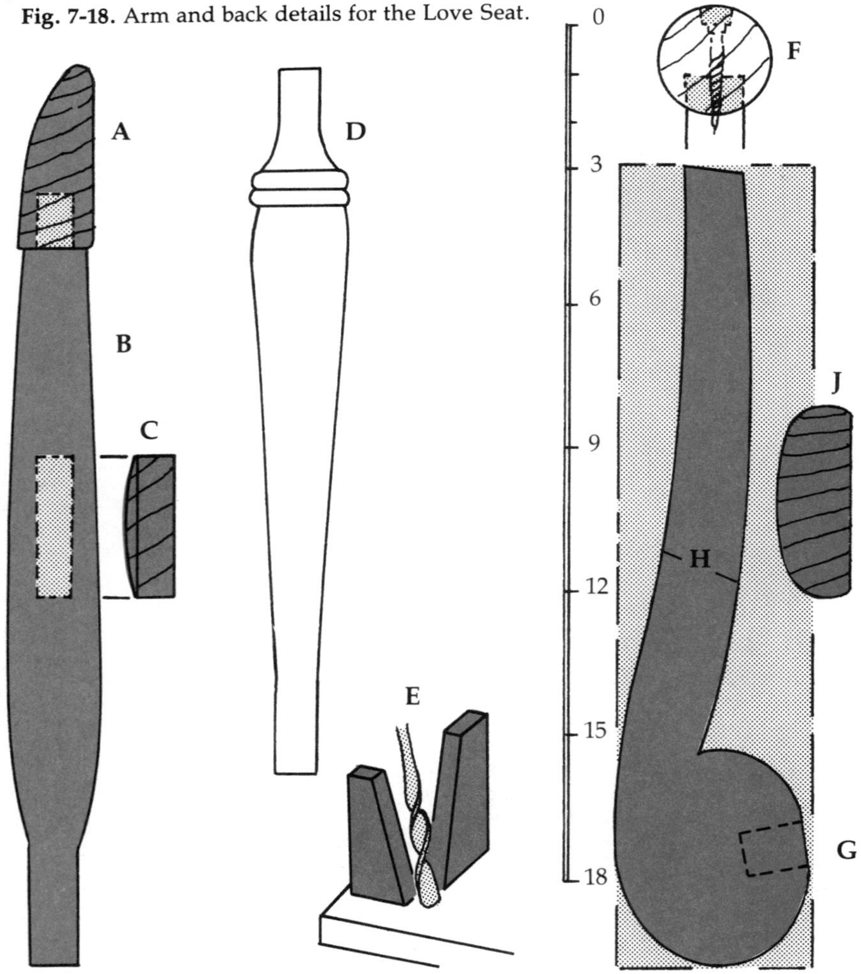

Fit the back rail to the spindles in the same way as the flat rails between the legs. It looks best and is most comfortable if you round the front surface and carry the shaping over its edges (FIG. 7-18C).

It is advisable to make the arm spindles (FIG. 7-18D) before making the arm. You need care to get the holes into the seat drilled at a matching pair of angles. The exact angles are not so critical as the need to get them the same both ways. Use templates cut to the intended angles, as seen from front and side, as a guide to drilling (FIG. 7-18E). With the arm spindles mounted temporarily in position, you can find the exact locations of the arm joints.

Start with a solid block of wood for each arm and lay out the joints before you do any final shaping, although you can remove some of the waste wood for convenience in handling. At the back spindles notch the arms in and hold them with screws (FIG. 7-18F). At the front, drill them to suit the supporting spindles (FIG. 7-18G).

When the joints have been prepared, draw the scroll shape of one arm and cut it (FIG. 7-18H). Use it to mark the other arm before you do any rounding. The side surfaces and the bottom shaping can remain flat in cross section, except for slight rounding of the corners, but you should dome the top surface (FIG. 7-18J).

For maximum strength, wedge the parts attached to the seat. Those downward can go right through. Fit the legs into fairly deep blind holes and foxtail-wedge them.

HIGH CHAIR

A high chair for a baby needs to stand on a broad base, to prevent tipping, and be provided with a footrest. Many versions were made and some of them have carried over to the present day. The simplest form is made like many normal chairs, but with the legs extended. The specimen chosen (FIG. 7-19A) makes use of plainly turned parts and a simple outline. Its size would suit a growing child, as well as a baby. By keeping the rail positions well up from the bottoms of the legs, adaption to a lower chair became possible. When the chair had served in its high position for each successive child of a family, the bottoms could be cut off the legs to make it suitable for continued use by larger children, who could then reach the ground.

The seat and floor area covered by the legs are squares, so except for the rail heights, the front and side views below the seat are the same. Draw this outline to get the angles (FIG. 7-19B).

Turn the four legs and pencil the hole positions in the lathe. Drill the rail holes, using the drawing as a guide to the angles. Use a square board for the seat and round the front edge well. Drill the seat so you can make a trial assembly of the under framing.

Cut the back board to a curve from a thicker piece of wood (FIG. 7-19C). Keep its lower edge thick enough to take the post holes without risk of splitting. You can round its ends and upper surface (FIG. 7-19D).

The two outer posts are stouter than the three inner ones (FIG. 7-19E), but otherwise they have similar shapes. Allow a little excess length at first. Drill the back of the seat for the posts. The posts all slope slightly to the same angle to the rear, but when viewed from the front the center post is upright and the others fan outward very slightly. Put the posts in their holes and mark their tops to the same height with a straightedge parallel with the seat (FIG. 7-19F). Use this assembly to get the positions of the holes in the back board and determine the angles to drill them.

Turn the arms and their supports parallel for most of their lengths (FIG. 7-19G). The supports can go directly into holes in the seat without reducing their size, but there should be a taper to a dowel into the arms. Round the fronts of the arms and reduce to dowel size into the outer back posts. When viewed from the front, the arm supports should slope outward at the same angles as the outer back posts.

You can leave the footrest until after the rest of the chair is finally assembled to reduce any risk of error resulting from changes of measurements taken at a trial assembly and those of a final one. Round the footrest's corners and edges (FIG. 7-19H). Support it with two small wooden brackets. Fit the footrest into shallow grooves across the legs, and fit the brackets against flattened parts below this (FIG. 7-19J). Do not cut too deeply into the legs, or they might be weakened. If you take screws into the footrest, you might be able to merely glue the brackets in place.

The sizes given were taken from an original, but obviously there is scope for variation. Much depends on the size of the child and table height. In particular, positioning of the footrest is best related to the leg length of the child who will use the seat, with due allowance for growth during the time the chair will be needed.

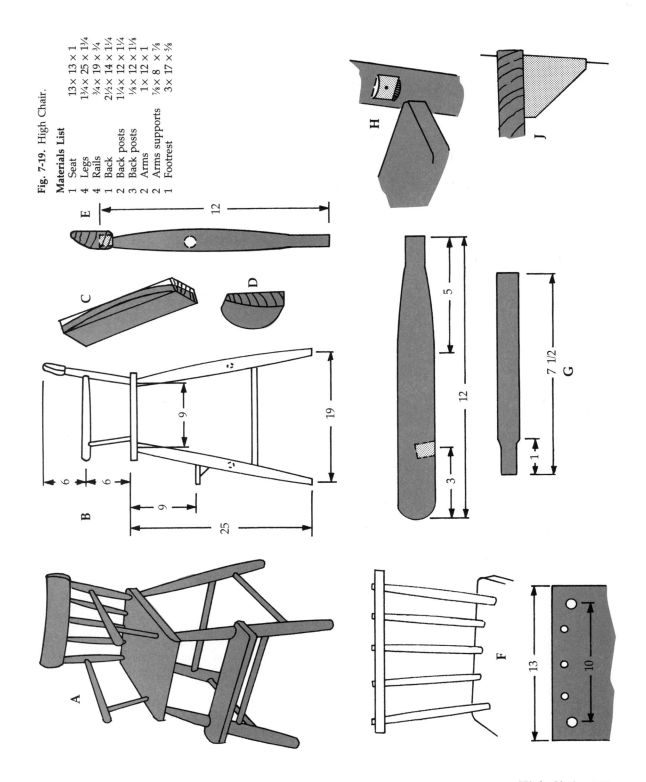

Fig. 7-19. High Chair.

Materials List

1	Seat	$13 \times 13 \times 1$
4	Legs	$1\frac{3}{4} \times 25 \times 1\frac{3}{4}$
4	Rails	$\frac{3}{4} \times 19 \times \frac{3}{4}$
1	Back	$2\frac{1}{2} \times 14 \times 1\frac{1}{4}$
2	Back posts	$1\frac{1}{4} \times 12 \times 1\frac{1}{4}$
3	Back posts	$\frac{7}{8} \times 12 \times 1\frac{1}{8}$
2	Arms	$1 \times 12 \times 1$
2	Arms supports	$\frac{7}{8} \times 8 \times \frac{7}{8}$
1	Footrest	$3 \times 17 \times \frac{5}{8}$

8

Cupboards and Cabinets

CHESTS AND OPEN SHELVES have their uses, but for the better and more attractive storage of the great many household items that accumulate, furniture that can be opened and closed from the front is more convenient. This meant that some early furniture took the form of cupboards and closets, either standing free or attached to the wall, while other items were like tables enclosed with storage space below, to form dry sinks and similar kitchen and domestic furniture, some of which developed into better cabinetwork pieces for use in bedrooms and the more important rooms of the house.

Open storage does not need to involve great precision in its making, but when it is developed into a form of closed storage by the addition of doors, there must be more careful fitting. The better forms of furniture with doors were usually the product of a specialist craftsman. One problem that came with the fitting of doors was the provision of hinges and catches or fasteners.

HINGES AND OTHER HARDWARE

Blacksmith-made hinges were usually large in relation to the door and mounted on the surface. A clumsy appearance was avoided by giving the hinges decorative shapes. Reproductions of these hinges are available and can be used for any reproduction doors (FIG. 8-1A). Hinges that went between the door and its stile were not long in coming into use. You can use these *butt hinges* for many reproduction doors. Some of the more primitive hinges were made from interlocking pieces of bent wire or by nailing on strips of leather.

With any hinge, it is the center of the knuckle that is the pivot point. The door swings on it. In most assemblies, the knuckle can be centrally over the gap between the door and its stile (FIG. 8-1B) and it will swing clear without trouble.

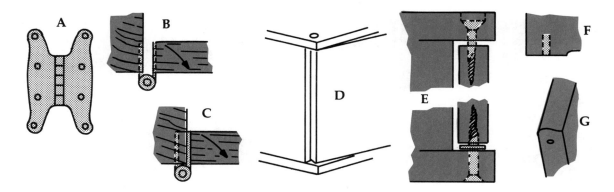

Fig. 8-1. Many early hinges were put on the surface (A). The position of the knuckle affects the way a door swings (B,C). A door may pivot on screws or dowels (D,E). Shaping the bottom avoids a washer (F). The door corner is rounded for clearance (G).

On some old cabinets, there is a very close fit of the doors, yet they swing clear without binding on the frame. Having the knuckle slightly toward the stile (FIG. 8-1C) helps in bringing the other side of the door clear of the frame as soon as it starts moving, and allows a closer fit.

You can avoid hinges by arranging the door to pivot on nails, screws, or dowels. The top and bottom of the cabinet should overlap and the pivots go through these overlaps into the doors (FIG. 8-1D). For the majority of furniture, the pivots are best made of stout screws, with the top one counterbored and plugged if the upper surface will be visible in the finished work. The bottom of the door must be lifted slightly so it swings into place without rubbing. You can use a washer on the screw (FIG. 8-1E) for this purpose, although on some old doors the bottom of the door was cut away, except for a small area around the screw (FIG. 8-1F). To give clearance as the door swung, its edge had to be rounded enough to clear the cupboard side (FIG. 8-1G).

The simplest arrangement of a door is to have a flat board overlapping all around (FIG. 8-2A), with hinges on the edge or between the door and frame. This could be modified to let the top and bottom overlap the door (FIG. 8-2B), providing some protection against dust entering. A further step was to set the door inside the framework (FIG. 8-2C), and this is the customary way of mounting doors in most good-quality furniture where there is no reason for using any other method, but it calls for the exercise of more care and skill in handling the door.

When a door overlaps the piece it is attached to, it is automatically stopped in the closed position. If it fits inside, there has to be a stop. A stop could be a single small block of wood near the center of the door (FIG. 8-2D) or pieces top and bottom for a tall door. Sometimes a shelf was arranged to be at a width that would also act as a door stop, but it was more usual for shelves to be set back a short distance.

In cabinets with a pair of doors, these might be arranged to meet at the center (FIG. 8-2E). Top and bottom stops brought the closed doors to the same level, then one door was secured with a bolt or catch to the frame (top and bottom usually), and the other door closed to it with a catch.

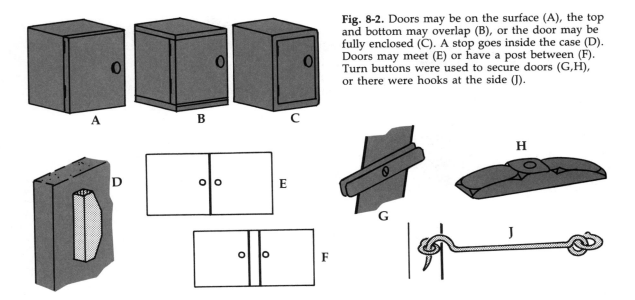

Fig. 8-2. Doors may be on the surface (A), the top and bottom may overlap (B), or the door may be fully enclosed (C). A stop goes inside the case (D). Doors may meet (E) or have a post between (F). Turn buttons were used to secure doors (G,H), or there were hooks at the side (J).

Many old double-door arrangements had a post between the doors (FIG. 8-2F), so each door was treated like a single one. The simplest catch then was a wooden turn button turning on a screw (FIG. 8-2G), with a single long one closing both doors, or a smaller one for each door. Turn buttons varied from unadorned plain wood to others that were whittled into decorative patterns or given shaped beveled edges (FIG. 8-2H).

Metal catches of simple form were imported or made locally. One common method of holding an overlapping door was with a metal hook and screw eye (FIG. 8-2J). Small sliding bolts would be appropriate in a reproduction and doors could be fastened with catches operated by a knob. However, the more ingenious type of modern door fasteners would be inappropriate, particularly if made of plated metal or plastic.

DOOR TYPES

The simplest door is a plain piece of wood. If the risk of warping is to be avoided as far as possible, it should be radially cut, so the end grain lines are across the thickness of the wood (FIG. 8-3A). If the width of a door is enough to need boards glued edge to edge, it is advisable to put battens across inside (FIG. 8-3B). You can slot-screw them to allow for expansion and contraction, or glue and screw them directly with a wood not expected to vary. Variation in the width of a door is undesirable and might need to be accepted if the door overlaps, but would affect fit of a door within its frame, so a different method of construction would be preferable.

In many items for kitchen or wash house, wide doors were made of many boards tongued and grooved together without glue (FIG. 8-3C). This method allowed movement in the width of each board without affecting the overall width of the door enough to matter. To give rigidity, the door was ledged and braced inside (FIG. 8-3D). The brace sloped upward from the hinged side and prevented the door from sagging. To do this it had to be related to the braces as well as

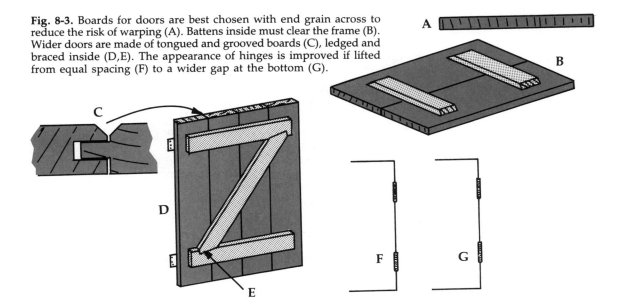

Fig. 8-3. Boards for doors are best chosen with end grain across to reduce the risk of warping (A). Battens inside must clear the frame (B). Wider doors are made of tongued and grooved boards (C), ledged and braced inside (D,E). The appearance of hinges is improved if lifted from equal spacing (F) to a wider gap at the bottom (G).

the boards, and it was usual to notch its ends into them (FIG. 8-3E). The natural tendency of the boards to settle caused the notched joints to be pushed tighter. If the brace was arranged the other way, the joints would tend to open. Ledges and braces were kept back from the door edges. Shelves or divisions had to be set back to give clearance inside. If strap or T-hinges were used on the outside, their positions were arranged so screws went through into the ledges.

A design consideration to be noted is the poor appearance of arranging hinges the same distance from top and bottom of a door (FIG. 8-3F) and the improved appearance if the lower distance from the edge is more than the top one (FIG. 8-3G). It is reasonable to make the bottom measurement about 1 1/2 times the top one, which should be 1/5 or 1/4 of the total depth.

Better doors were framed and paneled. A smaller door had a frame enclosing one panel (FIG. 8-4A), but dividing a larger door into two or more panels provided strength members between the outer solid wood framing, as well as keeping the panels down to a size more suitable for available wood. If there were two panels, the upper one was usually smaller than the lower one (FIG. 8-4B) because this arrangement looked better than two equal panels. Four panels might be similarly arranged, although some doors had the sides wider at the lower panels to give strength lower down (FIG. 8-4C).

The traditional cabinetmaking method of making a framed door had grooves plowed in the wood and the tenons in the horizontal members going into mortises in the uprights. In thin wood, the tenons were the same width as the grooves, but usually they were thicker and the inner edge was cut back to the bottom of the groove, while the outer edge had a haunch projecting the depth of the groove (FIG. 8-4D). The mortise was about three-quarters the depth of the wood (FIG. 8-4E). If you make doors in this way, leave some spare wood on the ends of the mortised part, so there is no risk of bursting out end grain when chopping the mortise or assembling the joint. Do no cut the surplus off until after assembly.

That joint suits a frame with square edges, but if you mold the inner edge or just bevel it to frame the panel, modify the joint to allow a mitered corner. Cut the mortised part down to the level of the bottom of the groove and cut the corners standing above it at 45 degrees (FIG. 8-4F). Then shape the tenoned part to match (FIG. 8-4G).

Although a modern panel would be plywood, the original panels were solid wood cut as thinly as possible, but even then thicker than the grooves. Two methods of fitting were used. If the front of the panel was to be level, the edges were beveled inside (FIG. 8-9H), but most old furniture has the panels beveled on the front. If you bevel neatly so the change from flat to bevel is the same all around, it gives the characteristic paneled appearance (FIG. 8-4J).

A development of a paneled door was the fitting of perforated sheet-metal panels in the doors of cupboards used for food, in the days before refrigerators. Zinc was commonly used. There is a modern machine-perforated version, but the original panels were perforated with a nail and the holes were arranged in patterns according to the artistic inclinations of the makers. Some quite elaborate pierced decorations are still in existence. In the simplest construction, the metal was merely nailed to the backs of the open door frames. In a better construction, the frame was made with rabbets toward the back and a small fillet was nailed in after the metal panel had been inserted (FIG. 8-4K).

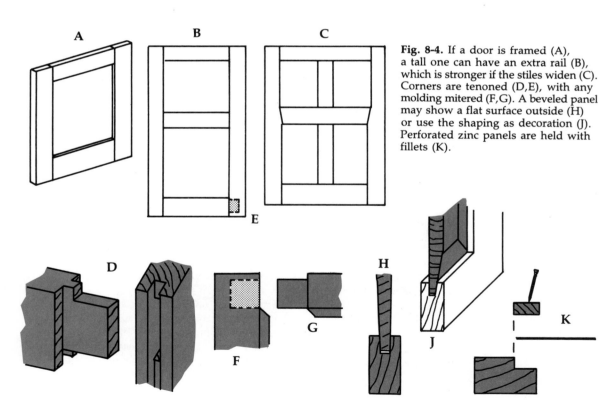

Fig. 8-4. If a door is framed (A), a tall one can have an extra rail (B), which is stronger if the stiles widen (C). Corners are tenoned (D,E), with any molding mitered (F,G). A beveled panel may show a flat surface outside (H) or use the shaping as decoration (J). Perforated zinc panels are held with fillets (K).

SMALL WALL CUPBOARD

Most early homes used small wall cupboards. One with perforated metal panels served for food storage in the kitchen, while others with solid doors served in living and bedrooms. Many developed from hanging shelves, to which a door was added in front. The example here is typical of many variations on a basic theme (FIG. 8-5A). In effect, it is a box with a door at the front.

On the sides, you can place rabbets for a rear panel and dadoes for the shelves. The dadoes can be either cut through or stopped for neatness at the front (FIG. 8-5B). Attach a bar across the inside of the top to take the main load when hanging. Deepen the rabbets in the sides to take the bar (FIG. 8-5C). Use screws through the bar into the wall to support the cupboard. You can supplement them with one or two other screws through the back panel lower down.

Make the top overlap the sides. The bottom can overlap, but it is stronger if it fits between the sides and is notched around, with a mitered strip at each side (FIG. 8-5D). Attach stiles to each side of the door with nails or screws through them, either covered with stopping or plugs or, if a smooth front appearance is to be maintained, glued with small fillets added to increase glue area inside (FIG. 8-5E). When assembling the cupboard, be careful to check squareness. The door opening must be true; a door only slightly out of square becomes very obvious.

To break up the plainness of the cupboard, fit a shaped piece to hold it above the front of the top (FIG. 8-5F). Use glue and screws from below. You can also place a glued fillet behind it.

A single-paneled door is shown with fairly wide framing for stiffness. The corners are mortised and tenoned in the way just described, and the panel shows the bevels at the front (FIG. 8-5G).

You can set the hinges on the surface for a kitchen cupboard or into the edges if the cupboard is made of attractive hardwood and polished. Traditionally, hinges were let into both surfaces (FIG. 8-5H), but it is less trouble to let into one edge only, adjusting the depth to suit the clearance needs. You must usually do some fitting when you hang a door. Make the door near to its final size, but hang it with one screw in each hinge. Note what needs to be planed off, then remove the door, plane it, and try again, until the clearance all around is the same and you can drive all the hinge screws.

You can use a turned wooden knob at the side opposite to the hinges. There is no need for a door stop because the door touches the shelves. You might be able to use the cupboard without a door fastener, but an appropriate type would be a knob with a shaft passing through to a turn button inside.

Cupboards had locks that screwed to the inside, and the lock bolt went behind the door frame as the key was turned. Use care in cutting the escutcheon hole. Give it enough clearance for the key, but do not make it too large. Measure the size of the key. Press the lock into position inside. The point of the post the key fits on will make a dent in the wood. Drill through to remove some of the waste (FIG. 8-5J) and clean out the slot with a chisel and file (FIG. 8-5K).

Some locks are supplied with a brass escutcheon liner, which makes a neat finish to the hole. This has a slight taper. If you cut the wood to match the smaller side, forcing the liner in will tighten it as it compresses surrounding wood fibers slightly. Escutcheon plates, which fix on the surface over the keyhole, are usually made of brass and held with small brass pins. For good-quality work, there are matching sets of hinges, knob, and escutcheon plate in an antique brass finish.

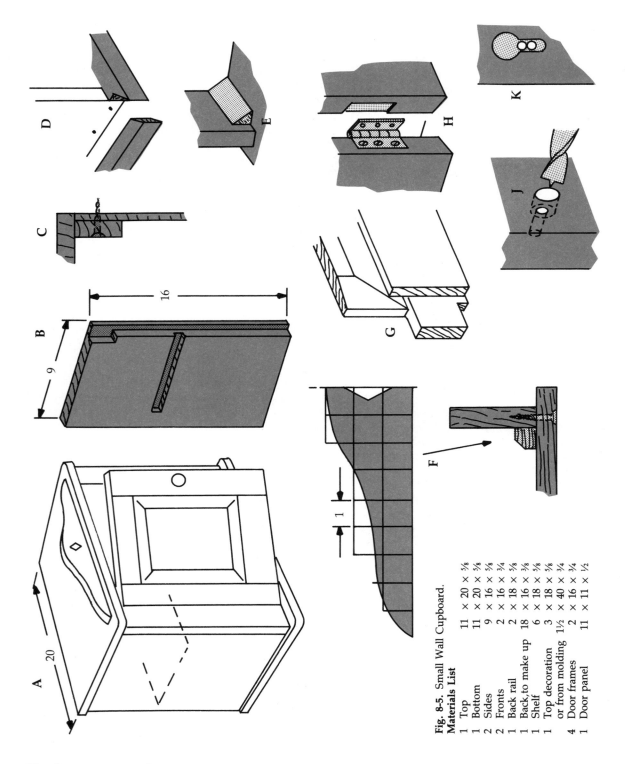

Fig. 8-5. Small Wall Cupboard.

Materials List

1	Top	11	× 20 × ⅝
1	Bottom	11	× 20 × ⅝
2	Sides	9	× 16 × ⅝
2	Fronts	2	× 16 × ¾
1	Back rail	2	× 18 × ⅝
1	Back, to make up	18	× 16 × ⅜
1	Shelf	6	× 18 × ⅝
1	Top decoration	3	× 18 × ⅝
	or from molding	1½	× 40 × ¾
4	Door frames	2	× 16 × ¾
1	Door panel	11	× 11 × ½

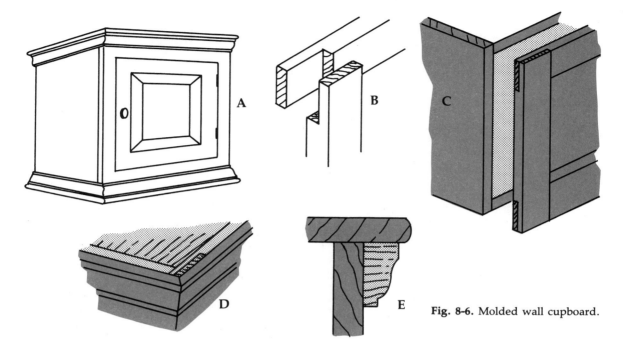

Fig. 8-6. Molded wall cupboard.

There was a furniture fashion in early Victorian days and before for moldings, and this was felt in America. You can make a variation of this basic cupboard with moldings around top and bottom (FIG. 8-6A). Make the framing at the front all around instead of only at the edges. Ideally, you should use mortise-and-tenon joints for the corners of the frame, but it would be satisfactory to use cross-lap joints (FIG. 8-6B).

Make the front edges of the top and bottom level with the sides and fit the front frame assembly against this. See that the front frame is carefully squared, but make its outer edges slightly oversize, and plane them level with the sides after fitting (FIG. 8-6C).

The molding will probably be a machine-made type, and any of the standard patterns will be suitable. Place the molding around the top and bottom edges, with mitered front corners (FIG. 8-6D), then add further strips with rounded or molded edges to give an appearance of greater bulk (FIG. 8-6E).

CORNER WALL CUPBOARD

A variation on the Small Wall Cupboard is one designed to fit into a corner. It is basically a corner shelf with a door, but it makes storage place in a situation that would not otherwise be of much use. Shelves and a door across a simple triangle do not provide much shelf area, and hanging the door to swing clear is then difficult. Most corner cupboards were made as shown, with narrow side pieces projecting at right angles from the wall to give more space and make the door action better (FIG. 8-7A).

Not all room corners are right angles. If the cupboard is to go into a particular position, check the corner with an adjustable bevel and make the parts to suit this if it is not a right angle.

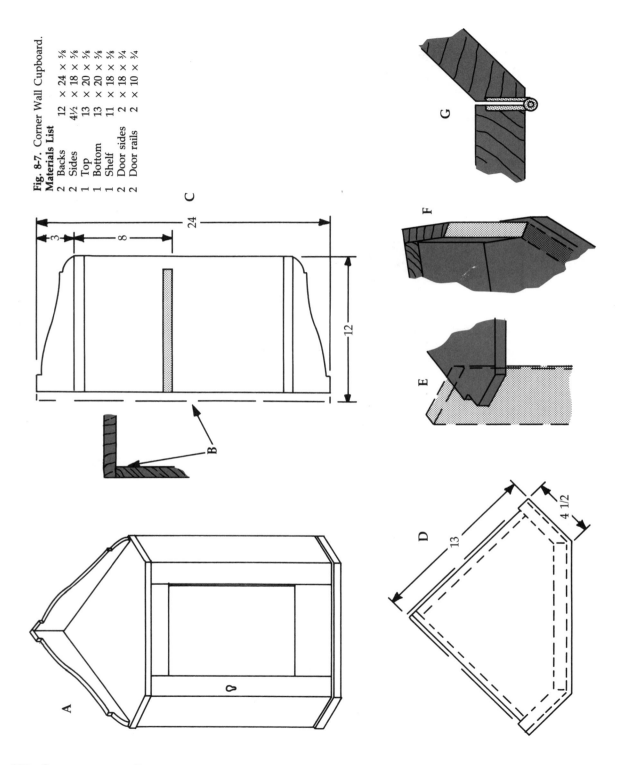

Fig. 8-7. Corner Wall Cupboard.

Materials List

2	Backs	12	× 24	× ⅝
2	Sides	4½	× 18	× ⅝
1	Top	13	× 20	× ⅝
1	Bottom	13	× 20	× ⅝
1	Shelf	11	× 18	× ⅝
2	Door sides	2	× 18	× ¾
2	Door rails	2	× 10	× ¾

Prepare the wood for the two back pieces first. One is narrower than the other by the amount that one overlaps (FIG. 8-7B). Fit the top and bottom into dadoes that can go right through, but stop the dado for the shelf (FIG. 8-7C). You can mark the profiles for the top and bottom edges now, but do not cut the shapes until after you have cut the joints.

Cut the top and bottom the same, with their grain across (FIG. 8-7D). Prepare these parts and use them to check the marking of the dadoes before you cut the grooves. Use them as a guide for marking out the shelf. Make the shelf to fit against the side pieces, but cut back enough to clear the door (FIG. 8-7E).

The side pieces overlap the backs. Cut them to fit closely between top and bottom (FIG. 8-7F). It is advisable to leave final trimming to length until you assemble the other parts and they can be tested in position. Cut the inner edges to give a parallel opening for the door. This means beveling at 45 degrees (FIG. 8-7G), unless the room corner is some way from a right angle.

Put the shelf in one of its dadoes and bring the two backs together. In addition to glue, you can use screws to join the backs and go into the shelf, since their heads will be hidden when the cupboard is hung. Fit the side pieces. Check that they are parallel with each other and that the door opening will be true.

Make and fit the door in the same way as for the earlier wall cupboard. You can have its panel showing the bevels on the front or give it a level surface on the front with some sort of decoration at its center. For Pennsylvania Dutch finishing, use a painted design. For another theme, mount a curved design on it.

Hanging is by screws through the backs inside and just below the top. A variation could be without any projection of the backs below the bottom. The cupboard could then stand on a corner table or be attached to the wall just above it.

STANDING CUPBOARD

A cupboard with a top at a suitable height for use as a table when standing can be made to match the hanging cupboards (FIG. 8-8A). Sizes are not critical and can be adapted to suit available wood. In a cupboard of this size, it is usually more convenient to arrange shelves to rest on battens so they can be lifted out than to fix them into dadoes or any other permanent manner. Most of the parts are plain rectangles, but the door is shown with tapered sides, although you could make them parallel. Note that appearance is improved by having the bottom door rail wider than the other two.

If you will make the back in the traditional way, it will have to be several boards, preferably tongued and grooved together. The alternative is plywood. In any case, make the back overlap the bottom and be set into rabbets in the sides.

Mark out one side and use it as a guide to determine the sizes of other parts (FIG. 8-8B). Make the two front pieces (FIG. 8-8C). Shape them at the bottom to form feet and cut the sides the same way (FIG. 8-8D). You can have square corners, but a stopped chamfer enhances appearance (FIG. 8-8E).

The bottom fits between the front pieces. For the strongest construction fit it into dadoes (FIG. 8-8F). You could have it go into dadoes in the sides, but it is simpler and stronger to put battens across underneath (FIG. 8-8G). The top goes above the sides and front. Put a batten across the back and more battens at the sides. At the front, cut a batten to fit across between the upright parts. Assemble all these parts and screw upward into the top (FIG. 8-8H).

Plane the edges of top level all around. Cover the joint with molding at sides and front, with mitered corners (FIG. 8-8J).

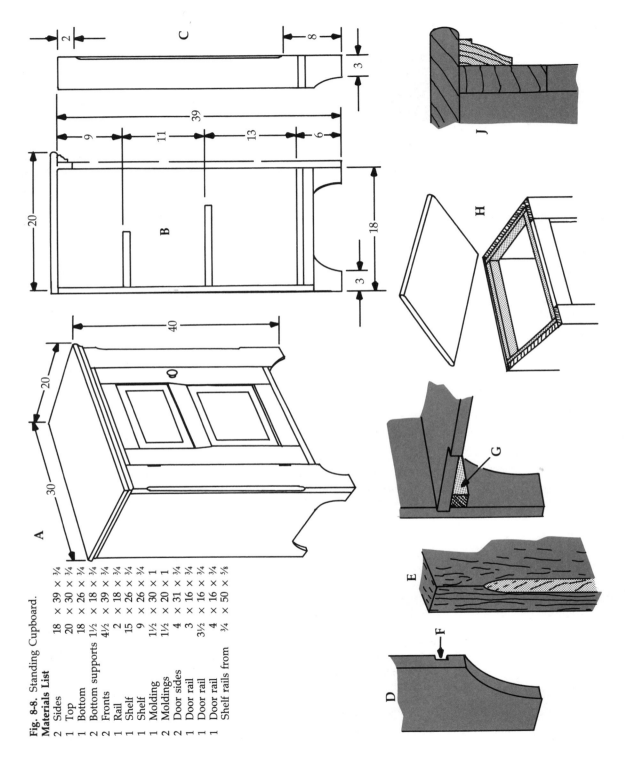

Fig. 8-8. Standing Cupboard.

Materials List

2	Sides	18	×	39	×	¾
1	Top	20	×	30	×	¾
1	Bottom	18	×	26	×	¾
2	Bottom supports	1½	×	18	×	¾
2	Fronts	4½	×	39	×	¾
1	Rail	2	×	18	×	¾
1	Shelf	15	×	26	×	¾
1	Shelf	9	×	26	×	¾
1	Molding	1½	×	30	×	1
2	Moldings	1½	×	20	×	1
2	Door sides	4	×	31	×	¾
1	Door rail	3	×	16	×	¾
1	Door rail	3½	×	16	×	¾
1	Door rail	4	×	16	×	¾
	Shelf rails from	¾	×	50	×	⅝

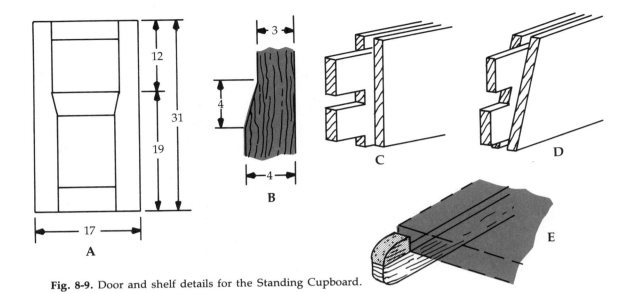

Fig. 8-9. Door and shelf details for the Standing Cupboard.

For the door (FIG. 8-9A), make the two sides and the center rail the same width, but the top rail narrower and the bottom one wider. Cut the sides so the upper parts are the same width as the top rail and there is a taper between the two sizes at the middle rail (FIG. 8-9B). Groove the parts for the panels.

You can use single tenons for the top corner joints, but the others are better with double tenons (FIG. 8-9C). Lay out the corner joints in the same way as for earlier doors. In the central beveled joints, cut the shoulders of the tenons to match the angles of the uprights. You can make the ends of the tenons at the same angles or cut them squarely. Make the sides of the tenons with the edges of the rail, not at right angles to the slope (FIG. 8-9D). Make the door slightly oversize. Pull the joints tight with bar clamps. You can use dowels across the tenons for extra security.

Two hinges should be sufficient, but if the door shows signs of flexing you can add a third. Be careful that all the hinge knuckles are in line if the door is to swing smoothly. Arrange door stops at top and bottom and fit a knob and catch.

In a cupboard of this size, it is inadvisable to have the shelves too wide; otherwise it is difficult to see what is at the bottom or on a lower shelf from the usual standing position. If there are two shelves, set the lower back about 6 inches, and the upper one 6 inches back from that. Mount small blocks on the battens to prevent the shelves from sliding forward (FIG. 8-9E), but still allow them to be lifted out.

DRY SINK

Water was not usually piped and had to be carried from the well or pump for household use. The basins, pitchers, or pans of water were put on a dry sink, which was a standing cupboard with a surround enclosing the top. The surround might have been lined with metal to prevent any spilled water finding its way below, although it was more often merely planked in wood. The lower part

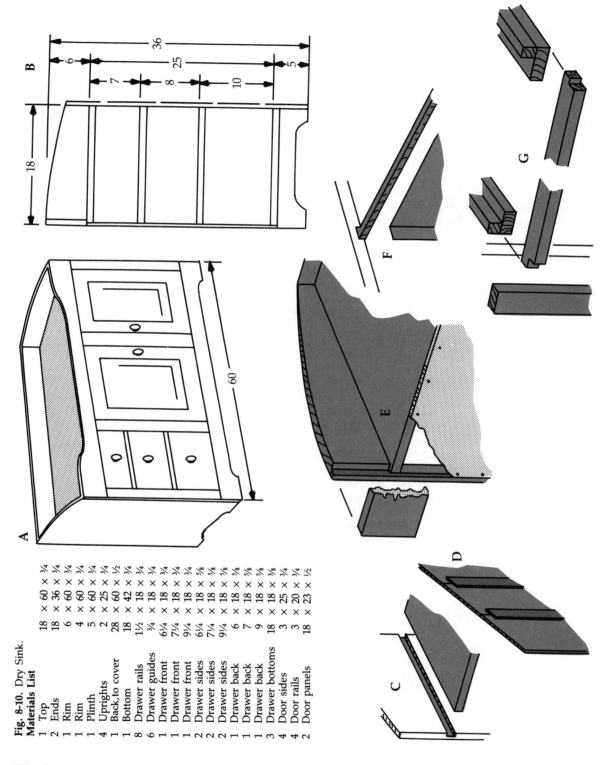

Fig. 8-10. Dry Sink.
Materials List

1	Top	18	×	60	×	¾
2	Ends	18	×	36	×	¾
1	Rim	6	×	60	×	¾
1	Rim	4	×	60	×	¾
1	Plinth	5	×	60	×	¾
4	Uprights	2	×	25	×	¾
1	Back, to cover	28	×	60	×	½
1	Bottom	18	×	42	×	¾
8	Drawer rails	1½	×	18	×	¾
6	Drawer guides	¾	×	18	×	¾
1	Drawer front	6¼	×	18	×	¾
1	Drawer front	7¼	×	18	×	¾
1	Drawer front	9¼	×	18	×	¾
2	Drawer sides	6¼	×	18	×	⅝
2	Drawer sides	7¼	×	18	×	⅝
2	Drawer sides	9¼	×	18	×	⅝
1	Drawer back	6	×	18	×	⅝
1	Drawer back	7	×	18	×	⅝
1	Drawer back	9	×	18	×	⅝
3	Drawer bottoms	18	×	18	×	⅜
4	Door sides	3	×	25	×	¾
4	Door rails	3	×	20	×	¾
2	Door panels	18	×	23	×	½

178 CUPBOARDS AND CABINETS

provided storage space and might have been enclosed with doors, although some longer dry sinks had a block of drawers as well. This was the form of the basic dry sink, but some were given upper cupboards as well, and the whole assembly served in much the same way as the sink, working tops, and cupboards of a modern kitchen do today.

In a modern home, a dry sink will not have its original use to fulfill, but it makes a good side table and storage place with the interest and character of a traditional piece of furniture.

You can make the example in FIG. 8-10A as is, or alter it to suit available wood or the space it will occupy. You also can make a smaller version without the drawers, or with the drawers and only one door. In some dry sinks, the top border is the same height all around, but others had the front cut down. If the reproduction is to serve as a side table or display stand, it will be better made with the cutdown front.

A dry sink is a functional item. Early specimens were very plain. Nailed joints were common. Therefore, you should confine any decoration to shaping edges. The usual construction was in softwood, such as pine, which was occasionally scrubbed. For modern use in a living room, the grain should be sealed, but a high gloss or painted finish would be inappropriate.

The ends provide the sizes on which most other measurements are based (FIG.8-10B). The top and bottom are parallel boards (FIG. 8-10C), which may rest on battens across the ends, but the top, in particular, will make a neater and stronger joint if it also goes into a dado.

In many dry sinks, the back was made up of boards nailed on, but for a better arrangement, rabbet the ends and use thin wood to make up the main area of the back. Tongued and grooved boards would be appropriate, or you can cover the boards inside with narrow strips (FIG. 8-10D), if you desire. The modern alternative, if strict compliance with tradition is not needed, is a piece of plywood. Nail the back into the end rabbets and onto the edges of top and bottom. Place the thicker board that borders the sink recess above the top and fit it into deeper rabbets in the ends (FIG. 8-10E).

The division between the drawers and the cupboards fits between the top and the bottom. In the simplest construction, it would be nailed in place, but using dado joints is better craftsmanship because the grooves prevent the board warping (FIG. 8-10F), which could cause trouble with the running of the drawers.

You can glue and screw the drawer runners in place, but allow for the front rails, which are strongest if they come behind the front uprights and meet the runners (FIG. 8-10G).

It is best to treat the front assembly as a unit that will be screwed to the sides (FIG. 8-11A). Cut away the board across the bottom to match the ends. Cut down the board at the top and round the edges well. Make its lower edge level with the underside of the top, so the top drawer comes against the top of the sink.

You can join the vertical pieces that come between doors and door and drawers, as well as at the ends, to the horizontal members with short tenons (FIG. 8-11B), although with thinner wood it would be simpler to use cross-lap joints (FIG. 8-11C), glued and strengthened with screws from inside. The most critical measurements are around the drawers. The edge of the intermediate upright must be level with the divider between drawers and cupboard, and the two posts should make a truly parallel space for the drawers. You can make the outer edges slightly oversize and trim after fitting.

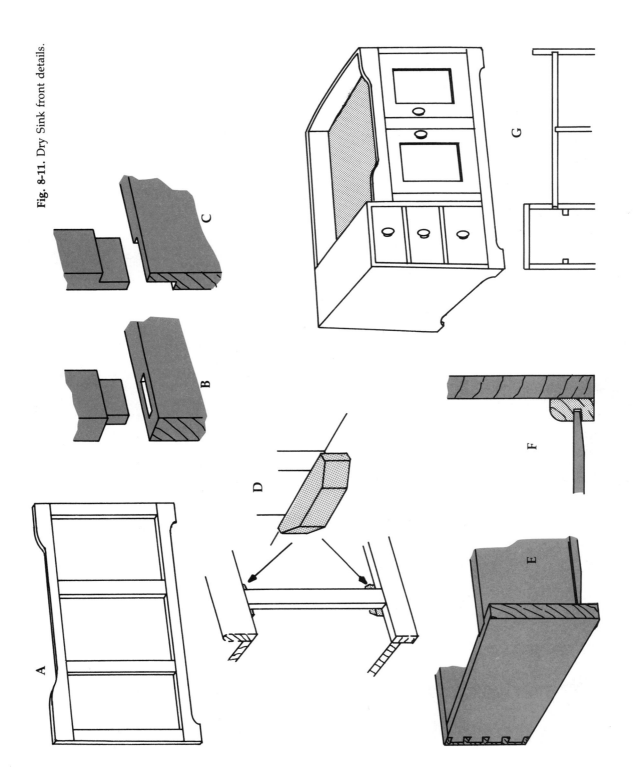

Fig. 8-11. Dry Sink front details.

Notch the rails between the drawers to fit behind the front uprights at a suitable spacing to suit the drawers and to fit closely against the runners (FIG. 8-10G).

Make up the doors with panels as previously described. Provide stops at top and bottom (FIG. 8-11D). You can put locks inside with keyholes below the knobs.

You can make the drawers in one of the ways already described. Many of the original ones had dovetails at the front. There might have been dovetails at the back, or the back might have fit into dadoes in the sides (FIG. 8-11E). Bottoms were made of pieces of thin wood with their grain across the drawer and fitting into grooves, either in the drawer sides or in strips fit inside. These strips gave a broader bearing surface, which was worth having to reduce wear, particularly when a softwood was used (FIG. 8-11F).

A variation sometimes seen took the block of drawers higher, so the sunk part to contain pans of water was over the part enclosed by doors, then the surface over the drawers could be used as a dry place for towels or cups and dippers. For that construction you will need to take the division between the drawers and the cupboard higher, with the sink top fitting into dadoes in it and another top provided at the higher level (FIG. 8-11G).

WELSH CUPBOARD

Settlers from Britain would have known the Welsh dresser or cupboard, which often acted as the main center of interest in a living room, with the best plates and other china displayed on the open shelves and the more everyday items, as well as table cloths and cutlery in the cupboards below. These were usual in many parts of England as well as Wales, and the name *Welsh* was usually applied to the design. Some were quite elaborate and made of fine hardwoods, but this first example (FIG. 8-12A) is a simple and effective design.

Ideally, you can cut the two ends from full-width boards, but it is more economical and a way of using narrower boards to join two pieces (FIG. 8-12B). You can simply glue the edges or reinforce them with dowels. You might need to make up the width of the tabletop of the enclosed part the same way. Fit it over the short parts of the sides and into dadoes in the ends, with reinforcing strips below (FIG. 8-12C).

Notch the bottom into the ends also, with strips below, then the front uprights cover the edges (FIG. 8-12D). Place the doors between the uprights, but so they overlap the bottom. Shape the ends and the front uprights to form feet, and it is advisable to put strips inside (FIG. 8-12E). They strengthen the feet and provide an increased bearing area against the floor covering. In some furniture, the tops of the doors come directly under the overhang of the top, but appearance is improved if you place a rail across, with another strip behind it to screw into the top (FIG. 8-12F).

Because the back will show through at the shelf levels, consider its appearance. A single piece of plywood would be inappropriate. Tongue-and-grooved matched boards with a bead over each joint were usual (FIG. 8-12G). If this wood matches the wood used in the main construction, the whole setting makes a good background to the item being displayed. You can have the boards go through from top to bottom, although it might be possible to use something simpler for the hidden lower part.

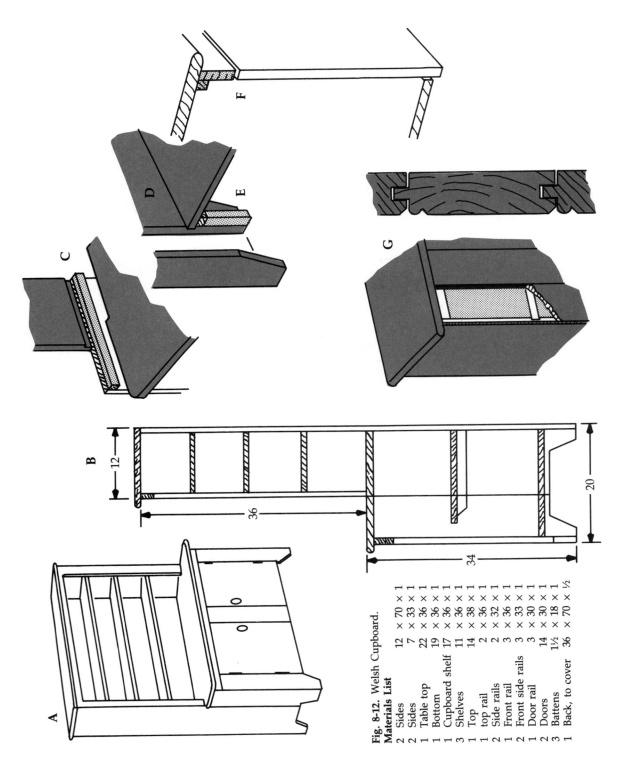

Fig. 8-12. Welsh Cupboard.

Materials List

2	Sides	12	×	70	×	1
2	Sides	7	×	33	×	1
1	Table top	22	×	36	×	1
1	Bottom	19	×	36	×	1
1	Cupboard shelf	17	×	36	×	1
3	Shelves	11	×	36	×	1
1	Top	14	×	38	×	1
1	top rail	2	×	36	×	1
2	Side rails	2	×	32	×	1
1	Front rail	3	×	36	×	1
2	Front side rails	3	×	33	×	1
1	Door rail	3	×	30	×	1
2	Doors	14	×	30	×	1
3	Battens	1½	×	18	×	1
1	Back, to cover	36	×	70	×	½

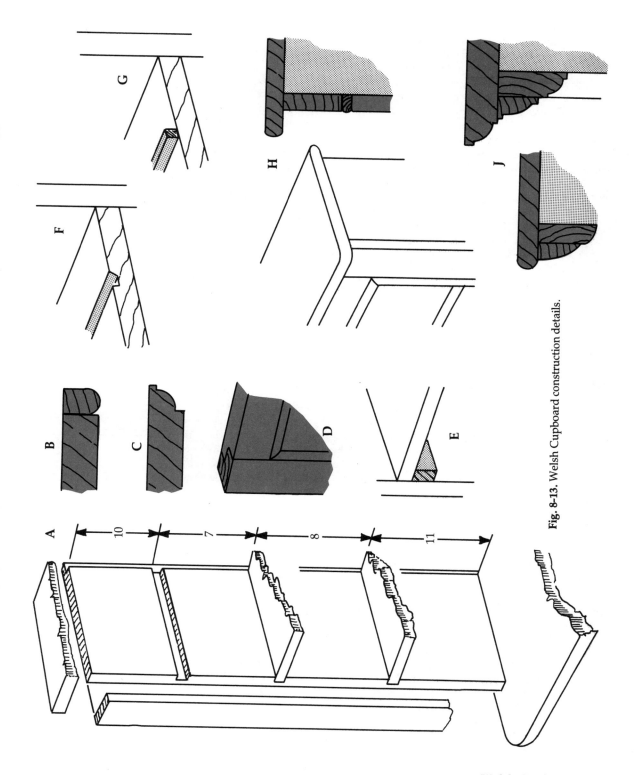

Fig. 8-13. Welsh Cupboard construction details.

The upper assembly has shelves arranged at intervals that reduce toward the top, with a space clear above the tabletop for anything expected to be put on it (FIG. 8-13A). Frame the front edges around with strips of wood, which look best with molded or beaded edges. You can apply a beaded strip (FIG. 8-13B) or mold the edge (FIG. 8-13C). Fit the top strip across, and miter any molding (FIG. 8-13D).

The shelves could fit into dadoes in the ends, but the cover strips on the front edges hide supporting battens and it would be sufficient to fit the shelves to them (FIG. 8-13E). This method also allows shelves to be removed later if necessary. However, for the security of valuable china so that accidental knocking could not dislodge the shelves, shelves should be screwed to the battens.

Groove those shelves that will support plates from a short distance from the back (FIG. 8-13F), or you can fit strips to prevent plates from slipping (FIG. 8-13G). For further safety, you can place thin pieces of wood across inside the front pieces.

What is done at the extreme top depends on the intended appearance. A simple overhang with rounded edges (FIG. 8-13H) will be appropriate to the generally simple outlines, but you can include molding (FIG. 8-13J). The top comes above the normal eye level, so any decoration there should suit an upward view.

For doors for the lower part, you can use ledged and braced, or framed and paneled boards.

FINE WELSH DRESSER

This type of furniture continued to play an important part in the equipment of kitchen and dining room. With more settled conditions and the availability of specialist craftsmen with more time at hand, there came Welsh dressers of good quality that served as main features of dining rooms, as well as functional pieces. A characteristic of some Welsh dressers is a curved top, but others kept to a generally square outline and got their decoration from shaped edges.

The specimen described here is of the second type, and the method of construction given is of cabinetmaking quality (FIG. 8-14A). You can obtain the same general appearance with a simpler construction, but a cabinetmaker always preferred fitted and glued joints to nailed or screwed ones. Although counterboring and plugging over screw heads might be found in some early furniture, the better pieces normally had no sign of this procedure, except where there was no alternative. Instead, the craftsman cut joints that fit so external surfaces were not marred by screws, nails, or plugs.

Make a drawing of one end to a fairly large scale, with details of shelves, drawers, dividers, and other horizontal members on it (FIG. 8-14B). From this drawing, mark all the important positions on the edge of a straight piece of wood to use as a rod for marking all upright parts so they match.

Some dressers were made so the top with shelves lifted off the other part, or they were made in two parts and doweled together. This one is made with the sides to the full height without a break. Make each side from two boards glued together (FIG. 8-14C). Also glue the tabletop to width from narrower boards. Make its ends to pass over the lower part of the sides, but to fit into dado grooves across the higher part (FIG. 8-14D). At the back, nail the boards covering the lower part to the top, but cover the upper part by a molded strip that takes the tongued ends of the exposed boards behind the shelves (FIG. 8-14E).

Frame the tabletop around the front and ends. Groove its edges for tongued pieces that go around and miter them at the front corners (FIG. 8-14F). Where the end pieces overlap the higher ends, cut off the tongue (FIG. 8-14G).

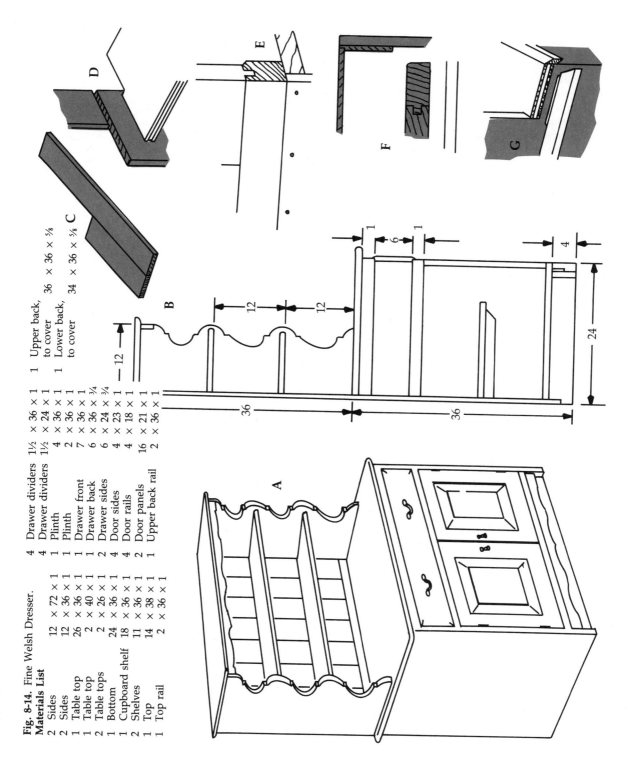

Fig. 8-14. Fine Welsh Dresser.

Materials List

2	Sides	12 × 72 × 1
2	Sides	12 × 36 × 1
1	Table top	26 × 36 × 1
1	Table top	2 × 40 × 1
2	Table tops	2 × 26 × 1
1	Bottom	24 × 36 × 1
1	Cupboard shelf	18 × 36 × 1
2	Shelves	11 × 36 × 1
1	Top	14 × 38 × 1
1	Top rail	2 × 36 × 1
4	Drawer dividers	1½ × 36 × 1
4	Drawer dividers	1½ × 24 × 1
1	Plinth	4 × 36 × 1
2	Plinth	4 × 36 × 1
1	Drawer front	7 × 36 × 1
1	Drawer back	6 × 36 × ¾
2	Drawer sides	6 × 24 × ¾
4	Door sides	4 × 23 × 1
4	Door rails	4 × 18 × 1
2	Door panels	16 × 21 × 1
1	Upper back rail	2 × 36 × 1
1	Upper back, to cover	36 × 36 × ⅝
1	Lower back, to cover	34 × 36 × ⅝

The bottom of this dresser should be flat on the floor with a plinth fitted around it. Do not cut back any part, but do not continue the rear edge to the floor. Fit the bottom of the cupboard on to battens to increase the bearing area (FIG. 8-15A).

Above and below the drawer there are two identical frames (FIG. 8-15B). Tenon their corners. The upper one goes directly under the tabletop. Fix it with glue and screws into the ends and the top. Screw the other one into the ends, although for the best work make it extra long to fit into dadoes on the ends (FIG. 8-15C). Assemble the two frames and check their squareness by measuring diagonals. Let the glue set before fitting them. They govern the shape of the drawer and should be carefully fitted if the drawer is to slide freely.

The shelf in the cupboard rests on battens (FIG. 8-15D) and is probably best left loose so it can be removed for cleaning. You could choose another shelf arrangement to suit your needs.

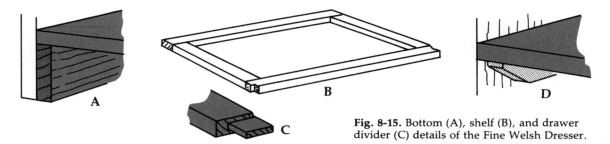

Fig. 8-15. Bottom (A), shelf (B), and drawer divider (C) details of the Fine Welsh Dresser.

At the front, make the edges of the frames above and below the drawer and the edge of the bottom to come level with the edges of the side (FIG. 8-16A). Set back the plinth under the bottom (FIG. 8-16B). It will carry a decorative overlay. Place the ends of the plinth to fit against the ends of the battens under the bottom, which you need to cut back to suit. Notch the plinth into the sides or cut it to fit closely in the final assembly.

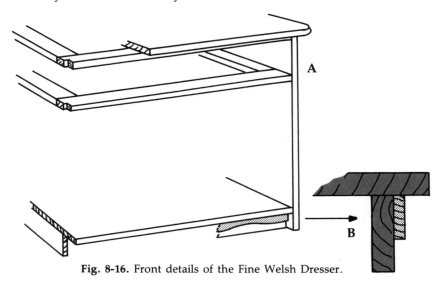

Fig. 8-16. Front details of the Fine Welsh Dresser.

Check dimensions and squareness of the lower body, but do not assemble yet. Avoid a trial assembly since this might cause loosening of joints. You can give the overlay on the plinth an undulating edge pattern or make it to a similar shape to the rail under the top. When the dresser is finished, you can stain the overlay darker than the rest of the wood to emphasize its shape.

Decorate the upper part of the dresser with scalloped edges. Some early furniture makers drew curves with a compass and left the shape at that (FIG. 8-17A). A step between reversed curves was usual. A better artistic appreciation is shown by asymmetrical curves between the shelves (FIG. 8-17B), with comparable curves around the fronts. A paper template is helpful.

Round the front edges of the shelves and cut them back to fit into stopped dado grooves (FIG. 8-17C). Groove them to hold plates. At the top place a rail with a shaped lower edge (FIG. 8-17D). Shoulder its ends to fit into grooves in the sides (FIG. 8-17E).

The top is one part where a skilled furniture maker might resort to screws, since this is not normally visible, but the best way of attaching it would be with a series of short tenons (FIG. 8-17F). In this case, cap the dresser with a fairly wide overhang of top.

Make the back of the top of several vertical boards, which you can tongue-and-groove; or thin boards may be only halved (FIG. 8-17G). With halving there is a risk that a board warping might open its joint with its neighbor, but tongued-and-grooved boards will limit each other's warping tendencies.

At the sides, fit the board into rabbets in the ends. At the top, nail or screw the boards to the back of the top board. At their bottoms, tongue the boards into the strip across the tabletop. These are the only parts that are not glued in the final assembly, since they must be able to expand and contract.

Up to this stage, you can make up certain subassemblies, but do not make any final assembly until it is certain that fixing parts together will not interfere with work to be done later to another part of the same assembly. For instance, you should do all the grooving for shelves and the making of joints for the upper part before you assemble the cupboard. You should fit the frames and the bottom of the cupboard between the sides before you add the tabletop or upper shelves.

When you have assembled the frame, check it in all directions for squareness, and leave it standing level for the glue to set.

Make the pair of doors in the same way as previously described, with the frame joints mortise and tenon, and grooves for the panels. In better work, the panels are not merely thinned to fit the grooves, but they are *fielded and raised*. This means that the center part has a definite edge so it shows a clean line, instead of a blend from flat to a bevel (FIG. 8-18A). You can use a suitable tool in a power spindle or router for this step, but to make a panel by hand cut in the outline of the raised part, either with a cutting gauge working from the edge, or with a sharp knife along a steel straightedge. This is important if you are to avoid disfiguring by grain tearing out. The amount of raising can be slight—1/16 inch might be enough. You can pare away some of the waste wood with a chisel (FIG. 8-18B), then use a rabbet plane to reduce the waste thickness (FIG. 8-18C). A low-angled shoulder plane is the best tool for working across the grain. With the depth worked, tilt the plane to make the bevel (FIG. 8-18D). Then thoroughly sand the lowered and tapered part, with the abrasive paper around a flat piece of wood to get an even surface. Try not to round the raised edge.

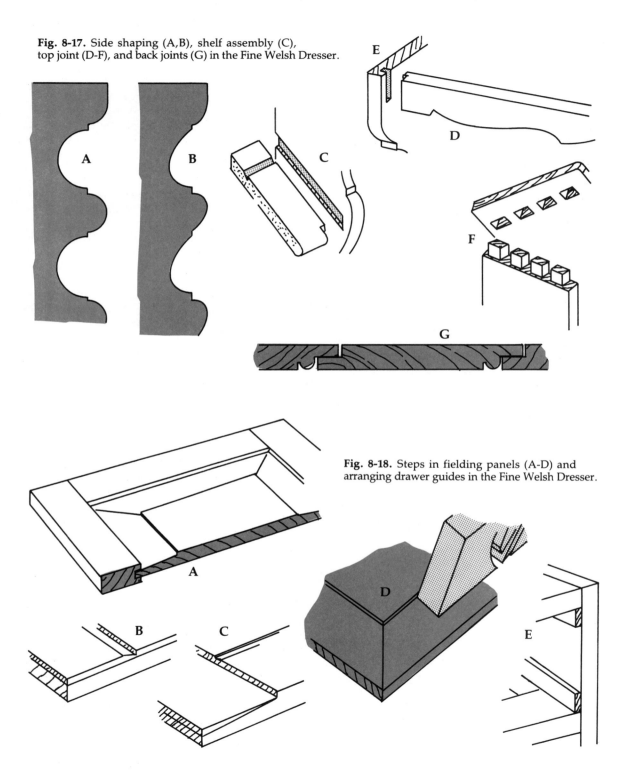

Fig. 8-17. Side shaping (A,B), shelf assembly (C), top joint (D-F), and back joints (G) in the Fine Welsh Dresser.

Fig. 8-18. Steps in fielding panels (A-D) and arranging drawer guides in the Fine Welsh Dresser.

You must have drawer guides fit inside on the runners, which are formed by the sides of the frame (FIG. 8-18E); otherwise there are no special preparations to take the drawer. Fit stops for the drawers.

The drawer for this piece of furniture has an overlapping front (FIG. 8-19A), otherwise its construction is similar to drawers described for earlier items. Prepare the front by working rabbets across the top edge and the ends (FIG. 8-19B). When this has been done, the projecting part of the back surface should fit in the opening in the frame. Dovetail the drawer sides into the front (FIG. 8-19C). Cut the bottom dovetail high enough to allow for a groove for the bottom to follow through the sides into the front (FIG. 8-19D).

You can dovetail the drawer back (FIG. 8-19E) or fit it in dadoes above the bottom (FIG. 8-19F). Slide the bottom in the groove from the back and screw it under the back.

Hinges for the doors could be ornamental ones on the surface, or butt type fit into the space between the doors and their stiles.

Knobs for doors on this type of dresser were nearly always turned wood, and they followed a fairly uniform pattern (FIG. 8-19G). They might be screwed from the inside of the drawer, but it was more usual for them to be turned with a dowel to glue into a hole.

You can provide separate catches for the doors, but one original wooden combined catch and knob was used. Extend the dowel inside the door and mortise it to take a wedge, which can be turned to overlap the stile and hold the door (FIG. 8-19H).

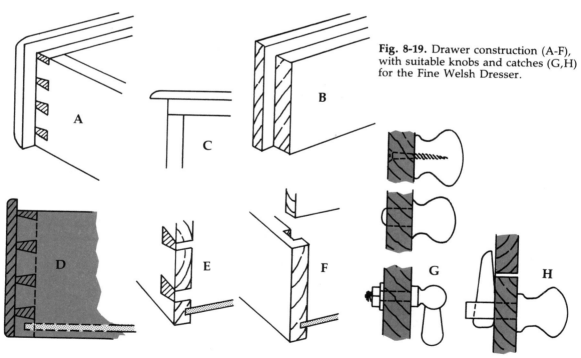

Fig. 8-19. Drawer construction (A-F), with suitable knobs and catches (G,H) for the Fine Welsh Dresser.

Index

Other Books in The TAB Furniture Woodshop Series

Do-It-Yourselfer's Guide to Furniture Repair and Refinishing—2nd Edition

Brush up on the latest woodworking techniques and applications.

Restore furniture to its original character and beauty—even make it better than it was! Precise directions cover everything from selecting a finish to using stains and fillers, from stripping the old varnish to applying the new, even restoring cane, metal, and bamboo furniture. Almost 200 two-color illustrations show you how to: make inlays . . . turn wood . . . rebuild panels . . . reupholster . . . reinforce joints . . . replace veneers . . . remove blemishes . . . imitate grains . . . ''antique'' surfaces . . . and much, much more!

Designing and Building Children's Furniture with 61 Projects—2nd Edition

A step-by-step guide to making all kinds of children's furniture and toys, from cribs, cradles, and desks, to a rocking horse, play house, and toy box.

Devoted entirely to children's furniture, this book shows you how to turn inexpensive materials into useful furnishings children will enjoy. You'll learn the basics of furniture making, along with some important woodworking tips and techniques. Packed with two-color illustrations and easy-to-follow instructions, this revised edition provides everything you need to construct useful, sturdy furniture that is as much fun to make as it is to use.

Designing and Building Outdoor Furniture, with 57 Projects—2nd Edition

Build beautiful, sturdy outdoor furniture and patio accessories.

This book is filled with practical, easy-to-understand instructions and detailed two-color illustrations. Even the novice woodworker will be able to make outdoor tables, chairs, benches, planters, and more. Advice is offered on tools, materials, and techniques. Fifty-seven projects are described in detail, from simple benches to a more complicated picnic table.

Designing and Building Space-Saving Furniture, with 28 Projects—2nd Edition

Unique ideas for saving money and space with built-in furniture you create!

Step-by-step directions, exploded drawings, detailed materials lists, and plenty of suggestions for project variations explain every aspect of making space-saving furniture. An excellent guide to designing and constructing built-in furniture, this book provides the novice craftsman with a complete course in measuring, marking, designing, and building furniture to meet specific space restrictions. Projects include complete instructions for building corner and hanging cabinets, room dividers, and units for kitchens, bedrooms, and other household areas.